Marx and Foucault

Antonio Negri

Marx and Foucault
Essays Volume 1

Translated by Ed Emery

polity

Polity Press
65 Bridge Street
Cambridge CB2 1UR, UK

Polity Press
350 Main Street
Malden, MA 02148, USA

ISBN-13: 978-1-5095-0340-7
ISBN-13: 978-1-5095-0341-4 (pb)

A catalogue record for this book is available from the British Library.

Library of Congress Cataloging-in-Publication Data

Names: Negri, Antonio, 1933- author.
Title: Marx and Foucault : essays / Antonio Negri.
Description: Cambridge, UK ; Malden, MA : Polity Press, [2016]- | Includes
   bibliographical references and index.
Identifiers: LCCN 2016028565| ISBN 9781509503407 (hardback) | ISBN
   9781509503414 (pbk.)
Subjects: LCSH: Marx, Karl, 1818-1883. | Foucault, Michel, 1926-1984. | Political
   science--Philosophy. | Economics--Philosophy. |
Sociology--Philosophy. | Philosophy, Marxist.
Classification: LCC JA77 .N44 2016 | DDC 335.4/1--dc23 LC record available at
   https://lccn.loc.gov/2016028565

Typeset in 10.5 on 12pt Plantin by
Servis Filmsetting Ltd, Stockport, Cheshire
Printed and bound in Great Britian by CPI Group (UK) Ltd, Croydon

For further information on Polity, visit our website: politybooks.com

Contents

Introduction

I am grateful to Polity because in 1986, shortly after I had been forced to leave Italy and found myself isolated, living in exile in Paris, I started asking myself how I saw the class struggle and the systems of government about to develop in the twenty-first century, which was fast approaching. The outcome of this thinking was a book entitled *The Politics of Subversion: A Manifesto for the Twenty-First Century*, which came out in 1989. Publishing it was an act of courage on the part of Polity, and I repaid it, I think, as it deserved, by offering a reading of the changes taking place in the composition of the working class. In that book I summarised the work on struggles in Italy and Europe that I had carried out in the previous decade, and I took the argument a step further, building on themes that were to emerge in the books which I co-authored with Michael Hardt a decade later: the trilogy *Empire*, *Multitude* and *Commonwealth*. The 1989 book therefore represented an early manifesto for the 'socialised worker' ['*operaio sociale*'], who was to be the protagonist of the struggles of the twenty-first century.

Obviously Polity had its reasons for being interested in me. I was being asked to intervene in the debate – which at that time had just opened in Britain and in the English-speaking world – on a 'new way' for socialism, as prefigured by Tony Blair's 'New Labour' project and soon afterwards by the new policy options outlined by Bill Clinton and the American Democrats. They too were interested in positions such as mine – namely that the traditional working-class corporations no longer played a progressive role – all the more so as my critique came from the left. They were interested because it offered them a way of legitimising the neoliberal policies by which we are now afflicted and sometimes crushed. However, there was no ambiguity on my part.

My manifesto argued a position that, in freeing itself from the crisis of a working-class representation that by now had become aged and impotent, opened the way for the construction of a new horizon of struggles, of antagonism and of a communist programme. This was precisely the opposite of what Blair was planning: in my work there was no renunciation of labour's struggle against surplus labour, no renunciation of the struggles of the cognitive, intellectual and precarious proletariat against a neoliberalism that wanted to mistreat these workers even more than liberalism had mistreated their fathers and grandfathers. So the manifesto published by Polity provided a broad account of the struggles of 1986 in France, the struggles of university and high school students, which had linked with the formidable strike of railway workers and urban transport workers: this was the first time you could concretely grasp the new unity between intellectual labour (in formation and organised as such) on the one hand and, on the other, the organisation of workers in the service sector – a sector increasingly invaded by cognitive and digital technologies. All this provided a good opportunity to understand how a new materialist analysis, applied politically in a class sense, could create a proposition for social struggles against capitalist command – and for how critique should work: not by seeking to impose (sometimes heroically; too often in vain) a past onto a present that had by now been thoroughly reshaped by the reforms and transformations taking place in command and in capitalist exploitation, but by shaking up this present, breaking it from the inside, and making possible the expression, in a rough and constituent manner, of the subjectivities that had been produced in it and were enclosed in it.

* * *

Philosophy connects with the history of the present – not as some distant superstructure, but by weaving itself into it as into a fabric. When we speak of contemporary philosophy, we often find ourselves in a situation very similar to the one we saw reflected in the *Manifesto for the Twenty-First Century*. Philosophy is sometimes a practice of power. From the middle of the nineteenth century on, philosophy has repeatedly applied itself to the task of either neutralisation or mystification, but always in order to exorcise the emergence of new social forces that were seeking to change the world. By this I mean the potentialities of subordinated labour in revolt. Their strength was too solid and visible for them to be denied; so it was rather a question of neutralising their insurgency or of recuperating (or subsuming) their potentiality [*potenza*]. We owe to the authors of western Marxism, and in particular to Georg Lukács, the growing awareness of the destructive intention of bourgeois ideology (in its philosophical form) in the face of the emergent social forces – or rather in the face of a working class that was in the ascendant. In continental Europe, for example, neo-Kantianism, in the various forms in which it expressed itself, played a fundamental role in the late nineteenth and early twentieth centuries in concealing and neutralising those new emergences of being. They were manipulated and, when everything went well, subsumed to a universalism that was incapable of grasping their productive force, which was creative of languages and institutions.

But – remaining in that area by way of example – it should be recognised that the reformism of the neo-Kantian social democrats, in their attempts to root out the subversive monster, in the end had effects that were entirely minor by comparison with the effects – in terms of devastation, or rather of inquisitorial exorcism – of the positions advanced by the vitalist and irrationalist currents of philosophy, in league with capitalist power. This process reached its peak in that twentieth-century synthesis between a metaphysical thought oriented towards being and an irrationalist tendency bent on the glorification of a totalitarian and eventual nothingness, as organised for example by the fascist thinking of Martin Heidegger. It is striking how the massive and ongoing growth in the power [*potenza*] of the working class and of the victory of the Soviet revolution was not accompanied on the capitalist side by any realistic evaluation, but only by a determination to destroy – which was as deep as the revolution had been radical. Fascisms and Nazisms, both in the realm of philosophy and in the realm of real life, offer this paradox: as reality becomes revolutionary, so philosophy becomes reactionary.

★ ★ ★

We had to pass through the tragedy of two wars and wait for 1968 for the resistance that had accompanied the victory against the forces of horror in the Second World War to be able to present itself effectively at the level of the search for truth. The radical negativity that the philosophy of fascism had developed had dragged down an entire philosophical tradition: there were now strands of modern thought that could no longer be decently taken up, for example neo-Kantianism. Or, when they were taken up (as in the essays of Rawls or Habermas), they looked like relics and leftovers of an non-recoverable past – philosophies of the university and of the state, renewals of a juridical and ideological formalism that no longer had the power to divert or de-nature, or to intervene in the new realities of class relations. And in the meantime these – as our manifesto pointed out – had already been changing radically. A different world now gradually took over from the reality of the working-class factory and of a society traversed by impulses, needs and behaviours that derived from the factory; and this was a world where exploitation was renewed on and through society and where new qualifications of living labour emerged from the wider society: intellectual rather than manual, cognitive rather than material, cooperative at a very high intensity – which in turn was measured no longer in terms of the space and values of industry but in those of communication and of knowledge.

★ ★ ★

A new generation of revolutionary political discourse was needed. There was an urgent demand for a radical shift in the epistemic paradigm, to match the new characteristics of the ontology of the present. This is the terrain on which I have now embarked, in order to deepen the discussion, and this is the terrain on which the present book – moving between Marx and Foucault – tries to trace a meaningful line, which might enable us to broaden our philosophical and political reflection. This is a difficult terrain because it is a 'post' terrain. In other words, defining it means that it is not enough just to look at the past and at the same time observe – however sharply – the present. To do it, one needs to gamble on the future and proceed (for all the risks that this entails) by using a *dispositif* projected onto the 'to come' [*a venire*].* This is even clearer to me today when I look back at my 1986 *Manifesto*. That book was already informed by understandings of, and debate with, thinkers of the standing of Althusser and Deleuze; it was already marked by a clear awareness of the changes taking place in the ontology of the present, particularly in relation to the world of production and hence to the dimensions of labour and exploitation – and yet at that time the view could only be partial, and the *potenza* of the anticipations that the analysis developed was inevitably limited. You had to work – or rather the world had to work – in order to advance, knowing that critical work itself – in these epistemic conditions – was not merely an act of observing but was a forward projection of oneself; it was not an operation of the mind but an adventure of bodies. In the 'post', moving forward into the postmodern – in other words into that dimension that we begin

---

* I.e. 'onto what is to come', the future: play on words in Italian between the phrase *a venire* ('to come') and *l'avvenire* ('the future').

to see more clearly today, spread out as it is in front of us and also within us, in that conflictual reality that concerns us intimately, both insofar as it is novel and insofar as it is total.

★ ★ ★

Let us go back to the 'paradigm shift' that theory had to set for itself as a problem around and after 1968. Here I would like to propose a game of historical–philosophical readings as a way of understanding that paradigm shift – a kind of play in which present-day characters act out a function that in another age was attributed to other characters – in the same way in which Renaissance theatre reworked characters that had been created in the comedies of Plautus and Terence. It is a philosophical game, designed to free us from the burden of those hundreds of volumes of the (universal and thus Eurocentric) history of philosophy that the silver age of the German university passed down to us as an inheritance all through the nineteenth century; a game that, precisely because it is a game, might free us from the burden of having to relive all that.

For example, how about Deleuze–Derrida–Foucault represented as a repetition of Hume–Kant–Hegel? Remember, this is just a game we are playing. But it is only in playing it that we shall eradicate the reactionary echoes that stand in the way of a new perception of history. Deleuze, then, *in primis*: the disarticulation of any notion of dialectical categories and solutions, just as Hume had been the destroyer of all possibility of causal categories and solutions. Or, again, Deleuze as a destroyer of any machine of individualisation, of any Cartesian consistency of the ego, just as Hume had been the destroyer of any form of substance; both of them inventors of an empirical and constitutive critique of imagination. This radical flattening of being, this refound surface of ontology destroys any neo-Kantian claim for the difference of intellect from experience; it uproots every subjective genealogy of being; and it opens onto the problem of the reconstruction of a new ontological terrain. And at this point enter Derrida. He emerges without timidity on that surface of being and offers it to us as a compacted materialistic constitution, taking from phenomenological thinking the relationship between perception, intention and language and constraining it within the concept of reality. The transcendental is taken by Derrida into immanence, the *phenomenon* to the *noumenon*, the thing *in se* [in itself] is unmasked and presents itself as world. Derrida succeeds in what Kant had prescribed and only partially achieved, as prisoner of a phenomenic project tied to a transcendental critique. Now, once we reached this point, that compacted world can be deconstructed. Here again Kant as critic appears on stage, but this time in constructive mode – a stage where concepts take on a shimmering aspect, a subjectivity immersed in an uncertainty of existence, a being that has something of a difficulty in coming into formation. And so the historical stage becomes filled with ghosts. Derrida does not hold them back; rather he brings them to the front, where (like Marx's spectre haunting Europe) they terrorise the logicians and phenomenologists who persist in the fixation of being – and the princes and kings who make light of the spirit and the passions in order to bend them to dominion. Finally here comes Foucault, who can be represented in this play as the author of a Hegelian operation as simple and radically innovative as had been that of the philosopher of Stuttgart: he addresses history as a material terrain and brings it back into a productive ontology that is lived as constitutive praxis. So is this, again, *Weltgeschichte als Weltgericht* – the history of the world as a judgement and justice of the world?

Here the play dissolves into pure fiction. This is because the constitutive praxis that constitutes and traverses the ontology of actuality is in no case superficial or noumenal or transcendental: it is, precisely, constitutive. It is, in Foucault, articulated between two poles: a historical one, the embodiment of a 'historicity' deprived of any theological origin and of any teleological direction; and one of subjectivation, liberated from the chiasm imposed by any dialectical process or *Aufhebung* [sublation], which are oppressive even when the dialectic attempts to be negative, Kojevian. Here we arrive finally at the post-1968. What started out as comedy reveals itself as tragedy.

★ ★ ★

Nevertheless, there are good reasons to try to broaden the picture and seek to understand the relationship between Marx and Foucault in terms of the development of European history, first of all by looking at the *Marx moment* and seeing it as a construction, in the fateful years that saw the insurgency of the Commune and the founding of the German Reich, of a philosophy of revolution that becomes a target for the guns of Power (and of academic philosophy). I have already made this point. But let us remember that this is not a unique and bizarre episode: it is the norm prescribed by the class struggle dominated by the ruling class. It is a reaction that repeats itself every time the struggles of the subordinated classes make power tremble. To take just one example – consider what happened after the Protestant Reformation: on the one hand, the repressive action of the Counter-Reformation; on the other, the watering down of the Reform itself, from within. And, when the peasants rebel under Luther's inspiration, they are massacred with his blessing. We could go on endlessly with examples of this kind of history – which still repeats itself today, when the springs of freedom blossom and are then closed by ferocious Thermidors and are repressed and executed in the name of 'order'. So too Marx and his theory: they are to be understood within the lived experience of the proletarian class struggle – and thus will inevitably be fought against and repressed by power and defamed by university censors. And now we come to the *Foucault moment*: after 1968 Foucault aligns himself with those who considered it necessary to reform the political and ideological system that was established after the Second World War, and especially against those who had tried to remove from democratic politics and from the class struggle all subversive thrust, all critical dimension, all theoretical decision for revolution – in short, all subjectivation. In this framework, he tells us, we have to change ourselves, we have to fight over our needs, in the micro, and take desires as a starting point for a politics of life against the Power that increasingly reproduces itself within and against life. Every reform changes our destiny. The subjectivation of the struggle reopens history.

★ ★ ★

But fortunately history (and especially the history of philosophy) is a 'battlefield' in which there is a clash between ideologies, or rather forms of life, abstracted into philosophical knowledge and transformed, becoming again concrete as experiences of a singular thinking and of active bodies. In this way the history of philosophy (just like history in general) presents itself as discontinuity, as excedence–actions–reactions, and, as in all battles, it leaves on the ground its corpses and glorifies its heroes. If we now go back and place ourselves again within the German philosophical debate that dominated Europe between the nineteenth and twentieth centuries – an experience whose reactionary quality we have measured and that leads straight into Heideggerian fascism – well, these ideas were of course not the only presences and outcomes on the scene at the time, especially when it comes to the philosophy of history. There are authors and forces (from Dilthey to Max Weber, not to mention Nietzsche) who take a position on the state's and the university's reaction against the class struggle and on the reduction of history to a destiny of command in unfreedom. These are authors (not necessarily progressive) who seek to understand the expansive nature of the historical process and who, in order to express it, coined the term

Geschichtlichkeit [historicity], snatching history back from theology and transcendentalism: affirmation of a concrete historicity, within which one should grasp not so much *historia rerum gestarum* [the history of things done] as *res gestae* [the things done]. These authors seek to locate themselves within an ontology of actuality and to live there a dialectic of unresolved and progressive oppositions: in so doing they try to mark the take-off of liberty – accepting the risks, all the risks, of a deed of liberation.

What dominates in this experience, at that stage in a German philosophy itself creatively opposed to the academy (take, for instance, the work of Dilthey), is a number of stylemes, reworked over a period of time and with positive tonalities. The first of these is the sense of the crisis and anarchy of values brought about by capitalism as it becomes established. Capital 'can make and unmake things as it wishes; it is like a beast with a thousand eyes and a thousand claws and without conscience, which may go wherever best suits it' (Dilthey, 1976, p. 245). A second motif of the confrontation with the forces of reaction is the strong evocation of the figures of the Enlightenment. Not of the Kant of the *Critique*, but of Kant as the bard of the revolution, Kant who proposes the Enlightenment as a progressive and unending terrain of and path to knowledge. *Sapere aude!* [Dare to know!] Third, there occurs – inevitably at this point – an experience of rupture, an expressive excedence that is able to go beyond the *Erlebnis*, beyond the lived experience, in other words is able to structure itself in the temporal comprehension of life and to project itself in its reproduction, in a *dispositif* that is reconstructive of the world of life. So the critique of historical reason becomes the basis for a constitutive genealogy. A fourth element is the qualification of this excedence: a qualification that seeks to be intensive and that produces subjectivation; a qualification that – equally – seeks to be extensive and reaffirms humanism, not so much as a universal, but as a common. This is the humanism that imposes itself at the moment when the 'death of God' ('the death of man') is declared, as a hypostatic subject of western metaphysics, bringing to the fore the image of an 'other' human being, people who constitute – without certainty, but with what energy! – their own work [*opera*] in history. By the end, what has been affirmed is the relationship between history and society. History is not contemplated but becomes a site of action; society is structured by action; historicity as a horizon and fabric of action is always traversed by a collective presence.

This theoretical experience of 'historicity' translates to France at the end of the Second World War: it is the so-called 'western Marxism' that transfers the ontology of historicity into French thought. Merleau-Ponty takes the Lukács of *History and Class Consciousness*, and incorporates subjectivity into history without making it an epiphenomenon and without hypostatising the subject:

> We give a form to history according to our categories; but our categories, in contact with history, are themselves freed from their partiality. The old problem of the relations between subject and object is transformed, and relativism is surpassed as soon as one puts it in historical terms, since here the object is the vestige left by other subjects, and the subject – historical understanding – held in the fabric of history, is by this very fact capable of self-criticism There is an oscillation from one to the other which, as much as we could hope for, reduces the distance between knowledge and history. It is along this road that Weber stops. He does not pursue the relativization of relativism to its limits. He always considers the circle of the present and the past, of our representation and real history, as a vicious circle. He remains dominated by the idea of a truth without condition. (Merleau-Ponty, 1974, pp. 30–1)

> It is Marxism that incorporates subjectivity into history without making of it an epiphenomenon, it is the philosophical marrow of Marxism, its value as culture and finally its revolutionary meaning, that are in themselves in solidarity. (Ibid., p. 47)

The two relationships – between consciousness and 'the produced' and between consciousness and 'productivity' – are held together. So in the French postwar experience we find conjoined those experiences that had stood against the neutralisation and the exorcism of the forces of resistance in the more recent history of capitalism and had made it possible to liberate the vitality of revolutionary knowledge [*sapere*].

* * *

I have to admit that I would never have succeeded in defining this philosophical journey and in making it my own if I had not had the possibility of travelling between Italy and France in the 1970s. Between those two countries, in those years, there was a strange complementarity: what happened in struggles in Italy in the 1970s translated in France into philosophy. In Italy we had lived a history, or rather an ontology, that was productive of struggles and a praxis that was constituting a new world: it was in the immersion in that experience that we found again the continuity of Marx's thinking and its interrelationship with the determinations that the new French philosophy was producing. Here understanding was the effect of a

passage: not only a passage from one country to another, but a historical passage through defeat – the defeat of struggles in Italy, the defeat
of socialism in Europe. We had already noted this in the *Manifesto*
published at Polity in 1986 – but at the same time there was a revival
of philosophical discourse that posed a constituent subject, namely
the full subjectivation of the new composition of the class at the centre
of the struggles and of the processes of transformation at that time.

In the texts that follow there will be references to this history, to this
development of a thinking of transformation that comes across from
Italy to France. I also offer two critical invitations: one, to do a rereading of these events and to rediscover them under the (vague, possibly
inappropriate, but nevertheless useful) label of 'Italian theory'; the
other, an invitation to reread and interpret the thinking of Gramsci
as an alternative path – albeit sometimes rather provincial, sometimes
futuristic – in short, to recognise in this author a kind of paradigm
(powerfully political and materialistic) of western Marxism.

* * *

At the start of the twenty-first century there has been much talk of
'going back to Marx' – in sociological research, in literary studies of
and on postmodernism, and particularly in historical and political
studies of postcolonialism, but above all in politics: not so much
in political science as in politics as it is discussed and lived through
active struggles, where people have rediscovered class struggle in the
fight against neoliberalism and have discovered for themselves the
arguments for the common in the struggle against financial globalisation. This is what has led to work on the critique of sovereignty,
government, law, and administration as key concepts of modernity – which was done observing how, behind each of these levels
of experience, lay rigid forms of the organisation of exploitation.
However, a return to Marx is only possible if we distance ourselves
from the Marx who was turned into dogma in the tradition of diamat
(dialectical materialism). And thus, if one is to replant one's political
economy into a *critique*, this requires a strong immersion in history,
a free political judgement, an ontology of the here and now, and
class subjectivation – all to be set as the basis of any new Marxist
doxa. Here the dialectic of exploitation can be described by reference to the actual historical conditions of the exploitation of labour
and of the extraction of financial profit, of the socialisation and
globalisation of capital, where the processes of emancipation, for
their part, bring to the fore new subjective figures and new forms of
struggle. That living labour that built the world has also rebuilt it –

and configures itself therein, in an original way, having acquired a new potentiality [*potenza*]. Living labour has become labour that is intellectual, cognitive, affective and cooperative. The abstraction of labour has brought into being a new antagonistic coupling: money and [Marx's concept of] 'general intellect'. I was already discussing this in the 1986 *Manifesto*. But now, starting from this new historical subjectivation of the proletariat, I was able to address the new suffering and the new slavery of labour; and I began to counter it with the new proletarian productivity. The novel of living labour will therefore have to be rewritten in terms of general intellect, just as Marx had described labour in his own time, giving us his account of the development of capitalism in *Capital*.

★ ★ ★

So let us return to Foucault and to the essays on his work that are contained in this volume. I would suggest reading them starting from the end, in other words starting with the last chapter, on the subject of a Marxist experience of Foucault – in short, a Marx *after* Foucault – and then reading back to the first title in Part III, 'On the Method of Political Critique'. A journey back in time from 2014 to 1977: a lifetime. Certainly a lifetime, because it was precisely in the 1970s that I perceived – from my reading of his earlier major works and from my proximity to Foucault's friends and research assistants (in those days I was attending the École Normale Supérieure and the Collège in Paris) – the importance of the *Lessons* he was delivering at that time. In 2014 my experience of reading Foucault in the light of Marxism finally came to maturity – in other words, far from claiming Marxian overlays in the thinking of Foucault, I see Foucault as a development – certainly an independent one – of a number of central analytical insights that were posed and developed by Marx. Here I am talking about the Foucauldian concept of 'biopolitics', which should be read alongside the Marxian concept of the 'real subsumption' of society to capital. Then there was the Foucauldian transition from disciplinary systems to systems of control – which for me clarify definitively the transition from the Fordist mode of production to post-Fordism; and many other things besides. One insight that stands out is the concept of the biopolitical as a fabric of reproduction of society and of circulation of goods (not only material but especially immaterial: knowledge, expertise, affects etc.) and as an open horizon in the production of forms of life. Each and all of these categories (and many others, also of Foucauldian inspiration) were used by Michael Hardt and myself in *Empire*, in *Multitude* and in *Commonwealth* to describe developments in the field of sovereignty and to build our narrative of the transition from the nation-state (and from the concert of nation-states) to the global (imperial) model; from the anthropological and political concepts of individualism to the definition of the multitude as a multiple ensemble of singularities.

But, beyond all this, a Marxist (even a strange and rather unorthodox Marxist such as myself) is indebted to Foucault for having opened a way to the solution of two fundamental problems: that of the definition of *Power* [*potere*] and that of experimentation, genealogies and movements of *subjectivation*. As regards Power, we know how Foucault defines it: an action on the action of the other. Here we are in the midst of that dialectics of capital that, in the same way it allowed Marx to build his comprehensive model of capitalism, also allows us – here as followers of Foucault – to see how capital and power also become unified conceptually and constitute a chiasm between two contradictory actions that are forced to join together and yet are intransitive: constant capital and living labour – a power relationship in which the dual nature of the functions never arrives at equiparity because only living labour produces value. The same applies to power: command and resistance form a couple whose constituents do not overlap. There is no contract that can reconcile these two realities, and there is no transcendence that can bring them together into a unity. What produces *res gestae* (history) is the movement of resistance in its clash with power, and this resistance sets down a marker for an eventual possible common progress of humanity.

The theme of subjectivation is, in various ways, quite complex. In my reading of Marx in *Marx beyond Marx* I particularly developed the theme of subjectivation in terms of knowledge [*conoscenza*] – knowledge of the tendency, a coming to awareness, science. As an approach it was insufficient, even though – in a period of Marxist cultural hegemony like the 1970s – it was easily understandable and efficacious. Foucault reproposes the theme and addresses it – certainly more correctly and in a totally materialist manner – as a problem of the body. Understanding, will [*volontà*], care, technologies – the body is at the centre of the research, of the diagnosis, and of the *dispositif* of action (in Marxian terms: of inquiry [*inchiesta*], of science and of tendency, of political consciousness and of struggle). So then: subjectivation as an action that operates on being and (collectively) transforms it?

* * *

Again, on this terrain the criticisms came pouring in, and they were not insubstantial. They came principally from two sides (leaving aside the infinite variations in between). One of the initial criticisms was to attack Foucauldian biopolitics as a late theory of being, conceived of as changeable or as actively constituted–transformed, when in fact this being and this mode of transformation would always have been produced by nature, in life. The conclusion is that this 'always' reduces any change, any transformation, to an insignificant particle: history should not overvalue what it can accomplish, it remains a variation in nature. The insistence on ways of life and on the transformation of *bios* is thus pure literature. This is the line that runs for example through Bruno Latour's critique, in his attempt to show the extent to which the anthropology of life bypasses (or exceeds and 'removes' in the Hegelian sense) the historicity of the world. Biopolitics is replaced by a 'cosmo-political'. A glorification of powerlessness to act? In some ways yes, it is still the negation of any subject, the affirmation of a 'process without a subject', and moreover the negation of any subjectivity – a kind of structuralism restructured on a naturalist horizon.

After that projection into a natural background that is infinite and indeterminate, the argument from the other side was that biopolitics has to do with the consistency of the individual and with the individuation of his parts rather than with the subjectivation of his potentiality [*potenza*]; and, in the history or transformation of biopolitics, what is placed at the centre is individuals, or rather *the* individual. This is the liberal reading of biopolitics. The authors who begin (with increasing arrogance) to venture onto this dual terrain are many. They are so different and yet so similar: different, indeed opposed in their definition of life – in Spinozan terms, one could say that some are fascinated by the substance and the others by the modes; similar in their denial of the central marker of Foucault's constructive *production*, namely history as the product of power and of resistance to power, historicity as the interwoven fabric of differences. In fact in both of these positions – in the liberal and individualistic and in the anthropological *à la* Latour – we find something identical: namely the deeply abstract concept of nature that exists in anthropology, and that of a nature that is individualised and isolated, as expressed by liberal revisionist writers on Foucault. But is not precisely this idea of nature and of profound identity, absolute in all its variations, the fundamental fetish of western ideology?

For me, the biopolitical lives – and is defined – through opposition to biopower, or (to put it in the terminology of Spinozist materialism) it is power [*potenza*] opposed to Power [*potere*]. This is the line that brings Foucault close not only to Marx, and not only to the western

Marxism in which we grew up, but to the tradition of productive materialism that incorporates into one single bloc a realist ontology and a transformative politics.

* * *

So why have I added more political chapters to those on Marx and Foucault in what is essentially a book about philosophy and is therefore, in a way, pure of contingencies? The question implies a wrong idea of philosophy – but I make it my own, insisting that now, for some time, the Marx–Foucault relationship represents, so to speak, a central contingency in contemporary philosophy's attempt to define an *ontology of actuality*. It is a matter of rediscovering Marx after Soviet dogma had turned him into an instrument of domination and thereby into a theoretical mess; after philology and structuralism had translated his work into an exotic fetish; after Marxism had been conceived (in the Frankfurt School's scholastics of exorcism) as a performative monster in a world darkened by domination and incapable of redemption – except when mystical or prophetic. It is a matter of bringing Marx back to militancy, of immersing him once again in the understanding of history, of rereading him in the context of political urgencies; of traversing the entirety of these activities with increased knowledge and with the will to transform. Existential 'engagement' is not enough: it is life, not existence, that is at stake here. Foucault pushes us to read Marx in this perspective. This is why, in the essays published in this book, between the chapters that attempt a rereading of Marx for today and those that propose a reading of Foucault for tomorrow, I have also included a number of political–philosophical texts mostly relating to the present: the aim was to illustrate how in the 1970s there was a radical break with the *Weltanschauung* of capitalism in the transition to the dominance of neoliberalism (these are articles that further develop the positions argued in the *Manifesto for the Twenty-First Century*). Second, I have inserted other writings that help to clarify the definitive crisis of the social democracies, which is caused precisely by their withdrawal from the task of a reactualisation of Marxism. The Marx–Foucault relationship is enhanced by this historical condition. So, taking this as our starting point, let us resume our critical work, our transformative activity and our desire for revolution – in short, what Marx taught us – bringing critique, with the further aid of Foucault, into the context of our contemporary times.

Part I

1

Why Marx?

Why Marx? Because a dialogue with Marx is essential for anyone developing the concept of class struggle at the centre and/or in the subaltern conditions of the capitalist empire and proposing a communist perspective today. The lessons from, and the discussion with, Marx are decisive for three reasons.

The first is *political*. Marxist materialism makes it possible to demystify all progressivist and consensual notions of capitalist development and to affirm, on the contrary, its antagonistic character. Capital is an antagonist social relationship; subversive politics locates itself 'within' this relationship, and immerses into it in equal measure the proletarian, the militant and the philosopher. The *Kampfplatz* [place of struggle] is 'within and against' capital.

The second reason why we cannot abandon Marx has to do with *critique*. Marx locates critique within historical ontology, which is constructed by, and always traversed by, the class struggle. Critique is thus the 'viewpoint' of the oppressed class in movement and enables you to follow the logic of the capitalist cycle, to understand its crisis, and by the same token to describe the 'technical composition' of the oppressed class and, eventually, to organise its 'political composition' in a perspective of revolution. The autonomy of the 'class point of view' is central to the critique.

The third reason for staying with Marx is that his *theoretical* elaboration made it possible, in the course of the twentieth century, to follow the deepening of the crisis of mature capitalism in its dual form (liberal and socialist), and at the same time to organise the liberation movements against colonial power and imperialism.

Today Marx's theory has to come to terms with a radically different world of work and markets, of division of labour and geography of power – in short, with a new configuration of the classes in struggle. We need to establish whether, in addressing the new figures of exploitation, Marx's theory can help with grasping their points of crisis, and then with liberating an appropriate imagination of the 'common'. After the defeat of Soviet socialism we need a new theory of 'common value'.

Within the limits of this chapter it is not possible to develop a comprehensive discussion on each of these points. Rather I shall limit myself to providing – on each point – an example drawn from Marx's *Capital*.

1

By examining Sections IV, V and VI of Book 1 of *Capital* (chs 10–20), where Marx defines relative surplus value and analyses the process of formation of the system of the 'large-scale factory', we can arrive at an understanding of the constitution of a *political point of view* in Marx, and at the same time at his definition of a class politics.

Now, since the transition from the extraction of absolute surplus value to that of relative surplus value radically changes the relations of magnitude between the two parts of the working day (necessary labour time and surplus labour time), this transition has to be followed by a revolutionising of the conditions of production, both in the forms of value creation and in the forms of the labour process. There is a shortening of the labour time socially necessary for the production of a commodity, so that a smaller amount of work has the potential to produce a greater quantity of use value. At this point we have a radical modification of capitalism: the assumption of a machinic aspect that, as relative surplus value develops, comes to invest and transform the whole of society. These are the terms in which Marx studies the transition from manufacturing to the large-scale factory and the ensuing subsumption of labour cooperation to the exclusive command of capital. This transition creates the conditions for a huge increase in surplus value and for the subjection of a multitude of workers to the discipline of capital, as well as a progressive extension of the employers' despotism from the factory to the whole of society. Thus the implementation of the processes of extraction of relative surplus value is not just about the division of the worker's working day between the necessary labour part and the surplus labour part: it also revolutionises from top to bottom both the technical processes of labour and the social groupings. While on the one hand the body of workers active in the factory becomes a form of existence of capital itself, on the other hand the division of labour in the factory has to be reflected in a matching social division of labour – which means that, also outside the factory, social life is gradually subsumed to capital, first in a 'formal' manner, and then in 'real' terms. Nature itself is completely subjugated to the capitalist mode of production, agriculture to large-scale industry, and so forth.

But this genealogy of relative surplus value and this expansion of big industry, both of which appear invincible, actually have a very bizarre historical origin. The fact is that capital, in order to produce, has to incorporate human material and it has attempted to do this in history (which always repeats itself) since its origins, enormously expanding labour time and extending the appropriation of additional labour power – the labour of women and children, for example, in the first phase of industrial accumulation in Europe. In such circumstances the very survival of the working class as a 'breed' was put at risk, so ferocious was the degree of exploitation. Marx speaks of a holocaust of the proletariat. Resistance is born. The very transition from manufacturing to large-scale industry – as Marx explains – is brought about by working-class rebellion. This is in fact what happened. At that point the state had to intervene, using the force of law, to oblige the capitalists to shorten the length of the working day. We might also add: to force them to understand that the life of workers is not just brute raw material but is vital activity, historically consolidated and qualified – and, on this basis, resistant.

When the resistance of labour power appears, the whole picture (as described thus far in these sections of *Capital*) changes. We have not only the historical event of the passage from the extraction of absolute surplus value to relative surplus value, there is not only the birth of the big factory, of the factory system, and of the mode of production of large-scale industry; what also becomes apparent, with the spread of this new figure of capital, is its internal structure as an antagonistic social relationship. Once one looks at it not solely from the viewpoint of the power of the capitalist but also from the point of view of the workers, of their resistance, of their potentiality [*potenza*], it becomes apparent that the categories that define capital are twofold. We can put this more succinctly: rather than as an 'objective organism' or as an irresistible despot, capital here shows itself as one partner in a game that has two players – and because, as Marx tells us, what the workers partially lose is concentrated in capital, and against them, it is as an enemy of the workers. On the one side is the exploiter, on the other the exploited.

Let us return to the 'dual nature' of the categories, not presuming to offer a complete picture but giving a few basic examples. We have seen from the definition of surplus value that surplus labour exists in opposition to necessary labour. But these definitions, these abstractions need to be related back to the materiality of the capital relation in order to be able immediately to measure its antagonism: when labour power reaches that point of the working day where it considers that it has worked enough to get the wages necessary for its own reproduction, it refuses to work further and has to be forced to do so. If this is the case, it follows that in the process of production the relationship between the labour process and the process of value creation, between the organisation of work and the organisation of exploitation, is always conflictual. Consequently, simultaneously with becoming more productive, labour power also has to be socially weakened, exposed to the overabundance and competition of other labour power, and, through this, subjected to a greater oppression. However, at this point labour power has reached higher forms of consciousness in the face of capitalist repression and, through its higher levels of productivity, has brought about a greater capacity for resistance. So – in Marx's narrative – labour is now in a position to impose reductions in the duration of the working day and increases in the overall wage bill. Relative surplus value is an outcome of the struggles.

Furthermore, the advent of a production based on the extraction of relative surplus value requires an intensification of cooperation by workers, since it is through the cooperation of labour power that labour productivity is increased. And if this cooperation always goes hand in hand with the capitalist division of labour, by virtue of this fact it poses itself as an element of contradiction in relation to capital. The antagonistic relationship that constitutes capital is, in this case, deepened in social terms. The capital relation, which always requires a combination of cooperation and subordination, is able neither to conceal the opposition nor to block its expression – so that the resistance to value creation in the labour process is further accentuated by the political consciousness that cooperation produces.

Furthermore, it is especially in the relationship with machines that labour power shows its potential power [*potenza*], because when the machine, in its relative independence, transmits value to the product, what it transmits still remains dead labour, while only the activity of the workers, of living labour, enables machines to be productive.

In short, capitalist despotism, both in the factory and in society, cannot rid itself of the use value of working-class labour, of labour power, and all the more so as the social productive power of labour progresses. The capitalist relation is therefore always subject to this contradiction, which can explode at any moment and which, on an everyday basis, banally but efficaciously, presents itself as the problem of wages. When the process of purchasing labour power on the capitalist market is enacted, it immediately becomes apparent that what happens there is an exchange of unequal magnitudes, an exchange that is conflictual. And whereas thus far we have stayed with a reading of chapters 10–20 of Book 1 of *Capital*, permit me now to recall how, in chapter 8 of Section III of the same book, Marx, by bringing the Factory Act into his theoretical analysis, makes it clear that, as regards the dimensions of the working day, in the factory there is always an antinomy, that of right set against right. He concludes: between equal rights, force decides. Put more strongly, in the precise terms of the critique of political economy, the situation is as follows:

> in the division between surplus-value and wages, which division essentially determines the rate of profit [...] there are functions of two independent variables, which limit one another, and it is their *qualitative difference* that is the source of the *quantitative division* of the produced value. (Marx, 1972, p. 364 = *Capital*, Book 3, Section V, ch. 22)

It was by viewing the wage as an 'independent variable' in the capitalist relation that I learned to do politics. And many others with me. This discovery of the antagonism, in other words of a contradiction that is not resolvable but could be acted on from the point of view of global labour power, and by the working class – this represented the essential *dispositif* from which political research, or rather 'co-research' [*con-ricerca*] together with the exploited, could develop; it could also extend in various ways – moving outwards from the organisation of the struggles in the factory to social struggles, from wage objectives to struggles over welfare, from the contestation of the restrictions of freedom imposed on the working-class struggles to revolution in the conditions of freedom of life... There were no objective laws to be met – rather it was a matter of developing that (material and political) independent variable that the production of the revolutionary struggle determined: constituent projects to be actualised, always within that liberation *of* and *from* work that, alone, constitutes society and history.

2

The quotation from Book 3 given above brings us to a discussion of the *critical function* that Marx's teaching produces: there we found a clear statement of the antagonism between capital and labour power as 'independent variables' that limit each other on the basis of their 'qualitative differences'. At this point we have a striking Marxian statement that is worth quoting: 'the real barrier of capitalist production is capital itself' (Marx, 1972, p. 250 = *Capital*, Book 3, Section III, ch. 15). If this statement is true, the entire critical *dispositif* of Marxism has to be read in its light.

By way of example we could look at the whole of Section III in Book 3 of *Capital* (chapters 13–15), which is devoted to a discussion of the 'law of the tendency of the rate of profit to fall'. I don't want to revisit the controversy that has dogged this formulation over the years; my point is rather to take from Marx's formulation, with its demystification of capital (for capital is the real barrier to development), the practical critique of capitalist development (which is both constructed and put into crisis by working-class resistance; so this is a critique that moves 'within and against' capital), and thus the autonomy of the working-class viewpoint.

What does the law say? It states that the average social rate of profit tends to decline in relation to the growing concentration of capital, in other words as a result of the relative increase of the totality of capital by comparison with the increase of variable capital, of living labour. 'Capital as the barrier' to its own development is thus not a pathological or occasional fact. Furthermore, having stated the law, Marx does not draw catastrophist consequences from it. Indeed, from an initial point of view, the law describes a huge advance in capitalist organisation:

> its most important consequence is that the law presupposes an ever-increasing concentration of capital and therefore a growing decap-italisation of the small capitalists. This is, in general, the result of all the laws of capitalist production. Stripped of the antagonistic character that capitalist production imprints on it, what does this fact, this progress of centralisation mean? It simply means that production loses its private character and becomes a social process – not formally, since production is social in every exchange because of the absolute dependence of the producers on each other and because of the necessity of representing their work as abstract social labour (money), but in real terms. Since the means of production are used as social means and thus not through

ownership by individuals but through their relationship of production, so too labour is carried out on the social scale. (Marx, 1972, p. 226 = *Capital*, Book 3, Section III, ch. 13)

Moreover, the purely tendential character of the law is accompanied by a series of efficacious countertendencies.

What, then, from a critical point of view, is the relevance of putting together the law of development and the law of the falling rate of profit? It is this: by so doing, one identifies, within development, the antagonist functioning of the fundamental relationship. The essential form of development will therefore be one of a clash between the existence of the working class within capital and the contradictory capitalist necessity both to associate itself to this presence and to repress it. Putting the law of development together with the law of the falling rate of profit means bringing this antagonism to the fore. The process of concentration reveals its fundamental importance, showing how capitalist reorganisation around the extraction of relative surplus value is nothing but a means of governing antagonistic poles: working-class resistance and the capitalist need to contain and constrain it for the sake of its own growth. From this objective antagonism to the one expressed in class struggle the journey can be long. However, it is qualitatively homogeneous. Marx's projection of the contradiction, in the law of the tendential fall in the rate of profit, shows itself not as the final index of a necessary crisis but rather as a first approach to defining a contradiction that affects not only the objective moment but also the mainstay of development: the relationship between capital and labour. As for Marx's immediate examples of the realisation of the law and of the effects of the deepening of the contradiction, namely his prediction that the reserve army of the unemployed will increase and the masses will become utterly impoverished – these examples have to be read against the experience of his time, in other words the experience of a working class that was still mainly confined in a movement of spontaneous resistance and was struggling to turn itself into a possible political power [*potenza politica*]. But, again, this prediction was neither deterministic nor catastrophist: 'an abstract law of population exists only for plants and animals, and even then only in the absence of any historical intervention by man' (Marx, 1977 [1863–7], p. 784).

So when the dimensions and quality of the class relationship come to be substantially altered by the events of the revolutionary struggles, the power of Marx's framework explodes in all the richness of its critical foundation. The rate of profit can fall independently of the competition between capital and labour; however, as Marx concludes in his comments on Ricardo, this is the only competition that can make it fall. Because when, in response to the struggle of the working class, capital is forced to move to very high levels of concentration and – in them – to the limit of a general equalisation of organic composition, then the proportion between the rates of profit will be the same as that between the masses of surplus value. Every other term will be removed.

But the story does not end there. The centralisation of constant capital, of capitalist power and, on the other hand, the socialisation of variable capital, of living labour, have increasingly become a reality beyond the outer temporal limits of Marx's thinking. The basic critical issue proved to be the understanding of the new figures of 'organic composition' of capital – that is, of the new relationship established between constant capital and variable capital, between dead labour and living labour, through their reciprocal transformation. In this situation of capitalist crisis and working-class resistance, what was the new antagonistic articulation of capitalist development? Developing the method of Marxian critique, it seems to me that the fundamental element that differentiates the current form of capitalist development from earlier forms is the fact that social cooperation in production (which in other times was produced directly by capital) has achieved a degree of autonomy. Let me try to explain.

In the history of the capitalist mode of production it has always been capital that has imposed the form of cooperation. The latter had to be functional in relation to the form of exploitation. Only on this basis did labour become productive. Even in the period of primitive accumulation, when capital incorporates the pre-existing forms of organisation of labour and subjects them to valorisation just as they are, it is capital that imposes the form of cooperation, and this cooperation implies the elimination of the relationships previously established. But today the situation has changed completely. Capital has become a financial power, engaged in the capture of surplus value that is 'socially' produced. Around this highly centralised process there develop antagonist moments of self-valorisation that are radically independent and that economic and political power attempt to hold together and to subject to capitalist despotism. The extremely high composition of capital is completely projected onto the social in order to control it. First automation and then computerisation have taken things beyond the processes of mechanisation and have imposed immaterial figures of control. Whereas on the one hand automation still partakes somewhat of the old political economy of value creation through machines, with digitalisation this threshold is crossed and the commodity becomes increasingly transparent. On the other hand, there begin to emerge sectors that are increasingly sensitive to the autonomy of social cooperation, to the self-valorisation of proletarian subjects, and to the growing presence of individual and collective microphysics. Therefore, in order to express itself, the productive activation of labour power will have no need of being put into connection with the means of production through being bought and sold by the capitalist. Or rather this is not the only case in which it will become productive. All this leads us to consider as a hypothesis (at an advanced degree of verification) that the antagonism between the social cooperation of the proletariat and the (economic and political) command of capital, while still taking place within processes of production, has now come to exist outside of them, in the real movement of the social. Social cooperation not only anticipates the economic and political movements of capital but also pre-exists them and asserts itself as autonomous.

Let me stress that, when I conclude in these terms our discussion of Marx's pages on the law of the falling rate of profit, it is not my intention – despite the pessimism with which others have addressed this law – to read major consequences into it. Nor do I want, as validation of my argument, to rehearse the literary exercise (which I practised on other occasions) of citing from the *Grundrisse* references to 'the social individual who appears as the great foundation stone of production and of wealth' and to 'this fixed capital that is man himself' (Marx, *Grundrisse*: The Chapter on Capital, Notebook VII) – although it is depressing that all too often they are regarded as 'delusional' rather than highly utopian ... Here my concern is merely to point out that (as the critique suggests to us) capitalist development has reached a level of extreme fragility, a disproportion of the components that constitute capital that will be difficult to restore to measure – and that, consequently, capital renews its search for a material foundation for a new period of exploitation. But

from the fact that capital posits every such limit as a barrier and hence gets *ideally* beyond it, it does not by any means follow that it has *really* overcome it, and, since every such barrier contradicts its character, its production moves through contradictions that are constantly overcome but just as constantly posited. And there is more. The universality towards which capital irresistibly strives encounters limitations in its own nature, which, at a certain stage of its development, will reveal it to be itself the greatest barrier to this tendency, and hence will drive towards its own suspension. (Marx, 1973, p. 410)

Why should we not use the Marxian critique as we seek a new point of support for the communist revolution?

3

The third reason for taking Marx as a reference point is that, through *theory* – which for us is also the development of the principles and examples that we draw from *Capital* – we can better build a bridge between the present and the future. Here again I offer an example, just as I did above – this time taken from Book 2 of *Capital*, where, through the analysis of the circulation of goods and of the socialisation of labour exploitation, we see hints of antagonistic upshoots in the construction of the 'common'.

If we assume that social labour has been subsumed to capital not only 'formally' (that is, in the concatenation of structures that maintain themselves in their individual specificity) but also 'really' (that is, in cooperation with a multitude of singular structures, henceforth unable to reproduce themselves separately), in short, if we assume that society has been subsumed to capital 'in real terms' – which means completely, and in a manner that modifies not only its external shape but also the forms of production and reproduction of society itself – it follows that we cannot consider these transformations (as often happens) only in terms of the 'fetishistic' and 'irrational'. (Admittedly, Marx himself sometimes takes the fetishistic point of view to extremes. For example:

> Thus we get the fetish form of capital and the concept of fetish capital. In M–M′ we have the meaningless form of capital, the perversion and objectification on production relations in their highest degree [...] As interest-bearing capital [...], capital assumes its pure fetish form, M–M′ being the subject, the saleable thing [...] It is the primary and general formula of capital reduced to a meaningless condensation. (Marx, 1972, p. 392 = *Capital*, Book 3, Section V, ch. 24)

But we would say that the character of 'fetish' is better constructed by Marx in Book 3 of *Capital* than in Book 1. We must therefore consider the subsumption of society to capital in real terms – that is, we must address the operation of the capital at the social level, and on that terrain we have to identify the forms of production of value, of extraction of surplus value, and thus the modes and articulations of labour power against capital.

This is why Marx returns to theories of the economic cycle – and in particular to the study of Quesnay's *Tableau économique* – to highlight (as appears very obviously in the cyclical formulae) the social character of the process of capitalist production. In the formula of individual and collective social consumption, Marx notes that, when we find ourselves in real subsumption, 'the transformation is not the result of a merely formal change of position pertaining to the circulation process, but of a real transformation experienced by the use form and value of the commodity constituents of the productive capital in the process of production' (Marx, 1997, p. 100 = *Capital*, Volume 2, Section I, ch. 3).

Here Marx repeatedly makes this same point, stressing that the constitution of global social capital represents a real and actual 'revolution of values' and that the result of this movement has an effect on the constituent parts of the value of the social product – in terms of both exchange and use. 'The movement of industrial capital is this abstraction *in actu*' (Marx, 1981, p. 185 = *Capital*, Volume 2, Section I, ch. 4) – where by 'abstraction' is meant capital's ability to recompose each revolution of value, every violent transformation, every attempt to become independent of a fraction of capital. This step is so essential in the analysis of capital (in other words in relating circulation and production to the matrix of value creation) that Marx says: once you get to this point, once you assume the complexity of capital, 'that requires a different method of investigation' (ibid.).

What is this other way of inquiry? It involves considering the categories of analysis no longer genetically, but as functions of antagonism, in the totality of society. It is only at this point that theory becomes a weapon in the class struggle. A similar approach had already been developed (as I mentioned above) in Book 1 of *Capital*. Now the method is deepened. It follows immediately from this that social capital should no longer be regarded as the result of a process of 'competition' that determines it. It is as if the laws that govern it were a consequence of the war that the small industrialists conduct against each other – no, really, the laws that guide global social capital are only those that are born from the antagonism, from the class struggle. The passage from formal subsumption to the real subsumption of society to the collective capitalist thus creates, as a first and fundamental consequence, a situation in which capitalist 'despotism' over the working class in the factory is extended to society as a whole, eliminating the 'anarchy' that initially seemed to be hegemonic in the play of the market. This anarchy produces *faux frais* ['incidental operating costs'] of production, which – along with all the complementary phenomena and utilities ('externalities') in general – have to be turned into 'positives' or otherwise eliminated, in order to configure the fullness of the social potentiality [*potenza*] of capital.

It is on this new basis that Marx takes from Quesnay the schemata of reproduction – a numerical version of those in the *Tableau Économique* (*Capital*, Book 2, Section III, chs 20–1). These schemata serve to balance (in the capitalist system) a first sector that produces 'means of production' with a second sector that produces 'consumer goods'. In order for the system to function smoothly, it is clear not only that total demand must equal total supply, but also that the demand for products for an entire section must equal the overall production of the same section. This is the case of 'simple reproduction', that is, of a state of affairs in which everything remains unchanging from year to year: if the constant capital consumed in both sections is equal to the production of the first section, and if the total income of workers and capitalists of the two sections (which must be entirely consumed for the conditions to remain unchanged) is equal to the production of the second section.

But when, in 'expanded reproduction' – where capitalists do not consume all their income but reinvest a part of it – all the proportions change, it seems harder to find that equilibrium. Indeed it is very difficult to secure, even if the capitalists continually try to restore it with new investment and new consumptions. In the history of the interpretations of Marxism, this step (expanded reproduction) has become a significant problem – because, from Rosa Luxemburg onwards, this Marxian formulation was not accepted as obvious. Indeed it seemed contradictory with the antagonism that, in Marx, was the heart of the categories of critique. So there were several attempts at historicising and giving new shape to these disproportions and imbalances. Luxemburg, in particular, showed how equilibrium would have been unachievable if, in the face of the consolidation of movements and struggles of social labour power, capital had not acquired for itself (in colonial exploitation) new sources of exploitation in order to rebalance the cycle.

Similarly, we note that, in expanded reproduction, there is a confrontation in new forms between two phenomena that we have already considered when we studied the law of the falling rate of profit – that is, on the one hand the growth in the size of the value of constant capital, and thus the massification of the organic composition of capital; and, on the other, the relative autonomy of the variable part from the constant part of capital, brought about by the increase in the productive capacity [*potenza*] of labour power. A fundamental consequence derives from this: expanded reproduction, the more capital massifies its composition, is increasingly afflicted by crisis. But this crisis takes place within a new figure of capital: now socialised, it has integrated production and circulation and has created a global dimension for its development. However, it has not succeeded in rebalancing the relations between the reproduction section of the means of production and the consumer goods section, between development and the overall wage; rather it has seen them going in opposite directions, where constant capital and variable capital are no longer able to find a stable state of coexistence. Here we see the final effect of the crisis of the classical theory of labour value: this does not mean that value is something that has its foundation outside of the exploitation of labour power, but that the dimensions, measurements and qualities of this labour power have radically changed and that, along with the form, in Marxist terms, the material also changes.

Why, at the start of this section, did we refer to the opening of a new theoretical space? Because in this crisis and in the deepening of the antagonisms, within the new concatenations of labour and against the capitalist exploitation of social cooperation, it might perhaps be possible to build *a new theory of labour value as a common potentiality* [potenza]. We know that nowadays we have a formidable increase in the use value of labour power, but on the other hand we also have the extreme violence of social capital, which tends to close it within exchange value, within the societal reorganisation of command for exploitation, in order to eliminate the resistance and autonomy of labour. But there is something of the 'common' that, within the social capitalisation of value creation, reacts strongly against being caged and attempts to express itself.

Great changes have come about in more recent capitalist developments. The first point to emphasise is that finance has now become a central element in the process of production. The traditional distinction between the management of money on the one hand and a 'real' production level on the other hand is no longer tenable, not only politically, but above all in practical terms, from a point of view internal to the processes of economics in general. Today capitalism maintains itself on rent. Big industry, rather than reinvesting profit, focuses on rent. And the circuit, the lifeblood of capital, is now called rent, and this rent plays a key role in the circulation of capital and in the maintenance of the capitalist system: I mean in the maintenance of social hierarchy and capital's unity of command.

Money also becomes the only measure of social production. So now we have an ontological definition of money as form, lifeblood, internal circulation, in which is consolidated the value constructed socially in the whole economic system. And here is where you have the total subordination of society to capital. Labour power, and thus the activity of society, is subsumed to this money that is measure and at the same time control and command. The political class itself is completely inside the process, and the forms of politics dance on this rope.

If this is the situation, it becomes logical and essential that the rupture – every rupture – should take place within this framework. We must – and I say this provocatively, but not too much so – imagine what it means today to make a soviet, in other words to take the struggle, the strength, the multitude, the common into this new reality and into the new totalitarian organisations of money and finance. The multitude is not simply exploited: it is socially exploited, exactly as workers once were in the factory. *Mutatis mutandis*, what is proposed here, at the social level (and in money), is the validity of the struggle on wages. Capital is always a relationship (between those who command and those who work), and it is within this relationship that the subsumption of labour power to money is established. But, precisely if the capital relation holds firm, the break is determined right there.

These starting positions can be used in interpreting today's crisis. The crisis is given as the need to maintain order by multiplying money (the subprime mortgages, and the whole scary mechanism that arose from them, served to pacify the workers, in order to pay for social reproduction from the point of view of a capital and a banking system that dominated this world). So we have to get our hands on *this thing* in order to destroy its capacity for command. There can be no equivocation on this point. Against any conception that tries to explain the crisis by referring to the split between finance and real production, let us hold on to the view that financialisation is not an unproductive and parasitic deviation of increasing amounts of surplus value and collective savings. It is not a deviation, in fact it is the form of accumulation of capital within the new processes of social and cognitive production of value. Financial crisis today should therefore be interpreted as a blockage of capital accumulation (by the proletariat) and as an implosive outcome consequent upon the failed accumulation of capital.

How does one extricate oneself from a crisis of this kind? Only through a social revolution. Today, in fact, a feasible New Deal can only consist of the creation of new rights of social ownership of common goods: a right that clearly opposes the right of private property. In other words, if up until now access to a 'common good' has taken the form of 'private debt', from now on it is legitimate to claim the same right in the form of 'social rent'. Ensuring the recognition of these common rights is the only right way out of the crisis. One last joke on this subject: there will be some (Rancière, Žižek, and Badiou have already said as much) who see these 'reforms' as completely useless, indeed as damaging for workers – well, why not try them? Why don't we suggest them to Wall Street?

Yet there is no worse illusion than that reappropriating the 'common' and putting it under democratic management is all it takes to build communism. In fact, in capitalist social accumulation there is a form to which there necessarily corresponds a homologous substance. So that capitalist common, that 'communism of capital', has to be destroyed. This destruction is the narrow gateway of any communist constituent process. A new theory of labour value should at any rate be rebuilt as of now, by excavating into the capitalist 'common' in order to critique its development and overturn its tendency – in the same way in which the Marxian labour theory of value served to show labour power as a potentiality [*potenza*] and to set the destruction of exploitation and profit as an objective of struggle, beyond surplus labour.

These four notes (and these three examples) are simply to say why Marx should still be a companion for those who have committed themselves to finding ways to organise resistance against capitalist exploitation, to build an ever growing autonomy of workers (in the cognitive cooperation of post-Fordist labour), and to enjoy, within and against capitalist socialisation, forms of common life. 'Why Marx?' What this question raises is the need for militant dialogue. These notes indicate avenues to be explored in the coming years.

2
Reflections on the Use of Dialectics

1 The dialectics of antagonism

Those of us who came out of the discussions on the dialectics developed in the so-called 'western Marxism' of the 1930s and 1950s–1960s will remember how in those days we exercised ourselves simultaneously with Lukács' *History and Class Consciousness* and the work of the Frankfurt School. In a strange hybridisation, what was produced in those days was a series of phenomenological descriptions and normative hypotheses through which life, society and nature, equally affected by the productive power of capital, were radically stripped of their potential. Notions of alienation were spanning the entire theoretical field: in other words, the entire phenomenology of action and the historicity of existence were thought to have been completely absorbed in the capitalist plan of exploitation and in the capitalist production of power over life. Technology was demonised, the dialectic of *Aufklärung* was thus completed, and the subsumption of society to capital was definitive. For revolutionaries, the only option was to sit and wait for the event that would reopen history; for those who were not revolutionaries, the only choice was *Gelassenheit* – quiet adjustment to destiny.

Of course, faced with this (sometimes ineffectual) understanding of the subsumption of society to capital, there was resistance. In western Marxism this was the moment at which, in the face of that conclusion, a critical point of view began to express itself, and for the first time an ethical–political attitude began to emerge that was accompanied by a theoretical *dispositif* in forefronting the 'subversive particularity': in other words an attitude that, despite the massive extension of capitalist power over society, instituted the opening of a

new form of dialectics. To the dehumanising dialectics of the capitalist relation of exploitation another (ethical and subjectivated) dialectic
was opposed, which opened up the social context in its entirety to the
expression of new resistances. There was a virtual affirmation of the
principle of a new figure of subjectivity, or rather of the production of
subjectivity; a dialectic opened by the 'critique' directed against the
closed dialectic of the 'critical critique';* a point of view that broke
with the placid, or pained, acceptance of the totalitarian arrogance of
capital in the two forms that enacted it – the liberal (and fascist) and
the socialist (and Stalinist).

So it was that in France Merleau-Ponty broke with the Frankfurt
phenomenology; so it was that, on the margins of the British Empire,
there arose, in the overthrow of colonial historiography, what shortly
afterwards we were to call the postcolonial point of view; and so it
was that, overturning the injunction to consider technology solely as
a terrain of alienation, the hypothesis emerged of a subversive usage
of machines by the working class and, within that, the workerist currents in Italy, France and Germany. The dialectic was, so to speak,
interrupted. And it was in the space of this interruption, in the hypothesis of a crisis of capital's ability to infuse the totality of society, that
the reappearance of the revolutionary subject, or, better, of a free
subjectivity, proposed itself as production – or rather as *expression.*

Dialectics moved from abstraction to reality. Dialectical development was located on the historical curve of the enactment of capitalist
development.

There was a prehistory to all this: a brief prehistory, which would
be worth examining. It brings us back to the renewal of analysis that
had taken place – not so much of dialectics in general as of its use in
'real Marxism', in codified materialist dialectics. In looking at this
renewal and its consequent operational instances, let us examine the
definition of dialectics given by some of the major theorists of that
time – in the instance recorded here, by Lucio Colletti in his com-
mentary on Evald Vassilievich Ilyenkov:

> In its most general terms, the Marxist theory of dialectics can be stated
> as a theory simultaneously of the 'unity' and the 'exclusion' of oppo-
> sites, in other words as a theory that seeks to provide at the same time
> both the moment of *knowledge* (that is, the possibility that the terms of

---

* Translator's Note: This is a reference to Karl Marx, *The Holy Family or
Critique of Critical Criticism: Against Bruno Bauer and Company*, originally published in 1845; see Marx, 1975 [1845].

the opposition or contradiction might be com-prehended [com-presi]*)
and the moment of *reality* or objectivity of the contradiction itself. The
theory can thus be summarised by two fundamental requirements or
instances. The first is that the specificity or difference of one object
from all others proves com-prehensible [com-prensibile], that is, men-
tally relatable to that different thing that the object is not, or to all that
residue that differs from the object. The second is that this understanding does not abolish the 'difference', that knowledge does not exhaust
reality in itself, in other words that the co-presence or resolution of
opposites in reason should not be taken for the resolution and abolition
of their opposition in reality. (Colletti, 1960, p. vii)

But this does not suffice. In the third chapter, entitled 'The
Transition from the Abstract to the Concrete', Ilyenkov concludes:

Science must begin with that with which real history began. Logical
development of theoretical definitions must therefore express the
concrete historical process of the emergence and development of the
object. Logical deduction is nothing but a theoretical expression of the
real historical development of the concreteness under study. (Ilyenkov,
1982, p. 200)

But this is still not sufficient. Marx's *Capital* is directly drawn into
the exposition:

The mode of ascent from the abstract to the concrete permits to establish strictly and to express abstractedly only the absolutely necessary
conditions of the possibility of the object given in contemplation.
Capital shows in detail the necessity with which surplus-value is realised,
given developed commodity-money circulation and free labour-power.
(Ibid., p. 283)

In 1960, the year in which Ilyenkov was translated into Italian,
another book was also translated: Michaud's *Theory and History
in Marx's* Capital. Its basic propositions coincided with Ilyenkov's
ideas, sometimes reinforcing them:

---

* Translator's Note: In the sense of 'taken together and understood'. The spell-
ing *com-presi*, used in Italian here, emphasises the etymology of *comprendere* ('to
understand') from Latin *comprehendere* – a compound of *prehendere* (to grasp)
with the prefix *cum* (with), which indicates togetherness. Thus the hyphenated
form *com-prendere* transmits in a flash the author's idea that 'to understand'
means 'to grasp together'. The English verb 'to understand' cannot render this
play on words.

Dialectics on its own is nothing; it makes possible the study of a movement but does not endanger this movement in any way; it would not
be able, by itself, to constitute the whole method, at least not in Marx
... It does not seem that dialectics alone gives the possibility of arriving
at any kind of reconciliation between theory and history. (Michaud,
1960, p. 140)

Immediately afterwards the thesis is restated:

Political economy becomes science only at the time of Marx, because
only the universality of capitalist production is able to *realise* those
abstract categories that allow us to understand not only capitalistic production itself, but also all the historical systems that preceded it ... The
characteristic of capitalism is to *realise* the abstraction of all economic
categories. (Ibid., p. 189)

And this problem is then developed in terms of extreme actuality (we
shall return to this below, when we address the current global crisis):

The theory of value, if it is separated from that of surplus value (which
is unthinkable for capitalism), presents itself as an abstract dialectics
that expresses the conditions of existence of every more or less developed society in order to enter into contact with others: it is not bound
to any particular historical form of society,

– but 'the value form in its most generic expression is precisely the
specific form that is assumed, at a given moment, by the capitalist
mode of production' (ibid., p. 197).

This kind of language is almost incomprehensible today. But with a
bit of attention you can see what is in play here: nothing less than the
recovery of contact with reality, the dissolution of the obstacle that a
fossilised materialist dialectics represented for the reading and transformation of reality. So the great effort here is the attempt to direct
abstract categories back to the determination of the concrete, to bend
the universal to the determinations of historical development. It is a
philosophical journey that proceeds alongside the 'de-Stalinisation' of
that period. The key categories of Marxist analysis (abstract labour,
value, money, rent, profit, etc.) are thus shifted with some force
from the theoretical context of nineteenth-century materialism – in
which they were formulated – towards a substantially new practice of
research. Henceforth abstraction will be justified only as 'determined
abstraction'. Determined by what? By the fact that it was periodi-
cally subjected not only to the analysis of the generic contradictions
that traverse each category, but also to the analysis of the concrete,

scientific and practical determinations of political action. From this point of view there is no doubt that the last phase of Marxist theoretical discourse (in the Russia of de-Stalinisation, but also in the West, both inside and outside communist parties) led the analysis of capitalist development further than what the Frankfurt School, or the ongoing legacy of Lukácsism, were capable of producing.

In 1968, however, the clash between these tendencies became unavoidable. Instead of finding a common ground in the context of that revolutionary occasion, the theoretical horizon separated definitively; on the one hand, the defeat of the movements was followed by the absolutisation of the dialectics of real subsumption, of alienation, of the unilateralism of capitalist domination, and the utopia of the explosion of the 'event', from Debord to the final results of Althusserianism in Badiou; on the other hand, that battle over difference, resistance and subjectivation opened issues that, although they transformed and pushed forward a deeper theoretical understanding of the development of capitalism and of the mechanisms of political resistance, did not succeed in recomposing and developing a communist perspective. In the attempt to move forward on this terrain, however, we placed ourselves on this last frontier of materialism. It seems that here a dialectics of antagonism might somehow be refounded.

2 Materialism as biopolitics

Thus, in the phase to which we have referred, dialectics opened up. While on the one hand it relied on a horizon on which the revolutionary event is an *Aufhebung* [sublation], on the other hand it rejected any out of the ordinary or mystical aura and presented itself as a *constituent experience*. To what extent can you still define as 'dialectics' that method that was making abstraction increasingly concrete (singular, in fact); and the antagonism of productive forces and relations of production, now non-resolvable in thought and insuperable in history; and the (aleatory) historical tendency, and truth, definitively entrusted to practice; and, finally, the effectiveness of the production of subjectivity, now become increasingly virtual? This is a question that is difficult to answer.

This is all the more difficult when one considers that the categorial abstraction, fixing itself now in the new figures of historical determination, proposed to method (in this latter phase, on the verge of the experience of a momentous transformation of capitalist development) a number of concepts that translated the phenomenology of capitalist development within figures and *dispositifs* that were entirely new. For example, the sequence 'abstract labour–value–money–...' found itself contracted into a figure of a financial capital that was entirely new; the process of real subsumption – namely the shift from production of goods to control over the life that was embodied in labour, the construction of the welfare state on the one hand and the institutional solidity of 'real socialism' on the other – presented capital as *biopower*; finally, the transformation of the law of value – I mean, when the temporal measure of labour was replaced by the power of cooperation and the mechanisms of circulation of productive services and of communication as agents of capitalist value creation – gave rise to a kind of 'communism of capital'.

Now, the analysis follows the transformations of living labour: it seems, however, that, in the face of social antagonism, the categories of power it has to address no longer have that dialectical flexibility that the old materialism had given them. The compactness of the categories of biopower seems to exclude any rupture. At this point, in this case, dialectics (that old dialectics in relation to which the resistances we have described had developed) seems to be rather reduced to an *apology for capital*. So what is left of dialectics now? Is the internal reform I described above sufficient (I mean, the insistence on the determined nature of the abstraction, the adoption of a specific point of view against the real subsumption of society to capital, etc.) – is that internal reform, that shift in emphasis sufficient to reconstruct dialectics as an effective method of research? Probably not. Because, while assuredly dialectics was no longer able to present itself as a 'method of exposition', this was not only because it had entered into crisis as a 'method of research', but because *the very ontology of materialism* had changed. Materialism today means the biopolitical context.

What was needed was no longer simply to pursue the passage from abstraction to determination, but to move within the space of determination. This is what happens especially when the law of labour value is thrown into crisis. The law of value functioned as a definition of the measure of exploitation, in other words of the capitalist appropriation of surplus labour. But now, by developing around the new relationship between production and reproduction the analysis of the changes that the exploitation of labour had undergone – in short, by penetrating the complex that capital had formed as it gradually closed the laws of dialectics on itself, imposed the copresence of opposites, realised successive *Aufhebungen* – we begin to understand how, in this context (which repeats in savage style the modes of primitive accumulation), a capacity [*potenza*] for exploitation is realised that is no longer about the expropriation of single labour (even when massified) but about *the expropriation of the common*.

The discovery of the common as a basis from which one could redefine an eventual communist political proposition, has a fragmented but continuous trajectory – starting from the analyses that studied the capitalist reforms of accumulation after 1968. The progressive transition of capitalist command from the factory (the Fordist organisation of industry and Taylorist discipline over the working masses) to the exploitation of the whole of society (via hegemony over immaterial labour, organisation of cognitive labour, and financial control) determines – in cooperation, in language, and in common relations (found in the so-called 'social externalities') – the new basis on which exploitation operates.

If this is true, at this point the matter is no longer one of running after dialectics for its ability to reconstruct the unity of development, whatever its contents might be. If the 'common' qualifies living labour as the basic tendency of its self-presentation on the stage of production, then antagonism itself will become a basis and an insuperable tendency – hence as a radical weakening of every dialectics of the 'co-presence of opposites', or perhaps, much more probably, as the impossibility of any 'universal' resolution of opposites. I mean, capital no longer has the possibility of internal reform and is now confronted with new types of class struggle. In fact, in the new conditions of accumulation, the common stands against any universal appropriation, any dialectical mediation, any definitive institutional inclusion. *Crisis* is everywhere. Antagonism is no longer a method but a given: *what was one has actually divided into two*.

Let us look at one example, in an attempt to interpret the *current global economic crisis*. Many readings of it have been proposed. Whether these readings came from the right or from the left, in all cases they assigned the causes of the crisis to the split between finance and so-called 'real' production. If we accept the new conditions that we have discussed above, which start from an understanding of the crisis of the theory of labour value and from the emergence of a new 'common' quality of living labour, then we can see that the financialisation of the global economy is not an unproductive or parasitic deviation of growing quantities of surplus value and of collective savings, but the new form of capital accumulation, symmetrical with the new processes of social and cognitive production of value. Today's financial crisis should therefore be interpreted as a 'blockage' of capital accumulation rather than as an implosive outcome of failed accumulation of capital.

How can we exit the crisis? This is the issue around which, again, the new science affirms itself as no longer 'dialectical' but simply as antagonistic. We can only come out of the economic crisis through a social revolution. Today, in fact, any proposition of a New Deal has to consist of building new rights of social ownership of common property, rights that are obviously in opposition to the right to private property. In other words, if until now access to a common good has taken the form of 'private debt' (and it has been precisely over the accumulation of this debt that the crisis has exploded), from today onwards it is legitimate to claim the same right in the form of 'social rent'. Forcing a recognition of these common rights is both the only way and the right way to exit the crisis.

3 From representation to expression

Let us now return to the statement that 'what was one has actually divided into two'. We have already seen the consequences we can derive from it when we interpret the current crisis. But let us try to take a closer look at things.

If we approach the explanation of 'one divided into two' from an inductive, genealogical point of view, we could note first of all that this opening of the dialectical relationship of capital is primarily due to the biopolitical excedence of living labour, when living labour expresses itself in the figures of cognitive and immaterial productivity. In this case, the closure of the relationship between constant capital and variable capital turns out to be non-operable from the capitalist point of view. Cognitive labour, and in general any immaterial labour (communicative, tertiary, affective, etc.) that is performed in the biopolitical sphere, cannot be completely consumed in the processes of capitalist exploitation: in relation to exploitation it accumulates not only value-creating residues (of constant capital) but also alternatives of expression, of development – in short, *dispositifs* of exodus. It is here that we find revealed the characteristics of the new era of capitalist production as an era of *crisis*, as an era of *transition* outside the continuity of capitalist development.

Characteristic of this exit from capitalist development are not only the difficulties that the dialectical *dispositifs* (now definitively entrusted to capital) encounter in closing the production processes; there are also those encountered by the cyclical movements of capitalist development in repeating themselves, in nurturing one another between phases of development and phases of recession, and in inserting into this passage moments of technological innovation and a new organisation of social relations. Thus we can add that all *homologies* between institutional structures and configurations of capitalist power on the one hand and, on the other, proletarian or multitudinarian movements, in their specific potentiality, are breaking down. And if certain (communist) philosophers believe that in spontaneity and in the free dynamics of movements there are no elements of substantial breaking with institutions and that therefore the (economic and political) cages of capitalist power remain, they are wrong (and also short-sighted in their thinking), because they do not understand that *all isomorphism of power and potentiality* [potenza], of control and resistance, has now collapsed. Not so much and not only because phenomenologically these relationships cannot be logically described, but because, even when they are, these relations are removed from the hegemony of the 'one' and are instead related to the alternative dynamics and to the exodus of the multitude.

It remains to be said that often the dynamics of the exodus of the multitude from capitalist command (and from its crisis-laden structures in real subsumption) are not recognised because of the illusion that proletarian movements can be purified and imagined 'outside' their real connections with historical process. As if the liberation, the rupture, the biopolitical transformations, albeit developing within society's subsumption to institutional and political biopowers, could arise as events uncontaminated by the materiality in which they are immersed. No, the break with capitalism, with command, with biopowers, happens 'inside' the world of exchange values, inside the world of commodities ... one cannot imagine an outside that is not built on the basis of this break. And, since thus far we have been talking about the 'common' as a place where value is constructed and that, precisely for this reason, is directly exploited by capital, we say that the only event, the only 'use value' that can be recovered within processes of liberation – construed as potentiality [*potenza*] opposed to power, as constituent power alternative to constituted power – is precisely that 'common' on the basis of which we move, on the basis of which people are both agents and product.

One last word. It is beyond doubt that the contamination between the determinations of resistance that have been produced in the thinking and political experience of Deleuze and Guattari and the historical meaning of the production of subjectivity that is readable especially in the last phase of Foucault's thought cannot be related to this new 'dialectics': it no longer has anything to do with so-called diamat ('materialist dialectics') but has everything to do with

biopolitical, cognitive and immaterial excedence and with a production that is internal to the biopolitical process of constitution of the
real. Allow me to recall what Deleuze replies to my question about
what it means to be materialists and communists (the piece can be
found in *Pourparler*): 'it means that communism is the production
of a people to come [*a venire*]'. That said, and having pointed out
how much we owe to the idea of 'to come', let us listen, within the
Deleuzian *dispositif*, to the same rhythm (we might call it dialectical) that is characteristic to Marx and Engels when they write the
Communist Manifesto or to Marx when, writing on the history of the
class struggle, he adopts that historicity that has its foundation in the
works of Machiavelli and Spinoza.

Recently there have been attempts to recover Hegel, especially
the young Hegel – from Jena to the *Phenomenology of the Spirit* and
to the 'Additions' in his *Rechtsphilosophie* [*Philosophy of Right*] (see
Axel Honneth on all this) – in order to rebuild a dialectics that is
open, arises from below, structures itself in terms of interactivity and
intersubjectivity, and still has the ability to configure a normative,
historically solid theory of justice. What we have here is a repetition of infinite attempts at recovering dialectics both as a research
method and as a form of exposition. But therein lies the difficulty:
dialectics cannot avoid constituting itself as 'representation' of the
whole process that leads to the affirmation of truth, when – as in the
current situation of crisis of capitalist development and of its cultural
and institutional forms – the word can only be related back to the
subjects' capacity for 'expression'. The common does not constitute
itself as representation but as expression. And here dialectics comes
to an end.

Let us not forget, however, that, if dialectics, as G. Lukács taught
us, is the theoretical weapon of capital for the development and
organisation of society, and if therefore its crisis opens to the expression of new theoretical needs in building a philosophy of the present,
these needs should still assume productive activity as the source of
all social configuration. Living labour and human activity on the
biopolitical terrain are at the basis of all subjectivation. The new
constitution of the common, no longer dialectical but materialist, is
articulated by subjective *dispositifs*, by the desire to escape from solitude and to realise multitudes.

3

Thoughts Regarding 'Critical Foresight' in the Unpublished Chapter VI of Marx's *Capital*, Volume 1

When you read Marx's unpublished Chapter VI having already studied Book 1 of *Capital*, you are struck by the theoretical power and the clarity of expression of some of the concepts that Marx was constructing more or less at the same time in Book 1, not in different terms but with another tonality. In what follows I would like to explore this theoretical power; I would additionally like to show that the relevance of the unpublished Chapter VI lies in the fact that some of those concepts become a source of significant later developments in Marxist political criticism and allow us to select a few theoretical *dispositifs*, or rather orient them towards a better understanding of capitalism today.* Indeed, Marx here often surpasses his own capacity for illustrating the perverse mechanisms of capitalist exploitation and, while he watches the tendency developing, he seems to locate

---

* Translator's Note: In order to offer a range of text comparability, for the unpublished Chapter VI we have included page references from three editions – Italian, German and English: Bruno Maffi's Italian translation (Marx, 1969a); its first German edition of 1933, which was accompanied by facing Russian translation (Marx, 1933); and Ben Fowkes' English translation in the Appendix to the Penguin edition of volume 1 of *Capital* (Marx, 1990). This triad of page references will follow the order Italian edition (I), German edition (G), and English edition (E). For the *Grundrisse*, apart from the English edition already used (Marx, 1973), quotations also come from the Penguin translation (Marx, 1993); for *Theories of Surplus Value*, they come from the English translation available in vol. 31 of the Lawrence & Wishart *MECW* edition (Marx, 1975), itself based on an earlier version (Marx, 1969b). Enzo Grillo's Italian translation of the former work (Marx, 1968–70) and G. Giorgetti's Italian translation of the latter (Marx, 1971) have also been consulted.

himself (in theoretical terms) in the 'to come' [*a-venire*] of class struggle against capital.

The chapters in which this 'critical foresight' is built are basically the ones that deal with the definition of absolute and relative surplus value (along with considerations regarding the development of technologies and machinery) and that therefore elaborate on the categories of 'formal' and 'real' subsumption'; the ones in which Marx constructs the concepts of 'productive labour' and 'unproductive labour' and stresses the position and function of science within capital's process of value creation; and, finally, the ones that touch on the concept and measurement of the productivity of capital and *perhaps* grasp, by digging into the social extension and density of capitalist exploitation, the image of a revolutionary subject that illuminates the contemporary horizon. My intention in what follows is not so much to deepen the analysis of these passages from the unpublished Chapter VI as to show how they help to extend the power of Marx's critique down to our time, into the era of postindustrial capitalism.

<h1 style="text-align:center">1</h1>

Here I am not interested in going over the definition of absolute and relative surplus value. Marx discusses this topic at length (pp. 3–58I : 454–73G : 966–1025E), then goes on to introduce the concepts of formal and real submission (or subsumption) of labour to capital (pp. 58–68I : 473–8G : 1025–34E). The definitions of the various forms of surplus value match those developed in Book I of *Capital*. Nor is it so important here (for the purpose of my research) to reiterate the criteria that distinguish formal submission from real submission. However, '[t]he real subsumption of labour under capital is developed in all the forms evolved by relative, as opposed to absolute surplus-value' (Marx, Unpublished Chapter VI, p. 69I : 478G : 1035E). Rather what we need to stress is that, for Marx, '[w]ith the real subsumption of labour under capital a complete (and constantly repeated) revolution takes place in the mode of production, in the productivity of the workers and in the relations between workers and capitalists' (ibid.). A *strong temporality* thus underpins the process – the time of a continuous revolution in which the 'organic composition' of capital changes in line with the movement of its components, machines and workers, science and use values. This temporal intensification is accompanied by a global extension of the capitalist mode of production:

> With the real subsumption of labour under capital, all the changes in
> the labour process already discussed now become reality. The *social
> forces of production* of labour are now developed, and with large-scale
> production comes the direct application of science and technology.
> On the one hand, *capitalist production* now establishes itself as a mode
> of production *sui generis* [of its own kind] and brings into being a new
> mode of material production. On the other hand, the latter itself forms
> the basis for the development of capitalist relations whose adequate
> form, therefore, presupposes a definite stage in the evolution of the
> productive forces of labour. (Marx, Unpublished Chapter VI, p. 691 :
> 478G : 1035E)

Under these conditions, subjected to this dynamic, capital strips
itself of any 'individuality'; it becomes *social capital*. But even more
important is the fact that the 'productive forces' immediately become
'social'. Mechanisation and technology ('determined', 'situated',
which renews itself precisely in real subsumption), far from being
only 'neutral' products of 'science', are on the contrary 'forces of
production' that, by invading reality, incorporate into their ambit not
only workers but also populations. Mechanisation takes possession of
life. Let us look at what machines are. Outside of realised capitalism,
Hegel teaches us, the instrument of labour is a means, a medium
to act on nature. Between man and nature is placed the tool, the
machine. But under capitalism a shift is created in the relationship:
the labour of the worker becomes a mediation between the machine
(the tool) and nature. The pervasiveness of technology in the world
of work becomes total. The instrument is no longer a use value for
the worker; the worker becomes use value for capital, for 'its' (capital's) machine (fixed capital).

> Once adopted into the production process of capital, the means of
> labour passes through different metamorphoses, whose culmination
> is the *machine,* or rather, an *automatic system of machinery* (system
> of machinery: the *automatic* one is merely its most complete, most
> adequate form, and alone transforms machinery into a system), set
> in motion by an automaton, a moving power that moves itself; this
> automaton consisting of numerous mechanical and intellectual organs,
> so that the workers themselves are cast merely as its conscious linkages.
> (Marx 1973, p. 692)

And again:

> In the machine, and even more in machinery as an automatic system,
> the use value, i.e. the material quality of the means of labour, is

transformed into an existence adequate to fixed capital and to capital as
such; and the form in which it was adopted into the production process
of capital, the direct means of labour. (Ibid., p. 692)

But, if this is the case, when this development is completed, two
social totalities come to overlap: the (constant) capital, which has
covered the whole of social reality, and the (variable) capital, which
is the source of valorisation of this social reality. These pages are
thus a powerful introduction to a 'biopolitical' description of the real
subsumption of labour to capital. To explain the premise: there is no
longer use value, there is no longer even nature – all social relations
(obviously those of production, but also those of reproduction and
circulation) are transposed onto the terrain of exploitation – in short,
life is subsumed to capital.
  In giving the above narrative of capitalist development from formal
subsumption to real subsumption, in addition to some of my older
writings – for example my texts collected in *I Libri del rogo* (Negri,
2005 [2006]) and in *Marx oltre Marx* (Negri, 1991 [1979]) – I have
borne in mind Claudio Napoleoni's (1972) fundamental commen-
tary on the unpublished Chapter VI; and I have done so because,
up to this point, Napoleoni's comments on Marx's pages are in
my view entirely correct. From what has been developed thus far,
Napoleoni draws a first and definitive conclusion, which is that in
Marx the subjugation of social labour to capital includes also the
machinery, the instrument of labour, both as a machine and as the
bodies of workers; from this he deduces, logically, that a machine not
used in a capitalist way should be *different* from one that is used in
a capitalist way and obviously that the bodies of the workers, which
compose themselves in a certain way in a certain form of capitalist
development, should compose themselves in a different way in a situation that is beyond capitalism; and this conclusion seems correct
too. However, this conclusion will be true only as long as one reads
Marx's deductions regarding real subsumption in a linear way. When
they are taken 'dialectically' (in other words, subjected to the historical determinations of the class struggle), it will no longer be possible
to consider the 'reification' of value in machinery or the 'alienation'
of the worker as closed worlds (this reversal constitutes the essential
breakthrough of the 'workerist' reading of *Capital*). Capital is, rather,
always a relationship of power, and machinery itself (subsumed to
social capital) is itself a relationship. This relationship cannot be
defined deterministically. It is struggle and conflict, it is a historical
assemblage – and hence open-ended – of victories and defeats: this is

where politics lives; and the changes, the effects of the struggle, the (workers' bodies') being 'within or beyond' the structures of exploitation, and the measures of this 'within or beyond' are variables, dynamics, ontologically defined with the passing of time. Machines run wherever there is struggle, as Marx himself said, and so do values, too: machines return to being a working class 'use value' in the struggle – a use value that the subsumption of labour under capital (the socialisation of labour, the scientific characteristics of its organisation) extends to the social struggle against capital. Here is defined conclusively the antagonistic relationship that constitutes the reality of capital – by removing all determinism, and also all idealistic or apocalyptic deviations, from the capitalist process that leads to real subsumption and to the 'reification' of social relations. The subsumption of society to capital *tendentially* represents, rather, a *biopolitical* terrain for emancipatory struggles.

NB. When I say *tendentially* I am not assuming a deterministic horizon; I move in the conflictual context of class struggles. On this terrain, after having registered the 'tendency' *ex post*, we have to verify the opening up of *dispositifs ex ante*. Therefore here biopolitical fabric (and/or potential [*potenza*]) and machines of *biopower* mean ontological openings of biopolitical *dispositifs*, desires, programmes, institutional machines – or else ontological accumulation of tendencies and structures of power over life. This is the field of class struggle in our present era – in other words in conditions of real subsumption of society to capital, which is now complete. Michel Foucault (in his late writings) and Judith Revel have worked especially on these issues.

2

This brings us to another important point that Marx writes about in the unpublished Chapter VI: the definition of productive and unproductive labour (pp. 73–92I : 480–90G : 1038–49E). Here again we shall read these pages in order to advance our understanding of our present time. Now, on the question of what is 'productive labour', Marx replies as follows: it is the labour that produces surplus value – in other words it is activity that valorises capital.

> Since the immediate purpose and the *authentic product* of capitalist production is *surplus-value, labour is only productive* and an exponent of labour-power is only a *productive worker* if it or he creates *surplus-value*

directly, i.e. the only productive labour is that which is directly *consumed* in the course of production for the valorisation of capital. (Marx, Unpublished Chapter VI, p. 73I : 480G : 1038E)

This view is heavily and polemically reiterated in those same pages:

> It is only bourgeois obtuseness that encourages the view that capitalist production is production in its absolute form, the unique form of production as prescribed by nature. And only the bourgeoisie can confuse the questions: what is productive labour? and what is a productive worker from the standpoint of capitalism? with the question: what is *productive* labour as such? And they alone could rest content with the tautological answer that all labour is productive if it produces, if it results in a product or some other use-value or in anything at all. [...] The only productive worker is one whose labour = the *productive consumption* of labour-power – of the bearer of that labour – on the part of capital or the capitalist. (Marx, Unpublished Chapter VI, p. 74I : 480G : 1039E)

These definitions seem to be in contradiction with my premise (developed in section 1 above) that productive labour and social labour are coextensive, both being subsumed to capital: this, in my view, is the essence of the tendentially biopolitical dimension of exploitation. I say 'seem to be' because I do not think that I am in contradiction with Marx on this terrain. Indeed it is obvious that I stand by the viewpoint of the critique of value: in principle, I do not consider *any* labour that produces 'utility' to be 'productive' – as do for instance Say, Bastiat and other economists, who understand 'utility' as any kind of service provided; in that case, paradoxically, every social activity should be considered as productive. But that is not true! However, around this question we must also immediately signal a shift in the verification of the theory of labour value. When the capitalist wants value, he wants it in the form of *surplus value* – to the point that, as we shall see later, *there is* indeed *no theory of value that is not* (as deduced from the definition) *a theory of surplus value* (in other words, deduced from resistance, or rather from the working-class struggle against surplus value). We can refer to Marx, to his draft *Theories of Surplus Value*, for clarification on this issue. But, to pick up the thread of my argument, how do we react to the fact that, with the real subsumption of work and society under capital, the labour process becomes, in its entirety, a process of valorisation? When Marx says that 'capital is productive' because it has invaded society and subjected it to the processes of production of surplus value, can the term 'productive labour' any longer have meaning, except insofar as all social activity is productive (which contradicts the previous reading of the concept of productive labour)? There is evidently a problem here.

Let us remove a misunderstanding straightaway. Occasionally in his writings Marx wonders whether labours such as those of priests, civil servants, soldiers, judges, lawyers and so on are 'productive'. He concludes that, rather than productive, they are 'in essence destructive', because these people – who

> know how to appropriate to themselves a very great part of the 'material' wealth partly through the sale of their 'immaterial' commodities and partly by forcibly imposing the latter on other people – found it not at all pleasant to be relegated economically to the same class as clowns and menial servants and to appear merely as people partaking in the consumption, parasites on the actual producers (or rather agents of production). This was a peculiar profanation precisely of those functions which had hitherto been surrounded with a halo and had enjoyed superstitious veneration. Political economy in its classical period, like the bourgeoisie itself in its *parvenu* period, adopted a severely critical attitude to the machinery of the State, etc. At a later stage it realised and – as was shown too in practice – learnt from experience that the necessity for the inherited social combination of all these classes, which in part were totally unproductive, arose from its own organisation. (Marx, 1975, p. 30)

There is no need to point out the historical acumen of these observations, which, while confirming the criteria of the 'long term', ridicule the 'eternal laws of tradition' vaunted by Tocqueville, the 'sycophant' of bourgeois power! The fact remains that today some of those infamous functions are turning out to be productive – albeit 'immaterial' and 'cognitive' – and are no longer exchanged for annuity, but for waged income. We continue to detest these 'ideological state apparatuses' and to consider them 'parasitic' – however, this is not the main point. Here what is new is the fact that real subsumption has gone far deeper than Marx himself could have imagined and that therefore we, too, must move forward in our analysis – maintaining our distaste for those bureaucrats and servants of ideologies and of the state who, even when they are rendered productive, nevertheless remain the dregs of society.

Let us readdress the problem: Marx does not leave us unarmed. We note how, after having restricted the concept of 'productive labour' so much, he then goes on to expand it. Since with the development of the *real subsumption of labour under capital* or the *specifically capitalist mode of production*, the *real lever* of the overall labour process is increasingly not the individual worker. Instead, *labour-power socially combined* and the various competing labour-powers which together form the entire production machine participate in very different ways in the immediate process of making commodities, or, more accurately in this context, creating the product. Some work better with their hands, others with their heads, one as a manager, engineer, technologist, etc., the other as overseer, the third as manual labourer or even drudge. And an ever increasing number of types of labour are included in the immediate concept of *productive labour*, and those who perform it are classed as *productive workers*, workers directly exploited by capital and *subordinated* to its process of production and expansion. If we consider the aggregate *worker*, i.e. if we take all the members comprising the workshop together, then we see that their *combined activity* results materially in an *aggregate* product which is at the same time a *quantity of goods*. And here it is quite immaterial whether the job of a particular worker, who is merely a limb of this aggregate worker, is at a greater or smaller distance from the actual manual labour. But then: the activity of this aggregate labour-power is its *immediate productive consumption by capital*, i.e. it is the self-valorization process of capital, and hence, as we shall demonstrate, the immediate production of surplus-value, the *immediate conversion of this latter into capital*. (Marx, Unpublished Chapter VI, p. 74I : 480G : 1039–40E)

Furthermore, with the development of the capitalist mode of production,

> the *objective conditions of labour* take on a different form owing to the scale on which, and the economy with which, they are employed (quite apart from the form of the machinery itself). As they develop they become increasingly concentrated; they represent *social* wealth and, to put the matter in a nutshell, their scope and their effect is that of the *conditions of production* of labour *socially* combined. (Ibid, p. 88I : 489G : 1052E)

Finally:

> *Science*, which is in fact the general intellectual product of the social process, also appears to be the direct offshoot of capital (since its application to the material process of production takes place in isolation from the knowledge and abilities of the individual worker). And since society is marked by the exploitation of labour by capital, its development appears to be the productive force of capital as opposed to labour. It therefore appears to be the *development of capital*, and all the more so

since, for the great majority, it is a process with which the *drawing-off of labour-power* keeps pace. (Ibid, p. 89I : 489G : 1053E)

And we could continue to flood our text with quotations from Marx.

But we are interested in a particular problem: What does it mean that the social labour process has, in real subsumption, transformed itself into the social process of valorisation, and vice versa? What does it mean that the social forces of production have been absorbed by capital and have become a 'force of production' of capital? It means two things. The first is this. When we consider the productive nature of labour, we are moving increasingly in the same *biopolitical* dimension to which the analysis of the process of real subsumption had brought us. These 'forces' that work productively in the labour process, within the 'socially combined' reality of the production machine – or rather of 'the collective factory' – are not 'individual' but 'social' forces.

But, in addition to this point (which we already began to see in section 1 above), this collective factory, which is both the precondition and the result of the productivity of workers in their conglomerations, is (and this is my second point) traversed and reorganised by science; and science too is incorporated in capital, but this indicates an ever more 'abstract' development of the potentialities of labour. About ten years before, in the *Grundrisse*, which was written between 1857 and 1858, Marx had even more acutely (and in almost idealistic terms) interpreted this scientific passage in the development of capital, placing general intellect as a final index of the process of real subsumption of society under capital and elucidating its potentiality as the revolutionary heir of the proletariat. (It was thus an *Aufhebung* [sublation] that was based on the assertion of the absorption of life into capital and therefore on the negation–inversion of that subordination – *Aufhebung* therefore as a solution to the crisis of the process of machinic socialisation and its transformation into a hegemony of cognitive capital – in this way the labour process and the valorisation process are conjugated together, in an innovative way.) To summarise our argument: in reading the unpublished Chapter VI, the second consideration that can help us advance a powerful Marxian 'insightful analysis' of the present is thus this grafting of science and cognitive labour onto the roof of the capitalist edifice built through the real subsumption of society. Today we would say: moving from the 'setting to work' of the whole of society through the exploitation of labour cooperation and of cognitive valorization to the creation of a new revolutionary subject.

NB. When we speak of 'productive labour' in real subsumption, we speak, in accordance with the development envisioned by Marx, of labour done by bodies of factory workers and labourers (manual workers) and workers of the mind cooperating socially, and we have to stress the transformation ('monstrous' and happy) that these bodies carry onto the new biopolitical terrain of class struggle. Naturally what is in play here is an antagonism between biopower and biopolitics; so out with all continuistic, determinist, eurodemoniac illusions! These bodies are 'monstrous' – but in fact what is 'monstrous' is the desire for the common in freedom and equality. (On this issue of 'monstrous' bodies, see the writings of Félix Guattari, Christian Marazzi and Matteo Pasquinelli.)

3

But if this is so, if the capitalist fabric – *tendendentially* biopolitical and cognitive in Marx's thinking, and *effectively* so in actuality – if, in short, within the fabric of capitalism the labour process has become completely one with that of valorisation, where does that leave exploitation? Or rather, how do we now identify those who exploit and those who are exploited?

There is no doubt that in some ways Marx leaves this question unanswered in the unpublished Chapter VI. Objectified labour, through the historical process of real subsumption, extends so broadly and assumes such a strong autonomy that the insurgence of subjectivity, of living labour, becomes increasingly difficult to recognise. Dead labour becomes a social body, an increasingly huge organic container of (and capacity to contain) living labour. To read certain pages of the unpublished Chapter VI, it almost seems that, once the 'social combination' of the productive forces has been achieved, the capitalist world succeeds in blocking the historical development of the class struggle. But this condition is only 'apparent'. (One should of course pay special attention to the specifically 'dialectical' value in Marx's words. 'Apparent' does not mean shadowy, superficial or insubstantial; it qualifies the material concreteness, ontological albeit mystified, of global capitalist power in the exploitation of labour power, and at the same time its ability to hide the potentiality of this power and its effects.) This condition is therefore apparent. Why? Marx would probably not even think of asking the question – the whole dialectical premise of his method reduces the question to banality. Not for us. But why? Because the relationship of exploitation is intrinsic and

intransitive – not external, not transitive vis-à-vis the labour relationship and the productivity of capital. To put it better: the alienation
of the conditions of labour, in the real subsumption of the society of
capital, continues and increases as capitalist development advances.
In the *Grundrisse* Marx notes:

> the fact that in the development of the productive powers of labour the
> objective conditions of labour, objectified labour, must grow relative
> to living labour [...] this fact appears from the standpoint of capital
> not in such a way that one of the moments of social activity – objective
> labour – becomes the ever more powerful body of the other moment, of
> subjective living labour, but rather [...] that the objective conditions of
> labour assume an ever more colossal independence, represented by its
> very extent. (Marx, 1973, p. 831)

So this colossal alienation produces a historical process through
which (alienated, objectified) labour, increasingly 'socialised', finds
its autonomy (now socialised precisely with regard to its primitive
individualisation) in relation to capital. We are faced with an 'inversion' of the concept of the 'social productive force' of capital that
manifests itself historically in the socialisation of living labour: a *subjective* 'inversion' that suppresses alienation, the reification of living
labour (here is not the place to distinguish these concepts, merely
to evoke them jointly in their descriptive and evocative capacities)
in dead labour. And it attributes to living labour a potentiality of
socialisation, now torn from dead labour. Through this inversion the
activity of individuals is endowed with a character that is immediately
social and productive.

Is this Marxian reversal of the effects of social subsumption
convincing in determining the recovery of the autonomy of living
labour as socialised labour, in other words as the figure of a *common
potentiality* of labour that has been exploited and oppressed up until
this point? To me it does not seem so; to me it seems rather that
the fact of not considering Hegel a 'dead dog' plays a bad joke on
Marx: it superimposes an intuition onto a reasoning, or rather it
imposes a bad reasoning, founded on the (outraged) claim of the
dignity of labour, onto a good reasoning, at other times expressed
(and with what force!): the foundational recognition of the antagonist potentiality that arises (immediately) from the experience of the
social exploitation of labour against the cruel abstraction of surplus
value. Here again, it seems (when we bear in mind the inversion
of the relationship 'alienation–socialisation') that one is dealing
with the passage from the *inside* (real subsumption, alienation in

production) to an *outside* (a whole socialisation of living labour and the fullness of its autonomy). But this is not the case: capitalism is fought both *within* and *against*; it does not permit an 'outside', and this is because the adversary of living labour is not simply the abstract figure of exploitation reshaped in the continuity of the circuits of the labour process, but the concrete figure of the capitalist who sucks out surplus labour. 'The *growth of capital* and the *increase in the proletariat* appear, therefore, as interconnected – if opposed – *products* of the same process' (Marx, Unpublished Chapter VI, p. 97I : 493G : 1062E). At the point where Marx's critique arrives, *there is no question of the labour process including the process of valorisation; rather it is the process of valorisation that configures and disciplines the labour process*, and labour value itself is grasped first of all from the experience of exploitation, under the shape of surplus value. Marx stresses the fundamental pre-eminence of surplus value in his works:

> The best points in my book are: 1. (this is fundamental to *all* understanding of the facts) the *two-fold character of labour* according to whether it is expressed in use-value or exchange-value, which is brought out in the very First Chapter; 2. The treatment of *surplus-value regardless of its particular* forms as profit, interest, ground rent, etc. (Letter to Engels, 24 August 1867, in Marx and Engels, 1975, p. 407)

Only now can we conclude:

> This destroys the last vestiges of the *illusion* so typical of the relationship when considered superficially, that in the circulation process, in the market-place, two equally matched *commodity owners* confront each other, and that they, like all other *commodity owners*, are distinguishable only by the material content of their goods, by the specific use-value of the goods they desire to sell each other. Or in other words, the *original* relation remains intact, but survives only as the *illusory* reflection of the *capitalist* relations underlying it. (Marx, Unpublished Chapter VI, p. 97I : 493G : 1062–3E)

Isaak Rubin comments:

> The usual short formulation of this theory holds that the value of the commodity depends on the quantity of labour socially necessary for its production; or, in a general formulation, that labour is hidden behind, or contained in, value: value = 'materialized' labor. It is more accurate to express the theory of value inversely [...] The labour theory of value is not based on an analysis of exchange transactions as such in their

material form, but on the analysis of those social production relations expressed in the transactions. (Rubin, 1972, p. 62)

Thus it is only the *against* that explains the *within*. It is the *antithetical existence* of the capitalist conditions of exploitation in relation to living labour that allows us to identify who is the one doing the exploiting and who is the exploited.

We could add a further consideration. We saw in section 1, as regards the concept of 'machinism' developed in the unpublished Chapter VI, how the Hegelian dialectic of the instrument has been transformed here: the instrument is no longer a mediation between the worker and nature; rather it is the worker who is the instrument between the capitalist and wealth (abundance of goods, and profit). Now, second, let us note that the instrument, in socialising itself, becomes profoundly transformed, or rather once again assumes its autonomy and reappears in the foreground. 'We see here how even economic categories appropriate to earlier epochs of production acquire a new and specific historical character under the impact of capitalist production' (Marx, Unpublished Chapter VI, p. 104I : 442G : 950E). These observations by Marx are useful to us as we conclude this brief *excursus* into the 'insightful' character of his critique of the economic categories of capitalism, as expressed in the unpublished Chapter VI. This foresight is not based on deterministic illusions but rather is open as a *dispositif* to the antagonist forces that construct the process of emancipation historically, in the course of the class struggle. Thus, if in real subsumption productive labour becomes a productive force of capital and if, by thus fulfilling the process and determining its inversion, the collective workers, formed through the social combination of the factors of production, recognise their own nature, transformed as they are into a 'common' actor of production – in short, if all this happens, we can conclude that in the 'biopolitical' figure of subsumption and in the 'cognitive' determination of production a new leading role is accorded to the proletariat (as collective instrument of production), namely that of taking a 'common potentiality' [*potenza*] into account, and therefore a 'common' *dispositif* is identified, which is radically ordinated towards a hegemonic claim for liberation from the domination of capital. The very instrument of production has potentially become able to liberate itself from exploitation and from command and to recognise itself as hegemonic in producing the wealth of the common.

NB. The class struggle, conducted within the real subsumption of society to biopower, seems to have to take on a particular tonality.

It is the 'antithetical existence' of the indebted body – mediatised, securitised and represented – that rises in indignation, rebelling, organising and struggling. It has to do this *within* this world, which has been reified by biopower, by 'single thought' [*pensiero unico*], always in new configurations of alienation (hence the inexorable urgency for cognitive and subversive 'co-research' to give a start to any project of emancipation); and it also has to do this *against* it. While we have clearly identified the 'within', the 'against' is the terrain of practice, now entrusted to constituent imagination and to militant practices. You can learn a lot in this regard from Frantz Fanon and in general from the first generations of activists and scholars of 'postcolonialism'. However, the problem today is how to organise the multitude – that is, how to engage the biopolitical networks of the singularities (digital and intelligent, cooperating and productive, critical of political economy and comunardistic, participant and democratically expert, etc.) in the establishment of a 'politics of the common'.

4

These last considerations allow us to return, avoiding the dangers of idealistic interpretations, to the section in the *Grundrisse* that deals with general intellect, which we have already mentioned, and to reread its location and development within Marx's thinking. We said that in the *Grundrisse*, written seven or eight years before the unpublished Chapter VI, Marx had advanced theses that would only achieve their full and material consistency in Book 1 of *Capital*. Already in the *Grundrisse* the problem for Marx was how to find a basis for overturning the effects of 'alienation' and 'reification': not to abandon them (as was suggested by Althusser, for example, when he defined them as products of Marx's humanistic adolescence), but to give them critical and materialist justification. These are concepts that, already before 1858, in Marx's early writings, represented – in an idealist manner – a perverse reality, the effect of capitalist exploitation. He denounced its repressive power and at the same time presented the occasion it offered for the dialectical passage – for negation towards an ideal overcoming. Now the renewed critique of political economy makes it possible to express this step in material terms: a passage that is historical, not dialectical, not necessary but effectually given; a passage through the hell of primitive accumulation, of both formal and real subsumption.

But to the degree that large industry develops, the creation of real wealth comes to depend less on labour time and on the amount of labour employed than on the power of the agencies set in motion during labour time, whose 'powerful effectiveness' is itself in turn out of all proportion to the direct labour time spent on their production, but depends rather on the general state of science and on the progress of technology, of the application of this science to production [...] In this transformation it is neither the direct human labour he himself performs, nor the time during which he works, but rather the appropriation of his own general productive power, his understanding of nature and his mastery over it by virtue of his presence as a social body – it is, in a word, the development of the social individual which appears as the great foundation-stone of production and of wealth. (Marx, 1973, pp. 704–5]

Utopia? Illusion? Maybe. In any event it is a forward shift in the whole 'insightful critique'. Shall we emerge from this transformed? Shall we emerge revolutionised? In 1858 'general intellect' is a powerful concept that allows us to grasp – within the intuition of real subsumption and of the aggregation or combination of social productive forces – the major determinations of the objective changes imposed by the *capitalist* revolution: the intellectual character of labour in the subsumption of society to capital. But here we still do not have a *communist* revolutionary subjectivity. For this to come about, it takes resistance, social recomposition, desire, struggles, and practical anticapitalist *dispositifs*. In any case this is a matter of establishing a relationship between the 'technical composition' and the 'political composition' of the proletariat. That said, it is only the first mature theoretical step in materialism (which occurs precisely in the decade from 1858 to 1867) that produces *in virtual terms* a revolutionary and communist subjectivity. For as long as this does not exist, the analysis remains hypothetical, locked in fragility in what is assumed, rhetoric in declarations and impotence in action. It is precisely in the unpublished Chapter VI that not only the theoretical transformation but also the revolutionary transformation begins to emerge. We are no longer only within the productive subsumption of society in capital; we are beginning to be *beyond* it. The transformation may be – and *virtually* is – revolutionary. After having been constructed 'within', the instrument, the subject, the *common ontology* of producing (a new reality of 'productive labour') come out 'against' capitalist command. Surplus value is no longer just a machine that produces an accumulation of capitalist power in the exploitation of society; it is also the opportunity through which the proletariat erects its revolt.

Shortly afterwards, the Paris Commune would reveal to Marx a first historical determination of this becoming – but more especially its first subjectivation.

Today, having endured a horrible centuries-long exploitation (made of misery and fatigue, and then, as if that were not enough, of ideological mystifications and religious barbarisms), we are finally able to give a name both to social surplus value (namely finance capital) and to *general intellect* (namely cognitive proletariat). This latter – in Marx's prescient imagination – is a potentiality that, in destroying alienation and reification in the name of the 'common', offers new possibilities for revolution.

4

Acting in Common, and the Limits of Capital

1

It was during the Second World War that the insight of Friedrich Pollock, elaborated during the Weimar era, came to be a reality – namely that the capitalist market cannot be considered in a simplistic and rhetorical manner as freedom (if not indeed anarchy) of circulation and as realisation of the value of commodities but, on the contrary, fundamentally as a unity of control over society as a whole, as 'planning'. This socialist concept, abhorred by capitalist economic thinkers, made a splendid re-entry into the categories of economic science. The concept of 'social capital' (and therefore of a capital unified in its social extension, within and above the market, and understood as a mechanism for guaranteeing the functioning of the market itself), as a kind of shorthand for an effective capitalist management of society, became increasingly widespread.

Particularly important in this regard was the debate that was taking place in the western communist left, about the nature of the Soviet Union. During the 1940s dissident workerist tendencies within Trotskyism developed the concept of 'state capitalism' as a way of defining the Soviet regime, taking the Thermidor of the Russian Revolution not as a contingent passage in the transition to communism but as a specific and progressive function of the reorganization of mature capitalism. In the Italian debate of the 1950s, a period of capitalist modernisation in the course of postwar reconstruction, the concept of 'social capital' was developed, notably by Raniero Panzieri – the Italian translator of the second volume of Marx's *Capital* and the founder of the journal *Quaderni Rossi*. It was on the basis of his analysis of the circulation processes of capital that Panzieri was able to develop the concept of 'social capital', demystifying notions of the 'free market' and also drawing in, in addition to the aforementioned Trotskyite dissident traditions, elements of European *liberal* thought – which, with Keynes, had made social capital and monetary planning the centre of democratic planning in Fordist development. But it was the Frankfurt School in particular (following in Pollock's footsteps) that took the concept of capitalist development as a whole and gradually formed the theory of the 'subsumption of society to capital' – from a structural point of view (the whole of society being included within capitalist domination), from a spatial point of view (from imperialism to the world system), and (with finer intuition) as an ongoing process of mutual translation between technologies and anthropological transformations. It was on this complex terrain, in relation to this social and dynamic ontology, that the thematic of emancipation and its consequent practices were advanced.

Conversely, and outside of that strong materialist methodology, in the western Marxism of the period between the two wars and immediately after the second, and among the heirs of the Frankfurt School (forgetful as they were of that other very rich anthropology that had been anticipated) the space of emancipation was rather built on (or, better still, reduced to) a moral (ethical) horizon and the space of liberation was written off as utopian. An idealist perspective imposed itself. The consequences of the theory of 'social capital' were addressed in a dialectics that did not relive the experience of exploitation. If, we were told, capital seemed more and more to embody the inhuman and *Aufklärung* [Enlightenment] translated into its opposite, then within this impoverished reading there arose a tradition that considered emancipation or liberation as an 'outside'. Here we are in the realm of metaphysics, where communism is by now presented as the product of a thinking that in absolute terms realises the universal, or as the inoperative reflection of a being removed from history. Badiou and Agamben have today taken on board those old frustrations, thus removing desire from life, without realising that those illusions consign the struggles for emancipation to impotence and defeat, to a destiny of obedience and pain.

But let us return here instead to the workerist thinkers [*operaisti*]. In Marx the concept of capital is always given – against all idealist positions that seek to present it as a unitary figure – as a 'social relationship'. Capital, capitalism, the dimensions of social command and so forth cannot be taken as a fixed given: the capitalist subsumption of society is the subsumption of a contradiction, an antagonistic relationship that continues to exist. But there is more: any epistemology

of capitalist development can only have as its starting point an antagonistic position that is *internal to* development itself. The analysis
is always 'within', and by the fact of being 'within' it will also be
'against'. And, while social command always implies an *other* over
which it is to be exercised, this relationship is 'intransitive', it shuns
any solution of the dialectics, any going beyond of the antagonist
movement; it imposes a movement of resistance that is not only ethical
but also epistemological. A number of consequences arise from this,
which I merely note here and to which I shall return later. The first
consequence – at a 'macrolevel' – allows us to read the development
(and crisis) of capitalism as an antagonistic process with a dynamic
marked by continuous, albeit varying, conflictual intensities. There
is always someone who wins and someone who loses within this
open-ended and unresolved process. The second consequence, at
the 'microlevel', is revealed by the continuous changes in the social
composition of the subject, in both technical and political terms:
the varying *densities* of the capitalist relationship drive the contradictions to figures that are increasingly singularised and irreducible. The
third consequence is that, from the relationship between intensity
and density that marks the antagonism, there emerge new *qualities*
of the subjects who participate in development. When, as happens
in post-Fordist society, the social relationship that constitutes capital
occupies the whole of society and determines its productivity, when
productivity becomes cognitive, immaterial, affective, cooperative
and so on, in short, a 'production of subjectivity', then the exchange
becomes ontological and we witness a deepening of the antagonism
that invests the subjects – especially the figures of living labour, who
increasingly recognise themselves as being capable of appropriating portions of fixed capital and able to develop productive efficacy
autonomously, on a basis of cooperation.

2

Before moving on in the discussion, allow me to stress here the
importance of Foucault's thought in driving research in this direction. It was instrumental both in redefining capitalist development as
the development of an 'intransitive' relationship between biopower
and subjective resistances and in introducing the analysis of the
anthropological transformations that follow on this intransitivity of
the relationship. Resistance (folding back on itself, producing autonomous subjectivities) increasingly configured itself as a production of

singularities, and the ontological instances of singularisation, which Deleuze had so clearly defined, found concreteness in Foucault's theory of the *dispositif*. The *dispositif* is the productive tension that is exerted on the subject; it is the tendency towards the development of the production of subjectivity within cooperative processes, and to their collective metamorphosis. The Foucauldian *dispositif* is a machinic *conatus* and a productive *cupiditas* that push forward the autonomy of the subjects in the resistance to capital – thus both within and against the capitalist relation. When we speak of the Marxism of Foucault we are referring to this machine of immanence that finds – no longer in the industrial structures of the class struggle but in the social texture of capitalist domination – the capacity [*potenza*] for resistance, for breaking, for alternatives. It is a new world becoming reality; biopolitical creativity in opposition to biopower.

3

Bearing in mind the conclusions arrived at in section 1, let us now move on to explore the theme of the 'limits of capitalism'.

In Book 3 of *Capital* Marx says that capital itself is the limit of capitalism. He arrives at this statement through a demonstration of the tendential fall of the rate of profit in the development of the organic composition of capital. If capitalist value creation (and thus profit) occurs through the use of 'living labour' (and through the exploitation or the extortion of its creativity), the more the mechanisation of work advances (and thus valorisation shifts and is flattened onto the constant elements of capital), the less the value of capital will increase, because the usage (exploitation) of labour power will be reduced.

In the nineteenth and early twentieth centuries, this law was often understood as being catastrophic for capitalist development. However, that was not how it worked out. The limit did not express itself in relation to, and in proportion to, the enlargement of the technological accumulation of the capitalist system; and the transformation of the subjectivities put to work widened rather than narrowed the field of accumulation, exploitation and command. This does not mean that the limit disappeared – it is still there, and capitalists are always dramatically aware of its imminence – but the limit has shifted and relocated itself in the light of the new subjectifications that have been produced. The result is that – as I have already pointed out in assessing the contribution of the Frankfurt School – the antagonistic character of capitalist development can be neither recognised nor revealed on the objective terrain: it can only be interpreted when one looks at those new subjectivities that development has produced – or, if you will, at the materiality of the new anthropological figures, which are singular and subjectively relevant – in short, at the anthropological transformations introduced by capitalist development itself, at the changes taking place in labour power, and at the new dialectic between immaterial labour power and the reappropriation of fixed capital.

By this I mean that, if the capitalist catastrophe arising from the falling rate of profit has not occurred, this is not because of capital's capacity to avoid it through successive waves of technological innovation, geographical expansion and updating and transformation of the instruments of command (the high profile of financial command by comparison with industrial policies is the latest manifestation of this). Rather, the catastrophe was reconfigured and postponed via the transfer of the capacity to produce and accumulate from bosses to workers; from the potentiality of constant capital to the diffusion of the processes of proletarian reappropriation of fixed capital. The limit of capitalism is here revealed by the extension of its domination, by the fact that it has subsumed the entire planet, but also by the fact that in this way, in the course of this process, it has been forced to surrender to the producers (who are increasingly singularised and grow ever stronger in their autonomous cooperation) the capacity to exist and produce outside of the homologating obsession of (capitalist) command and to build, chaotically but in alternative ways, their ontological independence.

4

Why is the problem of the 'limits of capitalism' re-emerging today? It seems at first sight that the problem arises simply in the political sphere, in other words that it is born out of the crisis of the relationship between capitalist development and democracy, that is, from the crisis of the democratic state, of the state of law, of the representative and parliamentary state. Are capitalism and democracy really incompatible, when understood from a constitutional point of view? They are and they are not; what is certain is that, in the current conditions, capital is not compatible with an egalitarian and progressive democracy. The crisis of social democracy should probably be read in this light.

However, these considerations are insufficient to define the difficulties currently observable in the relationship between capitalism
and democracy. It is beyond doubt that constitutional democracy
has difficulties when confronted with instances of equality that arise
from a productive world that is increasingly cooperative, and that
the economic order of private property is also in difficulty when it
comes up against those instances of the 'common' that are becoming increasingly present in the current state of production. What we
have is a cognitive labour power that is not consumed in usage, is
implemented in cooperation, and is not usable except in its cooperative and dynamic composition, therefore in its 'excedence' in
the face of all measurement and in its autonomy from all extrinsic
command. This is the 'common' character of the present-day force
of production power – linguistic, affective, cognitive, immaterial and
cooperative. The economic order of possessive individualism and
private property no longer has ontological consistency. On this point
modern constitutionalism and the world of life come into conflict in
an irreducible manner. We conclude, therefore, that this relationship
is in crisis for at least two reasons, which go far beyond the crisis of
the state of law [*stato di diritto*]: one is that money has overtaken [*ha
sopravanzato*] labour; the other is that technology has overtaken life.

5

At the end of this article we shall see how these two contradictions
find their cause in the tendential breaking of the capital relationship
itself: the oneness – of power, of money, of capital – has split into two
and cannot be put together again. But before considering this basic
element, let us open up the discussion on the problematics we have
sketched thus far.

That money has overtaken labour is clear when you analyse the
structure of financial capital: it has introduced ways of control-
ling labour power, which, as well as extending themselves socially,
place the capital relationship outside of any material measure. Profit
becomes very radically separated from labour; the law of labour value
has been completely dissolved. Globalisation intervenes in this tendency, extending it across the space of the whole world and making
it even more uncontrollable.

It is the possession of money – the financial convention – that
now becomes the regulatory norm of social and productive activities and therefore gives access to a 'property-owning reality' whose

efficacy is based solely on the most arbitrary monetary function. Property becomes paper-based, money-based or share-based, and mobile or based on real estate; its nature is conventional and juridical. André Orléan and Christian Marazzi – two writers whom I consider required reading in the present context – have correctly emphasised this transformation. The financial convention has to be viewed as a command that is independent of any ontological determination: this convention fixes and consolidates a 'sign of ownership' (in terms of 'private property') and holds even when it presents itself as an 'excedence' – not simply in relation to older and static determinations of labour value but also in relation to that continuous 'anticipation' and 'increase' that accompany it in exercising the financial capture of socially produced value and in operating at a global level. It should therefore be clear that, in this new configuration of the rules of property, the material basis of the law of value continues to exist. And yet we are not dealing here with individual labour – in reading the law of value – that becomes abstract, but with labour that is immediately social, common, and as such directly exploited by capital. The rule of finance is able to set itself as hegemonic because in the new mode of production the *common* has emerged as an eminent potentiality, as a substance of the relations of production, and is increasingly invading all social space as a norm of value creation. Finance capital follows on this growth of the common, seeks to translate it directly into profit, pushes securities and real estate rent, and anticipates them as financial rents. Another economist, Harribey, stated it well, in his discussion with Orléan: value no longer presents itself in substantive terms, it does not even show itself as a simple accounting phantasmagoria; it is rather the sign of a productive common, mystified but effective, which develops more and more intensively and extensively. Money has therefore overtaken labour and now looks at it like at a distant shore where it will not be necessary to land – in the illusion that this abstraction can last and that monetary speculation and the corruption of values can carry on forever.

And, second, technology has overtaken life. In saying this we highlight two elements: the first is the dissolution of the functional homogeneity that industrial activity created between technological development and the development of labour power. By contrast, today, within the structures of production (and no longer only industrial ones), the subjectification of labour power takes place in a manner that is less and less resolvable within productive command. In short, one is no longer seeing simply the theft of surplus labour by constant capital – one is also seeing the parallel appropriation of fixed capital by labour power. Technological command is no longer able to maintain a steady relationship with the autonomous cooperative socialisation of labour. Here we have a first paradox. It relates to *production*, and it consists in the fact that financial capitalism represents the most abstract and detached form of command at the very moment when it concretely invests the whole of life. The 'reification' of life and the 'alienation' of the subjects are produced by a productive command that has come to be – in the new mode of production, organised by financial capital – entirely transcendent, over a labour power that is cognitive. However, this labour power, when it is obliged to produce surplus value, precisely because it is cognitive, immaterial, creative and not immediately consumable, reveals itself as being independently productive.

This paradox appears fully when you consider that, given that production is essentially based on 'social cooperation' (in computer science, in care and welfare, in the service sector etc.), the valorisation of capital no longer clashes only with the massification of 'variable capital' but also with the resistance and autonomy of a multitude that has reappropriated to itself a 'part' of fixed capital (thus presenting itself, if you like, as a 'machinic subject') and of a continuous 'relative' capacity of organising the social networks of labour.

This paradox and this contradiction create a very violent opposition between 'constant capital' (in its financial form) and 'variable capital' (in the hybridised form it assumes, having incorporated 'fixed capital') – and thus tendentially implement the verticalisation of command and the breakdown of the representative structures of the state of law.

A second contradiction arises when we note that, as a result of these processes of appropriation – by workers – of fractions of fixed capital, capitalist command on the one hand extends and exploits the lives of workers, of society in its full extension, and thus defines itself as 'biocapital', and on the other encounters increasingly insurmountable difficulties in dealing with 'the bodies of the workers'.

Here the clash, the contradiction and the antagonism become fixed when capital (in the postindustrial phase, the era in which cognitive capital becomes hegemonic) must put directly into production human bodies, turning them into singular machines, no longer simply subsuming them as labour commodity. Thus (in the new processes of production) bodies become ever more effectively specialised and acquire autonomy, so that, through the resistance and the struggles of machinic labour power, there develops ever more expressly the demand for a 'production of the human by the human', in other words for the living machine that is 'the human'.

In fact, at the moment in which the workers reappropriate a part of the 'fixed capital' and present themselves, in variable and often chaotic manner, as cooperating actors in the processes of valorisation, as 'precarious' but 'independent' 'subjects' of the valorisation of capital, a complete reversal occurs in the function of labour vis-à-vis capital: the worker is no longer just the tool that capital uses in order to conquer nature – or, in ordinary terms, in order to produce goods; rather the worker, having incorporated the instrument, having metamorphosed from an anthropological point of view, reconquers 'use value' and acts machinically, in an otherness and an autonomy from capital that seek to become complete. Between this objective trend and the practical mechanisms of constituting this machinic worker we locate that 'class struggle' that we may from now on call 'biopolitics'.

6

These paradoxes remain unresolved in the action of capital. Consequently, the stronger the resistance becomes, the harsher becomes the state's attempt at a restoration of power. Any resistance is therefore condemned as an illegal practice of counterpower, and every manifestation of revolt is defined as destruction and ransacking. A further paradox – but this one is pure mystification – is that, in exercising the maximum violence, capital and its state need to appear as an inevitable and neutral figure: the maximum violence is exercised by instruments or organs that are 'technical'. 'There is no alternative,' proclaimed Mrs Thatcher. So here you are given to understand that, in the name of this inescapable command (which is rational in capitalist logic), technology overtakes life in forms that are extreme but nonetheless typical and generalisable. The case of the 'nuclear state' is characteristic here: in this model technology stands as a forceful guarantee of sovereignty, as a permanent blackmail of public power against any force or movement (especially in domestic policy) that wishes to or is able to impose itself on the 'legitimate sovereign'. These are probably the phenomena that polarise the capital relation and bring about the crisis of democracy even as a simple form of social democratic control over development.

The 'nuclear state' is a state that seeks to impose the sovereign 'exception' in physical terms, and to mould the statist notion of the 'autonomy of the political' within an insurmountable technological trope, as a guarantee of the predominance of capitalism and of the impossibility of going beyond it. Here modern sovereignty becomes definitively 'biopower'. Is this not a renewal, through the 'terrible power' of the 'nuclear state', through its technological functioning, of that tradition of sovereign power that, in history, characterised the tradition of absolutism?

In this last case, the nuclear state, the limit of capitalism is real and actual: it is the catastrophe of life itself. But this is an extreme case – not ontologically necessary albeit logically possible. This catastrophist dimension attracts reactionary spirits: Heidegger adopted this logic to extend the nuclear threat to the whole of life, generalising the effects of nuclear technology within the very concept of technology. In my opinion the potentiality of life and the joy of liberty can enable us to avoid such transcendental threats. To them we oppose ontological resistances, we pluck technology out of the hands of capital, and we embody it, not as a garb of slaves but as a bodily instrument of emancipation.

7

What, then, is the limit of capital? It is always to be found in that subjective place where the exploitation of labour is broken and the slavery of private ownership and of monetary overlordship is removed – in the place where we succeed in reappropriating not only technologies but also their command. And, since technologies are prostheses of the human, the problem is how to make technology a prosthesis of our resistance, of our revolt and our humanity. It is in the construction of the 'common' that we reappropriate technologies and become powerful; the historical process of capitalist development (at the very moment when it has raised capitalist power – in financial form – to an exaggerated and empty transcendence) has made possible an anthropological transformation that goes in the direction of a cooperative singularisation: not of a process of individualisation of possessive subjects but of a proliferation of cooperating singularities. Technological intensities, cooperative densities and singular qualities are the product of, and produce, new anthropological figures. The common is not a compacted organic entity but a cooperating ensemble of singularities. Here we recognise the subjective place in which the limit of capitalism is posed, because here is posed the intransitivity of that relationship that defined capital itself.

However, reviewing the process that we have described thus far from the point of view of those philosophers whom we have criticised for their idealistic and moral critiques of the capital relation, you might raise the following objection: How can there ever be a singularity, how can a limit ever be posed, if it is posed in a manner that is so impure, and in particular if it has soiled itself through the reappropriation of fixed capital? To this objection we reply clearly: there is no liberation, there is no subjectivity that is not completely charged with historicity and immersed in the violence of the capital relation. There is no place where humanity can ingenuously or desperately recompose itself or redeem itself. The 'universal human' who acted the idea of the common – after the overturning of 'real socialism' where shall we ever find him again? Or perhaps the bare human [*l'uomo nudo*]? But the bare human is only a maximum abjection produced by power, who has been stripped of all ontological dignity. The rebels, the resisters, the ethical human beings are always dirty, just like the Cynic philosopher (as Foucault reminds us), and take upon themselves the full load of historicity. Therefore what is the nature of that process of appropriation that arms subjectivity? It involves adopting, grasping, and using bodily, mental, linguistic and emotional prostheses – in other words, bringing back to one's own singularity some capabilities that were previously recognised as belonging only to the machinery that one worked with, and then *incorporating and embodying* these machinic characteristics, turning them into primary attitudes and behaviours of the activity of labouring subjects. In the separation established between the two subjects of the capital relation (the boss and the worker) there is, on the part of the singularity, a reappropriation of fixed capital, an irreversible acquisition of machinic elements that are subtracted from the valorising capacity of capital.

Now, every *reappropriation* amounts to an ousting [*destituzione*] of capitalist command. This process of appropriation, especially when conducted by the immaterial workers – who today are majoritarian in the processes of value creation – is very strong, very efficacious in its development; it brings about crisis. But there would be no crisis if we thought that it arose spontaneously from the processes of reappropriation and ousting. That is not how things are. The crisis needs a conflictual clash, a political reality that actively moves for the destruction not simply of the relation of exploitation, but also of the condition of enforcement that sustains it. In fact, when one speaks of reappropriation by the antagonist subject, one is not speaking simply of the changes taking place in the quality of labour power (which derive from the absorption of portions of fixed capital); we are speaking basically of a *reappropriation of the cooperation* that was incentivised in the capitalist restructuring of production and was then expropriated – and this is the essential drama of this critical phase. When it speaks of recuperation and reappropriation of fixed capital, far from expressing itself in terms that are tainted with economism, the analysis enters rather onto that terrain of cooperation that is now regulated by capital *in biopolitical terms*. *Ousting* capital from this function means recovering for labour power *an autonomous capacity of cooperation*.

5

Is It Possible to Be Communists without Marx?

Is it possible to be communists without Marx? Obviously, yes. Nevertheless, I often find myself discussing this with comrades and with subversive intellectuals of different backgrounds. Especially in France – and in what follows I am talking mainly about France. I have to confess, however, that I often find the question tedious. There are too many lines and contradictions that are rarely taken to the point of verification or experimental solutions. Often one is dealing with a rhetoric that addresses political practice only in the abstract. However, sometimes one comes up against people who actually argue that you cannot be a communist if you are a Marxist. Recently, for example, a leading academic – and one with a past involvement in various radical forms of 'Maoism' – told me that, if one continued to stick with revolutionary Marxism, which predicted the 'withering away of the state' and its 'extinction' after a proletarian seizing of power but which certainly did not achieve this goal, one could no longer declare oneself a 'communist'. I objected, replying that this was like saying that Christianity is false because the Last Judgement as predicted by the Apocalypse of St John has not happened and so far there has been no sign of the 'resurrection of the dead'! And I added that, in an era of disenchantment, the end of the world for the Christians and the crisis of the socialist eschatology seem to be two sides of the same coin, or rather they undergo similar epistemological injunctions – which, however, *are completely fallacious*. Certainly Christianity is false – but, I would suggest, for quite different reasons. And, if communism is also false, it is not because the eschatological hope never became a reality: I am not saying that this was not implicit in the premise, but that many of the 'prophesies' (or rather theoretical mechanisms) of Marx's communism have come into their own, so that today without Marx it is still impossible to address the problem of the struggle against slavery under capitalism. Precisely for this reason, I suggest, it would be important to go back from Christianity to Christ, and to return from communism to Marx...

Well, then? The withering away of the state did not happen. In Russia and in China the state became all-powerful and the *common* was organised (and falsified) in the forms of the *public*: statism thus emerged victorious, and what was imposed under its hegemony was not the common but a highly centralised, bureaucratic capitalism. However, it seems to me that, through the great communist revolutionary experiences of the twentieth century, the ideas of 'absolute democracy' and of a 'commons of human beings' [*comune degli uomini*] have been proven *possible*. And by 'absolute democracy' I mean the political project that builds itself beyond the 'relative' democracy of the liberal state, and thus as the index of a radical revolution against the state, of a practice of resistance and of construction of the 'common' against the 'public', of the refusal of the existing state of affairs, and a practice of the exercise of constituent power [*potenza*] by the class of exploited workers.

This is where the difference comes in. Whatever the outcome has been, communism (the communism that has moved in line with the Marxist hypothesis) has been attempted (even without being realised) through a set of practices that are not just random, nor only transitory: we are talking about *ontological practices*. Therefore the question of whether one can be a communist without being a Marxist should address first of all the ontological dimension of communism, and the materialist determination of that ontology, and its effective residues, and the irreversibility of that episode in actual reality and in the collective desire of human beings. Communism is a construction, as Marx taught us. An ontology. In other words, the construction of a new society by human beings as producers, by the collective worker, through an acting [*agire*] that reveals itself as effective because it is directed towards *the growth of being*.

This process was enacted in random fashion and the experiment was partly realised. The fact that it was defeated does not prove that it is impossible: indeed, it has effectually been shown that it is possible. Many millions of men and women have operated and thought, worked and lived within this possibility. No one denies that the era of 'real socialism' succumbed to and was traversed by horrible abuses. But were they such as to have completely cancelled out that experience, were they such as to have removed that growth of being that the realisation of the *possible* and the potentiality [*potenza*] of the revolutionary event had built? If this had happened, if the negative, which was real enough in the story of 'real socialism', had produced mainly a destruction of being, the experience of communism would have slipped away and would have dispersed into nothingness. But this did not happen. The project of an 'absolute democracy', the notion of building the 'commons of human beings' remain attractive and intact in our desire and our will. Does not this continued existence, this materialism of desire, perhaps demonstrate the validity of Marx's thought? And is this not the reason why it is difficult, if not impossible, to be communists without Marx?

In order to reply to the objection that statism is a necessary outcome of Marxist practices, we need to reframe our analysis: namely we have to assume that the accumulation of being, the progression of 'absolute democracy', the affirmation of freedom and equality pass through and incessantly experience breaks, interruptions and catastrophes, but this accumulation is stronger than the destructive moments that admittedly it has experienced. In fact this process is not purposeful or teleological, nor is it a move of the philosophy of history: it is not all that because this accumulation of being, which continues to live through the historical events, is neither a destiny nor a providence but is the outcome, the *intersection* of thousands and thousands of practices and wills, transformations and metamorphoses, which have acted together to constitute the subjects. That history and this accumulation are products of concrete singularities (which history reveals to us in action) and productions of subjectivity. We take them up and describe them a posteriori. There is nothing of necessity here; in the history we recount everything is contingent but concluded, everything is aleatory but completed. *Nihil factum infectum fieri potest* – nothing done can be undone: is there perhaps a philosophy of history where the living desire only to continue to live, and for that reason express from below an intentional teleology of life? The 'will to live' does not solve the problems and difficulties of living but presents itself in desire, construed as urgency and capacity [*potenza*] for a constitution of the world. If there are discontinuities and breaks, they reveal themselves in a historical continuity – a continuity that is always jagged, never progressive; but it is not globally and ontologically catastrophic either. Being can never be totally destroyed.

Another theme: that accumulation of being constructs elements of the *common*. The common is not a necessary finality – rather, it is an increase in being, for human beings wish to be multiplicity, to establish relationships, to be multitude: they are not able to stay alone, they suffer above all from loneliness. Second, that accumulation of being will be neither identity nor origin: it is itself a product of diversities and of consensuses and conflicts between singularities, an articulation of linguistic constructions and of historical determinations, a fruit of encounters and clashes. Here in particular it should be emphasised that the *common* does not present itself as the *universal*. It can contain the universal and express it, but it is not reduced to it; it is more extensive and temporally dynamic. The universal can be said to apply to each and every individual. But the concept of the self-subsistent individual is contradictory. There is no individuality, only a relationship between singularities. The common recomposes the ensemble of singularities. This difference, between the common and the universal, is absolutely central here: Spinoza defined it when, to the generic emptiness of the universal and to the inconsistency of the individual, he counterposed the concrete determination of 'common notions'. The universal is that which every subject can think in isolation, in loneliness; the common on the other hand is that which each singularity can build, can constitute *ontologically*, starting from the fact that every singularity is multiple but is determined concretely in multiplicity, in common relatedness. The universal is said of the multiple, while the common is determined, constructed through the multiple and specified there. Universality considers the common as something abstract and immobilises it during the course of history; the common draws the universal away from immobility and repetition – and instead builds it concretely.

But all this presupposes ontology. So this is where communism needs Marx: to implant itself in the common, in ontology – and vice versa. *Without historical ontology there is no communism.*

Can we be communists without being Marxists? Unlike the French 'Maoists', who never spent much time with Marx (I shall come back to this), Deleuze and Guattari, for example, were communists without being Marxists, but they were so in a very effective way – to the point that it is said that Deleuze, shortly before his death, was thinking of writing a book entitled 'La Grandeur de Marx' ['The Greatness of Marx']. Deleuze and Guattari build the common through *agencements collectifs* [collective assemblages] and through a methodological materialism that brings them close to Marxism but distances them from classical socialism – and certainly from any organic ideal of socialism or statist ideal of communism. Assuredly Deleuze and Guattari declared themselves communists anyway. Why? Because, although they were not Marxists, they were involved in those movements of thought that were continually opening themselves to communist practice and militancy. In particular, their materialism was ontological; their communism developed over *mille plateaux* [a thousand plateaux] of transformative practice. What they lacked was the history, the positive history that can often help in producing and understanding the dynamics of subjectivity (in Foucault, this *dispositif* was finally reinstated in critical ontology). Granted, that was sometimes positivist historiography, of course; but sometimes history can be inscribed within a materialist methodology without the chronological minutiae and the excessive insistence on historical events that are typical of any *Historismus* [historism] – and this is precisely what happened with Deleuze and Guattari. I stress the complementarity of materialism and ontology because history – which, in the perspective of both classical idealism and positivism, was certainly taken on board by philosophy, but only in order to be reduced to political or ethical hypostases and thus to be denied its ontological dimension – history, I say, can sometimes be tacitly but effectively subsumed when ontology creates particularly strong *dispositifs*, as was the case in Deleuze and Guattari. One should not forget that Marxism does not live only in science but rather develops itself within 'situated' experiences: Marxism is often made manifest by the *dispositifs* of militant activity.

Things go differently when, for example, we compare our problem (communism–Marxism, history–ontology) with the many variants of utopian socialism, especially the one that derives from Maoism. In the French experience of Maoism we witnessed the diffusion of a kind of 'hatred of history', which – and herein lay its frightening deficiency – revealed extreme discomfort when it had to produce political objectives. So, in fact, in the process of evacuating history, it evacuated not only Marxism but also politics. Paradoxically this was a repetition, but in the opposite direction, of what had happened in France during the period when the Annales School of Marc Bloch and Lucien Febvre was founded. At that time Marxism was introduced into philosophical discussion through historiography. And historiography became political!

The same is true of utopian socialism: one has to recognise that, in some of its experiences (outside of the Maoist variants), it offered materialist connections between ontology and history – not always, but often. So far as the French experience goes, one need only recall the formidable contribution of Henri Lefebvre. We have to understand, then, whether and to what extent, within this variation of different positions, there sometimes emerge positions that, in the name of the universality of the proposed political project, oppose ontological praxis – for example by denying the historicity of categories such as 'primitive accumulation' and consequently by proposing the hypothesis of communism as a pure and immediate restoration of the commons; or by devaluing the productive transformations that configure in various ways the 'technical composition' of labour power (which is a real and actual production of materialist subjectivity in the relationship between relations of production and forces of production) and by asserting that the root of communist protest is simply human nature (always the same, *sub forma arithmeticae*) – and so forth: this is clearly an ambiguous repackaging of idealism in its transcendental aspect.

For example, we have recently seen in Jacques Rancière an increasing tendency to deny any ontological connection between historical materialism and communism. In his research, in fact, the prospect of the emancipation of labour is developed in terms of an authenticity of consciousness; in consequence subjectivity is addressed in individual terms and any possibility of qualifying as *common* the production of subjectivity is therefore removed even before the start. Furthermore, here emancipatory action is detached from all historical determination and proclaims its independence from concrete temporality: for Rancière politics is a paradoxical action that separates the subject from history, from society, and from institutions even when, without that participation (that inherency that can be radically contradictory), the political subject would not even be statable. Thus 'politics' and the movement of emancipation lose any characteristic of antagonism, not in the abstract but on the concrete terrain of the struggles; the determinations of exploitation are no longer seen and, in parallel with this, the accumulation of enemy power, of 'police' – always presented in a vague figure, not as [*materia*] *quantitate signata* [quantitatively determined] – no longer constitutes a problem. When the discourse of emancipation does not rest on ontology, it becomes utopia, an individual dream, and as such is an irrelevance.

This brings us to the heart of the matter: the point where we ask ourselves whether (after 1968) there has ever been a communism in France that was tied to Marxism. There certainly was (and remains) one in the twin variants of Stalinism and Trotskyism, both of them protagonists in a now distant and esoteric history. But when it comes to the philosophy of 1968, here the rejection of Marxism is radical. I am referring essentially to the positions of Badiou, which are currently enjoying a certain popularity.

A brief clarification. When Rancière, in the immediate wake of 1968, developed (after having participated in the shared readings of

Capital) a heavy criticism of the positions of Althusser and pointed out how, in the critique of Marxist humanism (which in Althusser opened up into a critique of Stalinism only after 1968, and thus with something of a delay), there still remained the same intellectualist assumptions of the 'party man' [*uomo di partito*] and the structuralist abstraction of the 'process without a subject' – he was right. But should not Rancière today raise the same critique in relation to Badiou? For Badiou, too, the independence of reason, its guarantee of truth, the systematic nature of an ideological autonomy are in fact everything: only in relation to these conditions can one define communism. *N'est-ce pas, sous l'apparance du multiple, le retour à une vieille conception de la philosophie supérieure?* ['Is this not, under the appearance of the multiple, a return to an old conception of philosophy as something superior?'] ask Deleuze and Guattari (1991, pp. 143–4). In Badiou it is thus very difficult to understand where the ontological conditions of the subject and of revolutionary rupture are to be found. For him, indeed, every mass movement is a petty bourgeois performance and every immediate struggle, whether of material or of cognitive labour, of the class or of 'social labour' [*'lavoro sociale'*], is something that will never touch the substance of power – every enlargement of the collective productive capacity of proletarian subjects will be merely an extension of their subjection to the logic of the system; thus the object is unattainable, the subject is undefinable – unless theory produces it, to discipline it, to adapt it to truth and to raise it to the level of event, beyond political practice, beyond history. But these are lesser matters by comparison with what lies in store if we follow the thought of Badiou. In his view every framework of struggle, specifically determined, seems to be (if theory and militant experience attribute to it a potentiality of subversion) only a dreamlike hallucination. For example, to press the point of 'constituent power' would be, in his view, to dream of the transformation of an imaginary 'natural law' into a revolutionary political potentiality. Only an 'event' can save us: an event that is beyond any subjective existence that might determine it, and beyond any strategic pragmatism that might represent its *dispositif*. For Badiou, the *event* (Christ's crucifixion and resurrection, the French Revolution, the Chinese Cultural Revolution, etc.) is always defined a posteriori; it is therefore a presupposition and not a product of history. In consequence, paradoxically, the revolutionary event exists *without* Jesus, *without* Robespierre, *without* Mao. But, once deprived of an internal logic of production of the event, how will one ever be able to distinguish the event from an object of faith? In this, therefore, Badiou limits himself to repeating the mystical claim generally attributed to Tertullian: *credo quia absurdum* – I believe because it is absurd. Here ontology is swept away. And communist reasoning is reduced either to a stroke of madness or to a kind of business of the spirit. To spell it out, repeating Deleuze and Guattari:

> The event itself appears (according to Badiou) not as a singularity so much as an independent random point that joins or leaves the site, in the transcendence of the void or of truth as void, and no one is able to decide on the event's belonging to the situation in which its site is found (the undecidable). Perhaps there is instead an intervention, something like a throw of dice on the site, which qualifies the event and makes it enter into the situation, a power [*puissance*] of 'making' the event. (Deleuze and Guattari, 1991, pp. 143–4)

Now we can easily understand some of the presuppositions of these theoretical positions (which derive from a painful and shared self-criticism of past revolutionary practices). It was a matter, first, of destroying all references to the history of a 'real socialism', which had been defeated, yes, but was always stuffed with dogmatic premises and an organic disposition to betrayal. Second, they wanted to avoid establishing any relationship between the dynamics of subversive movements and the contents and institutions of capitalist development. To play with all of these, simultaneously *within and against them*, as the trade union tradition was proposing, had in fact produced a corruption of the desire for revolution and an illusion of commitment [*volontà*] to struggle. But to take these correct critical objectives and then conclude that any political, tactical and strategic attempt at reconstructing a communist practice and the effort of this exercise were excluded from the project of liberation; that neither a constituent project nor a transformative approach from within the material and immediately antagonistic dimension of the struggles is conceivable; that any attempt to take account of the current forms of domination, in whatever way it develops, is anyway still subject to and absorbed by capitalist command; and, finally, that all references to struggles within a biopolitical fabric, hence to struggles that consider the articulations of welfare from a materialistic perspective, are nothing but a vitalist rehash – well, to conclude, all this adds up to just one thing: *the denial of class struggle*. What is more, in the view of Badiousian 'extremism', the project of communism cannot exist except in a privative manner and within forms of subtraction from power, and the new community can only be the product of those who have no community (as indeed Rancière argues). What is particularly unpleasant in this project is the Jansenist purity it exhibits. But when the forms of collective intelligence are so despised – because all the forms of intelligence produced in the concrete history of mankind are reduced to the logic of the capitalist system of production – then there's nothing to be done. Or, rather, all that's left is to reaffirm the observation already made above, namely that *materialist pragmatism* (such as we know it, from Machiavelli and Nietzsche, from Spinoza and Deleuze) – that movement that is valid only for itself, that labour that refers only to its own potentiality [*potenza*], that immanence that focuses on action and on the act of production of being – is in any case more communist than any other utopia that has a difficult relationship with history and formal uncertainties vis-à-vis ontology.

We do not believe, therefore, that it is possible to talk about communism without Marx. Of course, Marxism needs to be deeply and radically renewed and reread. But this creative transformation of historical materialism can also take place as we follow the indications given by Marx himself and enrich it with indications deriving from the 'alternative' currents lived in modernity, from Machiavelli to Spinoza, from Nietzsche to Deleuze and Foucault. And, while Marx was studying the laws of motion of capitalist society, it is now time to study *the laws of* working-class labour, or rather *of social activity* as a whole and of the production of subjectivity within the subsumption of society to capital and the immanence of resistance to exploitation viewed globally. Today it is no longer sufficient to study the laws of capital; we have to work on the expression of the potentiality of the rebellion of workers everywhere. Still following Marx, what interests us is

> labour not as an object, but as activity; not as itself value, but as the living source of value. [Namely it is] general wealth (in contrast to capital in which it exists objectively, as reality) as the general possibility of the same, which proves itself as such in action. Thus, it is not at all contradictory [...] that labour is absolute poverty as object on one side, and is, on the other side, the general possibility of wealth as subject and as activity. (Marx, 1993, p. 296)

But by what means shall we grasp labour in this way – not as a socio-logical object but as a political subject? This is the problem, this is the object of investigation. Only by solving *this* problem can we speak of communism – and also, if necessary (as it almost always is), by getting our hands dirty. Anything else is intellectualistic chatter.

Part II

6

An Italian Breakpoint

Production versus Development

First, how did the Italian 'difference' begin to define itself in the philosophical framework of postwar Europe? It began when, at the end of the 1950s, groups of politicised intellectuals began to ask themselves what was the degree of immanence of labour within the development of capitalist technologies (the tragedy of fascism had come to its end only a decade earlier, the Cold War was raging, the new democracy was beginning to get to grips with capitalist economic development, and the socialist and communist masses were pressing on those in power but not managing to get space for themselves). What are the transformations that labour power imposes on machines from within the factory? This questioning continued to unfold in the face of the impetuous social development of the Thirty Glorious Years, and people asked themselves, moving from the factory to the society, what was the efficacy of human activity in the structuration of society. On the one hand, what was the effect of capitalist command (and of its technological instruments) on social life? And vice versa, what transformations did the social movements impose on the structures and institutions of capitalist command? In the face of a capitalist power that was extending rapidly into control over social life to the point of becoming a biopower, how broad and effective could the resistance be? How could one live and organise biopolitical relationships in such a way as to create forces alternative to biopower? I believe that these were the focal points around which an original political philosophy was taking shape in Italy in the tormented framework of heterodox Marxist debate, but it was a philosophy with deep links to the development of the Italian phenomenological schools of thought of the 1960s. These schools, which had counterposed the analysis of agonistic subjectivity to a whiny Heideggerian philosophy that nevertheless dominated the neoscholastics on the right and the last of the sirens of the Frankfurt School on the left – in other words, the phenomenology of Paci, Semerari, Melandri, and also the new critical positivism of Preti and Rossi-Landi – focused on the anthropological relationship between humans and machines, between productive activity and language, between perception and action, renewing the humanism of Merleau-Ponty and developing insights and perspectives that had already been elaborated by western Marxism (from Lukács to Kosik).

I think that some lines of research had already been indicated in the book *Radical Thought in Italy: A Potential Politics*, edited by Paolo Virno and Michael Hardt in 1996 (which contained essays written in the 1980s and 1990s). At that time, and subsequently, the themes defined above (originally conceived in the relationship between class movements and technological transformations) were intersecting with and drawing nourishment from contact with the philosophical literature of poststructuralism, especially (but not exclusively) French poststructuralism. Through this thematic hybridisation the above problems came to be central in the postindustrial, postmodern and globalist debate.

If this is the general framework within which the original adventure of the authors of the 'Italian difference' developed (and it would be important for researchers to do an analysis of these writers, as well as of the journals of the 'Khrushchev thaw' [*'disgelo'*] that fed into the discourse from 1956 until the late 1960s), let me now focus on a concept, or rather a slogan, that was central to that period of research and political activity and encapsulated in remarkable fashion both its rational nucleus and its *esprit de finesse*. I refer to the 'refusal of work' and what it really meant.

To this end, I shall reflect on some concepts that, although they do not relate directly to the question of the significance and meaning of the 'refusal of work', will be useful in arriving at a clarification. Here I would like to discuss some theoretical acquisitions that are relevant to our problem and were definitively expressed in *Empire* and subsequently developed especially in *Commonwealth*. (I apologise, obviously, for taking certain concepts as given, but if I had to trace the entire development of these concepts the argument would become too cumbersome). In other words, I would like to develop an argument around the forms in which *the ontology of human operations in the world*, or rather productive potentiality (as it is assumed in the social and political sciences), takes shape historically and in consequence is dominated (I mean subjected and exploited, disciplined and controlled) in this determined form, or else it puts itself in a position to revolt in order to liberate itself and (as the founding fathers used to say) to pursue happiness.

Labour and activity are the terms that one usually uses to define the unfolding of this ontological potentiality. These terms are understood here as 'labour' (manual, industrial, value-creating) and as 'activity' (generic). The philosophy, ethics and law of modernity have assumed that these terms are at the base of political economy and of every project of management of social production – at the origins of capitalism and for the 'to come' [*a-venire*]. Next, in postmodernity – as we argued in *Empire* – labour (value-producing, hence material industrial work) and activity (taken generically, in other words any productive activity that is intellectual and cognitive, immaterial, scientific, linguistic, emotional, etc.) tended to become one under the hegemony of the principle of activity. In the postindustrial and postmodern period, when we have the 'real subsumption' of society to capital or the full subjugation of *bios* to power, the canonical divisions of the thought (and mode of operation) of modernity – nature and culture, work and technology, factories and society, and so on – are no longer given. Contrary to what happens in the industrial era, it is now considered that force homogeneously invests both the natural and the social environment; hence the hegemony of 'immaterial labour' or of (generic) activity, inasmuch as they are directed not to individual productions but to social cooperation for the production of the common. (Let us be clear: 'immaterial labour' was a useful concept but was only indicatively correct. It expressed the urgency of getting rid of the essentialism of old discourses on nature and on work, both in naturalism and in labourism.) Therefore, at the moment when it was investing the totality of natural and social existence, labour was reduced: one can understand how, as a result of this genericness, production ended up being devoid of any pre-established rules, of any objective measure, and of any *telos* that was not conventionally constructed.

Why? Because the laws of economics, the organisational rules, the ethical–political norm, as Ricardo and Marx had defined them in their critique of political economy, had lost their efficacy. In fact, when the temporal relationship between necessary labour, surplus labour and surplus value is now irreducible to measure; when intellectual labour, knowledge and communication, in short the intangible elements, become increasingly central and indispensible, by comparison with the material elements, in the valorisation of commodities, and thus elusive to the discipline of the organisation of labour; and, finally, when the circulation of the factors of production becomes part and parcel of the cycle of production and reproduction of goods and destroys the spatial unity of production, then the realisation of the 'law of value' becomes impossible and the relationship between work time and the value of commodities becomes non-operative. This is what happens in the *first phase.**

Before considering the 'second phase' in our research, let me note that here, around the perception of this crisis, the question of a new 'form' of development opened at that point from the capitalist point of view: it was not acceptable that the conversion from the production of industrial labour to the hegemony of social activity should exclude all measure of production. I mean that capitalism was able very promptly to adapt to this new situation. It built new forms of accumulation, which were symmetrical to the new processes of social and cognitive production of value. It introduced new scales of value creation and measurement, which were entirely abstract, monetary and financial. For example, industrial value (profit) was replaced by the rules and measures of rent revenue. From 'energy' rent to 'real estate' rent, and finally to 'financial' rent, this was the path taken in the configuration of a new economic measure of generic human productive activity. Order was thus restored. In the total subjection to abstractly preconstituted values, to immobilised normative references, to privileges that some have described as 'neo-feudal' and to massive and absurd social inequalities, development was – so to speak – knocked back into shape. Of course this happens between one crisis and the next, because – as I pointed out previously – now all real value is inaccessible, and the temporalities of productive labour are unceasingly interrupted. Is it perhaps only violence that incarnates power and organises its continual permanence and recomposition? Is it biopower that fixes the governance of global assets?

I would like here – as a parenthesis, but not incidentally – to offer a critique of those fashions that present themselves on the stage of political culture pretending to be alternatives to the crisis of measure of development – that is, those cultural and political theories that, unable to think in terms of energy, potential or form, assume, as a model of reasoning and under the illusion of moving ahead, a particular image of the crisis and how to overcome it. Thus to capitalist development they oppose degrowth (i.e. the weakening of the relationship between culture and nature), or rather, to put it better,

---

* I apologise for this cavalier reference to the theoretical categories of classic political economy and Marxist critique – but it, too, reproduces the spirit of the time and the theoretical climate in which that 'Italian difference' was born.

to the historicity of the political and productive relationship they oppose 'nature' – as if it were possible to disinvest it, in other words to free nature from that massive investment that it has undergone and often independently reproduced; as if it were thus possible to disentangle the lived world from those social practices that have transformed nature itself and have seen it responding positively – and we can list among them, not least, the new tropes of sexuality, the effects of feminism, the enjoyment of a correct apparatus of welfare, the new usages linked to advances in medicine and biotechnology and so on. However, in the border areas between the social and the natural, in the regions in which the lived world is more obviously articulated with the natural world (very differently from what we find in inane antigrowth politics and the mechanisms of ecological extremism), we need to react to the 'crisis induced by the affirmation of biopower (through the subsumption of society to capital). In fact the hypothesis of a 'return to nature' is not an alternative but is consequent, symmetrical to the capitalist hypothesis of its integral 'domestication'. The discourse, here as elsewhere, then returns to production – that is, how are we going to invent values and organise forces that allow us to separate, to uproot not nature from production but the production of 'humans for humans' [*'dell'uomo per l'uomo'*] from capitalist development (thus freeing ourselves at the same time from all parasitic antigrowth utopias). The hypothesis we shall try to demonstrate here is one in which labour no longer valorises industrial capital and social activity no longer generates exploitation through rent. We shall have to ask whether it is possible to build a society in which production by workers no longer ends up in the valorisation of capital, that is, in the development of biopower. Production against development: can one justify this slogan on theoretical grounds? (Let us be clear that, when we say 'production against development', 'against development' does not mean 'degrowth' or being against growth in the production of goods. It means being against taking the market as the criterion of production and competition as the agent of its management, and thus against qualitative logic and the capitalist quantification of development. Is it possible to have such a thing as a non-capitalist logic of the market? Is it possible to have a planning (of humans for humans), taking for example the thread of goods indicated by welfare as a qualitative direction and a quantitative multiplier of production? In this sense *production* is no longer against development but is *for the common*.)

In younger days I tried to understand what 'to struggle against work' meant. It was not an invitation to laziness, to idleness, to doing nothing. Instead it meant to refuse (and to try to break) that organic oneness, that *synolon* [composite whole, fusion] which, in exploitation, in capitalist development, unified (contradictorily but efficaciously) living labour and dead labour, the toil of being exploited and capital. The workers too were prisoners of this duality in their consciousness brought about by the wage relation. It was no accident that Marx had indicated the end of capitalism as the moment in which the working class itself would be destroyed. When exploitation reached the point of acting at the social level and alienation was diffused everywhere, in order to struggle against exploitation and alienation it was necessary to struggle against work, against industry and against society too; in other words, not only against exploitation but also against alienation, and consequently against those corporations that nourished themselves and grew overbearing by negotiating the measure of exploitation; against those socialists who, wishing to take the place of capitalists, deluded the workers by calling 'public' those same goods that the bosses possessed privately and that capital exploited however it wished, even when the bosses chose to call themselves 'socialists'; and against the state that guaranteed and glorified the subjection of the masses (and sometimes exemplified this subjection in extreme and purging ways, massacring those same masses in so-called patriotic wars that were monstrous and cruel). My generation lived that history. Whether the battle that the working class of that time conducted against work was won or lost, I do not know. But I do know that, from the end of the 'short century' (whether you locate it in 1968 or 1989), capital was forced to replace (as the subject of value creation) industrial labour with generic social labour – and industry was replaced by the market, and class was replaced by people, and the corporation by the individual, and the state by global society. Given the balance of forces that the working class had effected by moving against industrialism, capitalism could not have done otherwise.

Much had changed – and almost nothing had changed. Almost nothing, for example, when one viewed things from the point of view of exploitation. Certainly the 'horny-handed' factory workers had given way to computer workers; Detroit had given way to IBM and Apple; 'jobs for life' had been replaced by precarious workers, and a thousand other kinds of people who toiled and emigrated across entire continents ... only to toil even more and so on, and the ecologists replaced the socialists. But one still found oneself there, in biopower, and that was true even if the wage packet had been replaced by the credit card and the wage had been replaced by debt. Certainly the mobility and flexibility of generic working-class activity

were relatively preferable to the monstrous monotony and repetition
in the prisons of Fordism and so on. However, even though a lot had
been transformed, almost nothing had changed. One noted in particular that now the slavery of exploitation did not hit the individual
as much as it hit cooperation; it did not strike only individuals, but
struck the multitude of singularities; it did not extend itself over the
daily working hours in the factory but on the entire length and duration of life – not only on private life but also on the commons. Now
it was life, life in common, that was subordinated to the money of
the bankers and to the finance of states. The theoretical 'real subsumption of society' within capital, this had now become fully – in
practical and historic terms – *biopower*. What a terrible misery for
that old working class that was now subordinated to the new figure
of command, for that old working class that from now on is called
poverty! And yet what a terrible force now emerges here! The new
generations of cognitive labour have won such an autonomy in work
that only with great difficulty will they be subjected to capitalist
command – and also the old classes, their poverty, put in this condition, have no other road than to destroy their own misery, to take
their leave of capital, to make an exodus from that common machine
of oppression.

But what is this 'common'? Here we arrive at the *second phase* in
our line of argument. We know that the water, the air, the sea, and
(according to the Bible) also the land are common. However, none
of this belongs to us any more. The accumulation process of capital
progressively appropriated these natural resources right from the
start. But we are more interested in the common that is produced by
humans, because this, like the natural commons, has on the one hand
been reabsorbed into, and by, the organisational structures of capitalism but on the other represents itself as a human common living that
is in some senses impossible to expropriate. Certainly the very *milieu*
in which we live and reproduce ourselves has been expropriated by
capital. Certainly capitalism today is a *capitalism of the commons*. We
have already said this: cognitive capitalism, global finance, life itself,
which is organised and exploited as such – this is the new figure of the
commons. All of which is masked in archaic titles of private or public
property, and the whole in any case subsumed to capital. But what
capital has not succeeded (and will never succeed) in appropriating is
the energy of labour power, or rather of that force of production that
is today called cognitive activity, knowledge, invention, of that multitude of singularities that produces the common. The common is in
fact not only the totality of the wealth produced but also the force of

production par excellence. One can certainly affirm that today there cannot be production without a production of the common and that the common constructs it.

So let us return to ourselves. While the way in which the potentiality of common production is put into shape – or the way in which the common energy that today constructs concrete historicity reveals itself – frees us from the need to begin with an a priori distinction between human order (*bios* [life, mode of living]) and the notion of a natural order (*zoē* [life vs death]), this condition does not free us from the need to repropose, for this common, the same separation that living labour demands from dead labour and the production of humans for humans imposes, against capitalist valorisation. Only in this way will it be possible to recognise in our singular existence the form of the common, and therefore to construct the experience (which can also be the urgency) of giving a face and political force to this common. Is it possible that this constitutive relationship, which is proposed in the name of the multitude, will be the new name of democracy? It is up to us to verify it. But it can only be verified through a social revolution; a democratic revolution, in which the terms 'revolution' and 'democracy' are compatible. Any project of democracy today can only found itself on the construction of new rights of reappropriation and of social ownership of common goods. And I should add that the form of this reappropriation will have no choice but to refuse the concentration of power in favour of a diffusion of power; it will have to reject all hierarchical (and/or competitive) forms, institutionalising the common as the content of a governance in which people share in a spirit of cooperation, a governance capable of promoting and absorbing ever newer communities of producers: thus a democracy of producers, against work and activity, both of them equally exploited, against development (and against 'degrowth').

So now let us return to us – in other words to the 'refusal of work', understood now as a theoretical defining point of the Italian 'difference'. During the decade from 1956 to 1966 there was, within Italian Marxism (and not only there), a real Copernican revolution against the Soviet tradition of diamat [dialectical materialism], which accelerated its dissolution after the twentieth congress of the Communist Party of the Soviet Union. After 1956 there was a real and proper change of paradigm in revolutionary thinking. What becomes hegemonic now is a new anthropology and a new sociology (expressed by an experience of militant activity exercised directly in the factories), which are no longer simply those of *Homo faber*, of the productive individual in industry and generally in the relationship with machines (they are no longer simply this, even if we are still dealing with a thinking turned against all thanatologies of a more or less Heideggerian stamp).

I would like to recall this in biographical terms. Our problem, in those years, was that of reinventing the anthropology of labour. The 'refusal of work' was not at all a voluntarist act but an operation that occurred within the system of machines; it was not a cultural operation for the transformation of nature, but a new, natural–cultural constitution; it was no longer simply a political act but an act that was constitutive of another humanity. Here I would like to invite people to a research that might traverse (as we ourselves did) the sociology and the anthropological philosophies of the early twentieth century. We had found, for example, a powerful solicitation in the phenomenology of Maurice Merleau-Ponty, whose thinking invited a hybridisation of phenomenological practices and Marxist analysis. There was a new humanism that was being constituted here, after the death of the human being [*dopo la morte dell'uomo*], a humanism that was communist. Habermas for instance notes this, and polemically, when he reminds us that in Merleau-Ponty there is the fundamental idea of a subject that already constitutes a socialised and integrated organism capable of speaking and acting even before it relates itself, in an objectifying manner, to something that exists in the world. It is the realism of a social and non-alienated transformation of the (common) labouring subject; this is what has the power to break with exploitation and thus with capitalist development, to make the production of humans for humans. In Italy the people who were pressing this phenomenological 'hyperdialectics' were Enzo Paci, Giuseppe Semerari, Enzo Melandri and others. It was, as we have said, a new humanism after the death of the human being. On the one hand, you had the Heideggerian reading and all kinds of catastrophist and eschatological pessimism in the thinking of the relationship between technology and human constitution; on the other hand, you had a conception that took as indestructible the relationships of culture–nature, human–machine, and socialised worker–biopolitical structure and proposed an anthropology that was liberatory, a new praxis within this relationship.

The essays by Panzieri and Tronti and, even more, Alquati's powerful early articles in the first issues of *Quaderni Rossi* offered a precise definition of the 'refusal of work', describing the production of working-class struggles (their forms and their cycles) against capitalist development (in its forms and cycles). This experience permits us to relaunch research on the ontology of operating (*operare*), on the relationship between critical phenomenology and the practice of militant and revolutionary intervention. Naturally, these themes also reopen the problem of the relationship between true knowledge and the ethics of transformation.

7

On 'Italian Theory'

If, out of that confusion of theoretical perspectives, of philosophical projects, of initiatives and new political practices built and developed between the 1960s and the end of the century in Italy... if out of that confusion we didn't have people trying to construct a thing called 'Italian theory' (whether plural or dialectical), there would be nothing to say – just as the Americans have done by putting together, into 'French theory', Derrida and Deleuze, Bataille and Foucault, Althusser and Lyotard, without claiming a common, shared heritage but simply mapping a context, a territory, an era. In Italy, apart from its being difficult to identify an area that could be covered by a single label, the situation is complicated by the fact that that particular territory and that stretch of time were marked not so much by a thinking as by a fairly dramatic political conflict. The philosophy was born and established itself within that conflict. The origin of what was to become Italian theory thus has features that are difficult to trace to any common historical and theoretical condition. The academic world was totally extraneous to it, and the social world was divided by political and class conflicts virtually tantamount to civil war. In the early days of that confused situation you certainly could not claim to have identified a political theory; at most, in its interstices, you might be able to identify some tools of political struggle. The toolbox comes before everything else.

At the origins there was the critique of Gramscianism and its Togliattian interpretation. This interpretation claimed to be a philosophical tradition and saw itself as hegemonic and based on supposed national–popular characteristics in Italian history, but not disdaining to pick up, along with the flags that the bourgeoisie had dropped in the mud, also the political understandings of sovereign acting [*agire*] and social mediation proper to the ruling classes of yesteryear. Historicism was a mix of continuity of the state and socialist innovation: a giant Tocqueville enthroned on Togliattism. The background against which the historicism of the Italian Communist Party [PCI] is articulated is vast and deep. It tends to invest capitalist development with a critique that is not a progressist alternative – the alternative is postponed to a point where development will have extended to the whole of society, where the dualisms of Italian history will have been removed, where corruption within the system will have been eliminated, and where a fine national–popular society will have shown itself to be ripe for socialism. This saccharine ideology began to be countered by critical voices in the second half of the 1950s; a central figure among them was that of Franco Fortini. With Brechtian and Benjaminian antecedents, but especially Giovinian–Luckácsian, he offers a scathing critique of the Gramscian notion of the 'national-popular' and of the Crocean historicism with which Gramscianism had ended up being identified. His critique also incorporates layers of the culture of the Catholic left of the time – of Felice Baibo and many others, and also of a certain liberal radicalism that was Gobettian in origin. But fundamental was above all the fact that, from within this critical upsurge, there emerged and spread a new type of grassroots militant, who brought Marxism back to life through the use of factory inquiries and extensions of those inquiries into society at large. Right from the start these people carried within them a desire for a radical alterity. It was a kind of militant sociology, markedly so in the case of Montaldi and Alquati; but it also involved intellectuals of the standing of Pizzorno and Momigliano and extended beyond sociological research to the medical and psychiatric practices of Basaglia, Terzian, Maccacaro and others. A new politics was created through battles against power – a new philosophy in militant activity with the exploited.

Despite having come from a long-standing background of communist cultural militancy, Raniero Panzieri was a product of this alternative culture. He translated into Italian Book II of Marx's *Capital* (on circulation). In the course of this work he was drawn to the Frankfurt School's interpretation of mature capitalism proposed by Pollock. He began to investigate 'social capitalism' – in other words, to attack the deeply pessimistic image that the theory of the Frankfurt School had arrived at in its latter days, of a world that is compacted and univocally formatted by capitalist power. The initial fascination of the method (a capital that engages the whole of society; production that extends into circulation; the human who becomes machine) was followed – as Panzieri himself tells us – by a blockage of research; but above all a blockage of movements, of struggles, of processes of emancipation. From the start, the reaction of *Quaderni Rossi* to this image of a blocked capitalist society – with which the high priests had rightly or wrongly identified themselves, in a line of thought that goes from Max Weber to Adorno and Horkheimer's jointly authored *Dialectic of Enlightenment* – engages the factory and society, working-class life and the life of the city, as territories of the class struggle and as a political reality. It is starting from this biopolitical perception that the toolbox begins to get organised.

One might add here that Panzieri and his friends were not alone. Even in certain academic quarters the reaction to the twin influence of Togliattian Gramscianism and Frankfurt pessimism was starting to take shape. Both in the area of phenomenology (Enzo Paci and Aldo Semerari) and in the area of a pragmatic and neopositivist philosophy (Preti and the protolinguist Rossi-Landi), there was an insistence on the importance of the phenomenological 'relationship', and in renewing an attachment to late Husserl or to second-period Wittgenstein there was a call for a radical break with all forms of residual Hegelianism. Personally I think that this theoretical background was much more important, in the elaboration of thinking about alternatives, than what academic historiography claims to have been the contribution of Della Volpian critique. It was not on the basis of an arrogant and irrational logicism (the belief that logic is the purest form of philosophy, of which the latest manifestation was Colletti) that one could reinvent the philosophical framework of a critique that invested life. The Italian phenomenological heresy was much more effective for this purpose.

With Mario Tronti the break with the Frankfurt School's interpretation of mature capitalism is radical. Here it is not denied that capital has entirely colonised society; what is denied is that this is an economic and necessary phenomenon – that the very concept of capital is unitary, transcendental, the foundation of both politics and life. No – capitalist value creation is done on and against the resistance of the working class. The undoubted subjectivity of capitalist initiative, of 'constant capital', of the capitalist owner is answered by the subjectivity of 'variable capital', of the worker-capital; power is answered by life. In short, Tronti offers us a Marx readapted to political struggle in the present, reproposing subjective characteristics of variable capital. The subjectification was radical: it made a break with all the brands of Hegelianism present in the Italian knowledge market at that time – it rediscovered the antagonistic nature of the capital relation, and thus the hardness of variable capital, within the general concept of capital. The recovery of the original Marxian insight becomes complete with the affirmation that what produces capitalist development is struggles and what builds history is organised labour power. The subjectification deepens to the point of considering, against the entire Leninist tradition, that the strategy of historical destruction of bourgeois society belongs directly to the working class, while what belongs to the party, to the intellectual leadership, is only the possibility of elaborating a tactic, a way of managing the relationship between state and struggles. The social democratic mechanism that saw the capitalist tendency of development as producing the conditions of the socialist revolution is deconsecrated, and the elaboration of the tendency is viewed in terms of the subjectification of the working class. The theoretical element is born within a politics that engages life and discovers in this the *dispositifs* of the destruction of capitalist domination.

The subjectification of the political rupture develops therefore within the struggles. Here, in the rupture, an ethics emerges. It shows itself in the immediate overturning of the function of the intellectual, in a Weberian *Beruf* [practice] that is completely reversed, antagonistic rather than functional, a participant in the destiny of the working class rather than a producer of ideology from above. It is the overturning of theory into practice. Ethics is rather the recognition and defence of a resistance that cannot be subsumed to any dialectics, whether of capital, of the state, or of the party. Ethics is the foundation of a negative dialectics, where the subjective class antagonism recognises the breaking, or rather the impossibility, of any capitalist mediation in strategic terms. It is from here, however, precisely in this rupture, that we have the ability to live and to define a tendency that affirms itself in the struggles, a production of subjectivity that plays out over a long time frame. The concept of tendency qualifies what is in fact a gnoseology and epistemology of acting. A kind of biopolitical approach unfolds not simply as a cognitive potentiality [*potenza*] of capital and of its development, but as a politics that is both in life and of life. There are at least three points that stand out here. The first involves an analysis of wage systems that spill over from the factory into society, engage it in its generality, and define the present social state and its ongoing crisis. In this transition from factory to society the analysis of the wage rearticulates the relationship between needs and social production, between consumption and collective behaviour, between the organisation of the factory and the organisation of the family and of 'civil society'. A second area of analysis concerns the political composition of the 'waged sector'. Here the history of modes of production takes up Marx's broad-brush account from original accumulation through to industrial society, from formal subsumption to real subsumption, and within this historical nexus it defines the lines of reading institutional forms and figures. The history of modes of production is a history of the modes of domination. This is where workerist [*operaista*] theory connects directly, at its birth, with French regulation theory and with the economic phenomenology of development of the German neo-Marxists (Hirsch, Offe, etc). Capitalist subjectification and proletarian subjectivity live in a common articulation, broken by struggles, reproduced in a continuous institutional self-configuring of the process. The theory is further developed on a third ground, namely that on which the technical composition of labour, of the working class, comes to deepen itself in the analysis of the human–machine relationship, with all the richness of the transformations that this relationship implies. It is particularly in this area that German sociology and anthropology are taken up and immediately transformed into tools in the organisation of the struggles.

There is therefore an entire generic horizon in which and on which life and biopower come into conflict. This opposition is at the base of the development of the new political philosophy in the 1960s, against all historicism and every continued existence or revival of a dialectical Hegelianism. We are talking about an atmosphere that was widespread in European thought. This rupture of western onto-teleology also found a recognition in Habermas. Habermas' first steps in his break with the horizon of powerlessness that was the legacy of the Frankfurt School consisted in the rediscovery of the Hegel of Jena, and hence of an open mechanism of social interrelation. That fracture was to be dramatised, according to early Habermas, and resolved through communicative mediation. What was being proposed was a kind of latter-day, flaccid neo-Kantianism. That is exactly what the innovative Italian conception of struggle denies. Phenomenology, no longer simply of capital but of a capitalism that has engaged life itself – in other words, the Frankfurt framework – is assumed here too, but turned to a definition that is antagonist to biopower: it does not find an intellectual solution. The sense of this crisis can be recovered only through an ethical immersion, an epistemological break and a new political orientation. The analysis moves top down; it is conducted from the inside; it does not admit caesuras; it assumes subjectification as an essential ground to all philosophical reasoning.

The antagonistic link between relations of production and forces of production, between subjectification of capitalist domination and subjectification produced by the behaviours of social labour power is accentuated and gradually rendered dramatic through the transformation of the power relations within this antagonist polarity. On the other hand, capitalism increasingly engages life in terms that are 'extractive' of surplus value, whereby the whole of society, the whole of life, have become productive – but on this same terrain one perceives the tendency of productive society to regain an autonomy that is increasingly significant and important. The biopolitical context is therefore opposed ever more obviously by a biopower – and the resistance configures itself, in the tendency, in terms that are increasingly autonomous, constituent and institutive.

But the tendency soon comes under attack. It is accused of proposing teleological substitutes and historicist contexts to the critique of any possible *Aufhebung* [sublation]. But this charge does not affect its target: in the new philosophy the only possible teleology is that of the point of view of action, and the only historicism admitted is that of the recognition of its historicity. Conversely, the idea is that the assumption of a negative dialectics has no solutions – the phenomenology of *Krisis* [crisis] becomes mystical. This is the central breaking point of Italian alternative thought in the late 1960s: to the pragmatic and tendential exit from *Krisis* and its radically immanentist and humanist determination, to the fixing of biopolitics as a productive fabric is opposed a sort of exorcism – no longer the weak, transcendental exorcism of neo-Kantianism and of the linguistic and communicative philosophies (this was the moment of the Habermas–Apel controversy), but one that is eschatological, mysteriously transcendent. The struggles, which at that time were more powerful than ever, were opposed at the theoretical level by the so-called 'autonomy of the political' and at the practical level by the effectiveness of *raison d'état.* The crisis of paradigm in modern philosophy, which the new philosophy had interpreted in political terms, anticipating in Italic dialects and in the struggles that horizon of thought that the French poststructuralism of the second half of the twentieth century presented in open manner (and developed through various and multiple perspectives), is here brought back to the nihilist ontology and ethical impotence of Nietzsche as interpreted by Heidegger – worse, to a Hartmannian wasteland. The effective outcome of this 'critique of critical criticism' is to consolidate a biopower with no possible alternative, whereas it is precisely in this phase that the new philosophy begins, from within the broken dialectics, to constitute an ontology that is productive of the common, in other words to fill out the critique of the real

subsumption of society to capital through the discovery and the establishment of a constituent power of the common. This is where this
constituent power, brought back to ontology, widens to form a real
and actual materialist basis, critical of capitalist development. Already
then, at the start of the 1990s, Hardt and Virno were emphasising how
much the practical critique developed by Italian thought on struggles
had been translated positively into French poststructural philosophy.
It was no accident therefore that the neo-Heideggerian critique and
the mysticism of *Krisis* thinkers ended up being totally extraneous to
that same poststructuralist brand of thought – but above all alien to
any vision of biopolitics and of the production of subjectivity.

Let us stop there. Put crudely, what happened after that seems to
me simply a summing up and accentuation of what had happened
thus far. In that tangled context of problems and contradictions,
Italian theory appears as yet another 'weak' historiographical schema
that vaguely grasps the temporal and local determinations of the
historical process and then leads them forward to a cowardly pacifica-
tion – with some extremely heavy consequences: first and foremost,
that of diverting the attention of the researcher from the contradictory
phenomenology of biopower by maintaining a confusion between the
categories of immanence and of transcendence. This is where the
political theological is still on trial. This is where, for example, political–theological critique, after having glimpsed, in utopian manner,
a community in the making, refuses subjectification not so much as
resistance and antagonism but as materiality, institution and historicity. Biopolitics is therefore configured here as a place that exhausts
itself in a power vacuum, in a nakedness that is another name for
void of time and history. Second, Italian theory ends by intimat-
ing the emptying out of every historically determined point of view,
ethically situated and politically oriented in knowledge and in acting
on the political horizon. Also from this point of view, the historicity of the struggles, the thresholds of production of subjectivity, and
the constructed tendencies are systematically reduced and censored.
Third, in Italian theory, in the pacifications it seeks to register, the
possibility of taking any rupture of the biopolitical relationship as an
emergence–insurgence of new autonomous potentialities is excluded.
Biopolitics is presented here as a terrain that is not located in the
negative dialectics but suppresses it, that does not pose the ontological relationship as a polarity but takes away its potentiality and denies
the intransitivity of the antagonism it includes. Fourth, as a result,
the final crisis of western onto-teleology would leave us in the impossibility of determining a space, of rehabilitating a temporality, and of

building a subject that could find in history a common constituent horizon. It was in order to carry out this work that the new criticism was born in practical terms in the 1960s and later reorganised itself in philosophical terms: to give nobody the possibility of denying the subject.

But subject means subjectification. Was there anyone who thought that in the struggles, in the dynamics of the clash between biopower and biopolitical subjects, in the transformation of the concept of the working class into that of cognitive and precarious subject – or rather into that of multitude – was there anyone who thought that collective subjects – call them identities, substances, individuals or whatever – could again appear on the stage? Of course: not even this kind of defamation was missing in the attack on the new philosophy. But the more the new philosophy was confirmed, the more, on the ontological terrain, subjective and determined emergences (Spinoza would have labelled them infinite ways of being) were qualified as singularities. And the concept of production could not be grasped except in terms of cooperation between singularities, as assembly of singularities, which were otherwise unproductive: singularities defined both by the invention power of their cognitive nature and by the potentiality of the affects put into production, but above all defined by their pooling into a common cooperation of the biopolitical potentialities of which they expressed the tendency. Their existence is common, and there can be no existence outside of the common. They are productive multitude. Solitude is a dark story. Only the common is productive, but it is productive because it is composed of infinite singularities that associate together continuously. The arguments of individualism, on the other hand, continue seeking space, re-emerging equivocally in relation to the new philosophy, in other versions of the Italian theory – both *zoē* and *immunitas* [exemption] maintain the individualist reference as the principal reference. Not to mention those writers who have taken fear – today called *katechon* [duty, principle of restraint] – and have made it the Hobbesian driving force of individuality in turning to the state for security.

Of course, subjectification is productive and produced in the same measure. But this antagonistic relationship is 'extractive', in the two senses of that insoluble duality that negative dialectics proposes. On the one hand, biopower extracts from the totality of the people its wealth and its legitimacy; on the other, the singularities, promoting themselves as a common potentiality in productive cooperation, expropriate biopower of its ability to govern. Here, after 50 years, the new philosophy is returning (beyond all fanciful notions of an 'Italian theory') to ask itself what kind of sociology and what kind of political economy might act as 'toolboxes' that could be used to rebuild – in these new conditions – a militancy of the common that can recover and develop the subversive force of the early days – in the formation of the common.

And, as regards the Italian theory, no bad feelings: *omnia munda mundis* [to pure men all things are pure].

8

The Constitution of the Common and the Logics of the Left

1 Defining the left

Once upon a time there was an academic neo-Enlightenment (Norberto Bobbio's, for instance) that defined the left as the bearer of values of equality, while the right would be the bearer of values of freedom... but the ideal would be to keep them both together. We can leave tales of this kind to Habermas, the only ideologist still to pursue them. But, ever since this notion of equality–freedom was taken up by Tony Blair in his reform of the Labour Party, the project has ended in nothing – or rather in catastrophe. At the present we are witnessing a series of self-criticisms so widespread that it is not surprising to find even the likes of Pierre Rosanvallon and Anthony Giddens among its spokespersons. In fact, in this period of triumphant neoliberalism, the distinction between left and right had become subtle and shifting. The left defends the welfare state as long as the cost is not too burdensome on the public debt (in other words on the desire to maintain the hierarchical order of society); and the right demolishes the welfare state as long as public order and security are not endangered. The monetary dimension became essential to managing social inequality behind a rhetoric of equality–freedom. In military matters the idea of a distinction between left and right has become even more hypocritical: while the right leads imperial wars and invasions of territories, the left contributes to those wars through humanitarian bombings from the sky. Anyway these distinctions too are superficial: the ideological transcendentalism of the propaganda on both right and left is a very brutal practice that makes no distinctions. Please note: my flattening of the left on the practices of the right really is not a caricature; actually it is not far from reality. Whatever way you read the concept of the left, there seems to be little space for it in the system of imperial governance. The project of a movement 'of struggle and government' (the old paradigm of the left) no longer works, because when you are up against imperial governance the capture power of the institutions is stronger than any attempt to renew the order of society and to democratise its administration.

I do not think, however, that the concept of the left has become meaningless or useless. On the contrary, the left can become important when conceived of as a constituent potentiality.

2 Obama and the illusions of reform

Why did we like Obama? Because both in the democratic primaries and in the presidential election he had expressed the constituent intention (not only as a 'form' of his project but also as a 'strength' of his politics) to use his executive powers so as to transform American society. That has all turned out to be illusory. Faced with the problems raised by the financial crisis, Obama has not found an adequate response to them, except by renewing trust in the financial institutions that dominate world politics and that had been the cause of that crisis in the first place; faced with the wars unleashed by George Bush, Obama not only failed to extricate himself from them, but actually stepped up the military and policing aggression. As regards welfare policies, and in particular questions of healthcare reform, Obama has only complicated the first reforming steps with crippling retreats and compromises.

But the problem is not Obama (even though obviously he is). The problem is the inability of the left to keep its promises once it has been swallowed into the system of power. Where does this limit lie? The left does not succeed in reopening the struggles while it is in government. Should we conclude that the weight of the structures of power has now reached such a level of complexity that elections can never match the necessary timings of reform? Or rather, are there other reasons (not only institutional) that render left proposals for reform illusory?

To answer these questions we have to remember that in both the United States and Europe there has been a big expansion of executive power over the past 30 years. Everywhere the executive bureaucracy has developed structures that duplicate the other two powers or compete with them: in the United States the legal officials of the executive dominate the judiciary; the executive's Office of Legal Counsel has become more powerful than that of the attorney general; the economic experts of the presidency dominate the legislative powers. In Europe, for some time now, government has been hollowing out the power of parliament through legislation by decree; ministries of the interior and the police have been put beyond any kind of control. The powers of war and the running of the army represent perhaps the most dramatic moment of this transformation. Why, then, given this disproportion of the powers of the executive in relation to other powers, has Obama not been able to develop his projects for reform? Obama has not put an end to the use of powers that, in the Bush era, had operated in the form of exception; so why has he not been able to use them effectively? To what extent is Obama himself a prisoner of that executive structure of which he should be the boss? Of course, Obama is not a revolutionary but rather a person who came into power with the intention of carrying out some modest but significant reforms. The same could be said of the left in Europe: the last example of strong left-wing reforms goes back to the first two years of François Mitterrand. Since 1983 the left in power has never succeeded in renewing society through reformist projects.

To answer these questions, I think that we first have to note the difference between the effectiveness and success of the reforms of the right (Reagan, for example) and the ineffectiveness and failure of the reforms of the left – and analyse it. We believe that the right is able to make its reforms because democratic constitutions prefigure this possibility only for the right. Democratic constitutions, both the older ones and those built after the Second World War, were constructed within a framework of liberalism. The only opposing example, in other words the only radical left reform, Roosevelt's New Deal, does not prove the contrary, nor do the triumphs of social democracy in the immediate postwar period in Europe. In those cases it was the disaster of the capitalist economy and the war that had just ended that imposed those reforms: they were not reforms but transient and reversible compromises.

Conversely, it can be noted that the transformation and expansion of executive power in the United States, which began under the Reagan administration, was not only carried through by the Republicans but also perfected by Democratic administrations. The policies of the White House under Clinton and Obama have also furthered that concentration of power in the executive to which we have referred. Even in Europe the movements of the left have not been able to impose onto executive power a force that could break through in the direction of reform.

3 The three powers in crisis

There have been attempts (and in Italy one is currently under way) to bring about new constitutional equilibria and reformist openings through the use and mobilisation of the judiciary. Such attempts have also been pursued in the United States and have sometimes succeeded: the jurisprudence of the Supreme Court in the 1930s and 1960s contributed to social reform and to libertarian and antiracist changes in the constitution. But, as I said before, this was due to exceptional conditions of economic crisis or to situations of conflict that put the social order radically in danger. Things then immediately changed, and the judiciary once again recognised itself as conservative. Leaving aside the crucial role played by the US Supreme Court in the election of George Bush in 2000, one might simply point to the recent decision to allow unlimited contributions by big business to the election campaign, on the grounds that such contributions are a protection of the constitutional right to 'free speech'. In Europe too there are, as I said, attempts to consider the judiciary as a constituent machine. What is being renewed here is an old Jacobin utopia, never efficacious and always ambiguous. In Italy in particular, the reforming power of the judges produces a deformation of the constitutional place allotted to the judiciary: when judges operate in non-conservative ways, they do so in a way that mimics political power. And this produces no end of disasters.

It is alarming to see how the places dedicated to reforms, namely parliament and the legislature, have been gradually emptied of their functions. The crisis of democratic representation seems today to constitute the point of greatest weakness in western systems of the organisation of power. The legislature now has a very weak, almost non-existent capacity to propose social budgetary projects, and above all to be effective in the control of military affairs. Its primary role is now to build support for, or create obstacles to, the proposals of the executive. The main activity of which the US Congress is capable, it seems, is to block the initiatives of the executive and to obstruct government. In this light, when the left puts its faith in legislative power (and often this is the only space in which it is present), either it is deceiving us or it is under an illusion about its effectiveness.

As always in these cases, the sense of alienation that citizens have about the political parties (which are the backbone of parliamentary representation) continues to grow. And this distrust is particularly marked when it comes to parties of the left. Some complain that the role of parties has become extraordinarily complicated in the transition to the twenty-first century: in addition to the classic problems of the representation of civil society, the political parties have had to deal with problems of public debt, migration, climate change, energy policy, and so forth, so that within this complexity their ability to represent issues should have expanded and specialised. But in reality it tends to disappear. Seen in this light, the parliamentary system seems to be totally inadequate, particularly because it is under siege from the lobbies. But how are we to reform it, how are we to renew it? Doing so would require new forms of representation, a new civic terrain of discussion and proposals, and new subjects formed through a constituent process that develops from the bottom up. But how are we to initiate this process? The left, whose responsibility it is to achieve this, tells us nothing about it. Debates on the electoral aspects of parliamentary representation have become incomprehensible and pointless. In Europe, when it comes to questions of electoral law reform, you can no longer distinguish between irony and cynicism. In any case people seem to forget that money plays a major role in electoral politics, both through the moneys contributed by the economic potentates and through the media, which are always an expression of the economic potentates. Their claims to represent society disappear behind the power of money. And so the road to corruption paradoxically becomes almost unavoidable, and this is particularly true for the left. In short, the left parties seem particularly unable to arrive at a proper relationship with civic society. We ask again: Why?

4 Conservatism of the left, reformism of the right

Left-wing parties have increasingly become parties of complainers. In Europe they complain about capitalism's inability to secure work for the people; and the destruction of the welfare state; and imperial military interventions. They also complain about the corruption of their own representatives and about their lack of representative legitimacy. The only position that they are capable of taking aggressively is a defensive recourse to the constitution: they protect an imagined past, consecrated by an antifascist rhetoric and by a constitutional compromise with the capitalist powers. They are affected by an 'extremism of the centre', which they often remember as an idyllic past. As for left-wing intellectuals (if such a thing can still be said to exist in Europe), they complain about the corruption of the constitution and about how the structures of representation have been voided of content. The same thing is happening in the United States. For example, Bruce Ackerman worries that the expansion of the power of the executive poses a danger of dictatorship. Sheldon Wolin claims that the democratic content of the US Constitution has been voided to such an extent as to create an 'inverted totalitarianism': whereas previously the totalitarian state controlled the structures of capitalism, in 'inverted totalitarianism' it is the capitalist structures that directly control the structures of the state. In Europe Rosanvallon, one of the fathers of the so-called 'third way', now admits the impossibility of a state that controls the power of finance. And Anthony Giddens laments the excessive power of media giants, denouncing their totalitarian effects.

We have arrived at the (somewhat paradoxical) point where it is only the populist movements – such as the Tea Party, the Northern League and others – that address problems of transformation or reform of the constitution. As regards the Tea Party in particular, although a part of it has undoubtedly taken on the standard rhetoric of the Republican Party in defence of the constitution (with literal interpretations and a return to the intentions of the founding fathers), the grassroots level of the movement recognises that representation has ceased to function and that parliament no longer represents it. So it is calling for a constituent assembly. The programmatic contents of the Tea Party are largely reactionary and often explicitly racist, but its basic political assumptions are correct. You could say the same perhaps of the principles underlying the populism of the [Italian] Northern League. These too are often reactionary and racist, but they are effective when they point to the crisis of the representative constitutional system. The institutional left, on the other hand, has not understood the depth of the crisis of representation and has not grasped the need for constitutional reform. In Italy in particular the left has not yet understood that the recent referendums were not defensive but were actually innovative in constitutional matters. Finally, one of the great contributions of the 'Spanish revolution' of 15 May has been to focus critical energy on the crisis of representation, not in order to restore some imagined legitimacy of the system but rather to experiment with new forms of democratic expression – *democracia real ya*. The Occupy Wall Street movement also advances this critique of representation and this demand for democracy. The camps at Puerta del Sol and on Wall Street are seeking a constituent process.

5 Can the left become a constituent power?

This should probably be the starting point of our discussion, namely that the left perhaps does not have the ability to grasp the radicality of the problems that democratic politics must now confront: the problems of a constituent power. These are the things on which public debate should now be opened. I believe that the only future for the left lies in the opening of a constituent discussion. So let us start by listing the major problems of a constituent *dispositif* in today's world.

The first problem arises from the fact that liberal democratic constitutions are founded on private property, whereas in today's world production takes place in ways that are increasingly marked by the common. Innovation and the expansion of the forces of production are based increasingly on free and open access to public goods, knowledge and information, while on the other hand the enclosure of the common into private hands reduces and hinders productivity. Capitalist accumulation is now organised in financial terms; capital exploits wealth that is socially produced and captures it principally under the form of investment incomes. Thus, in our time, the social nature of production comes more and more dramatically into conflict with the private nature of capitalist accumulation. This is the first point to be addressed by the constituent politics of a left alternative: it should be framed in terms of the expression of the common and should seek to fix the criteria for a 'production of humans for humans'. In this framework the first objective obstacle is therefore private property and rent revenue. Constituent power has to organise an opening up of common goods to social productivity and the reappropriation of the financial structure of production in order to direct it to common goals. The reproduction of life should prevail over the accumulation of capital, and welfare over financial revenues.

The second problem today, or rather the second theme of attack of the constituent power of an alternative left, is that of the cognitive value of labour. Here the problem is how to develop, constitutionally, policies of self-formation and common education that extend over the whole structure of production. University policies and communications policies have to go not only beyond the current state of privatisation-related misery but also beyond the level of the public organisation of education, to become engines in the construction of the common and of social integration. It is on this terrain that the left has to prove its existence and its political will. Right-wing populism can be defeated on this terrain, through the expropriation of the means of production and communication that are now in the hands of both private and public capital. Freedom of expression is measured through the ability to make truth a commons, and the freedom to produce is measured through the ability to make life a commons.

The third point around which a left alternative needs to organise its constituent capacity is the need to move beyond political representation as a profession. This is one of the few slogans of the socialist tradition that can be put back at the centre of our civil condition. Building up the instruments of direct democracy is a fundamental necessity, and it has to extend over matters of the security of common life and over functions of protection and control of both 'privacy' and social relations. It is clear that the functions of justice also need to be brought into the arena of direct democracy by doing away with the illusion that, in virtue of their economic privilege and social class, professional magistracies can offer guarantees of independence and vision.

A fourth fundamental point is the need to create a federalist programme, in other words with the decentralisation of power across territory. The crisis of the nation-state can only be resolved by developing federal forms of government that are close to the base, spread throughout the territory, and able to act on all aspects of society and production – in short, on the governance of common life. Modern sovereignty is over. The left, as a figure internal to the struggle between powers in modernity, symmetrical to and complicit with the right, is also over. If the left still has reasons to exist, its future lies not in aspiring to join the power groups of the ruling elites, but in grassroots democratic participation in a constituent process that remains always open-ended.

The last urgent point of attack in the definition of a left alternative is the capacity to match governance on an ongoing basis to the changes taking place in the social system. Any system of constitutional rules must be able to be modified quickly when the need arises. It needs to be able to keep pace with changes in productivity in an economic system that takes as its purpose 'the production of humans for humans', and to stimulate and deepen the participation of citizens in the functions of governance.

6 The social reappropriation of the common

The current phase is characterised by a crisis of all those sections of the left that do not see themselves as constituent. We live in a period of struggles against the economic and political crisis of capitalism – struggles that are increasingly revolutionary in spirit. The insurrectionary movements in the Arab countries – and also in Europe – are turning against the political dictatorships of corrupt elites and against the political and economic dictatorships of our superficial democracies. I do not mean to confuse the one with the other, but there is clearly now a desire for radical democracy that is mapping a 'commons of struggle' on various fronts. The struggles today present themselves in various ways, but they are unified by the fact of recomposing peoples against new poverties and old corruptions. These are the struggles that move from moral outrage and multitudinarian *jacqueries* towards the organisation of an ongoing resistance and the expression of constituent power. They are not simply attacking the liberal constitutions and the illiberal structures of governments and states – they are also developing positive slogans such as guaranteed income, global citizenship, and the social reappropriation of common production. In many ways the experience of Latin America in the last decade of the twentieth century can be seen as the preamble to these objectives, also for the central countries of highly developed capitalism.

Can the left go beyond modernity? Here the question is, what does it mean to go beyond modernity? Modernity has been capitalist accumulation under the sign of the sovereignty of the nation-state. The left has often been dependent on this development, and so has been corporate and corrupt in its activities. However, there has also been a left that has moved within and against capitalist development, within and against sovereignty, within and against modernity. It is the logics of this second left that interest us, at least those that have not become redundant. If capitalist modernity is entering a state of irreversible crisis, antimodern practices that may have been progressive in the past now have no reason to exist. If we still want to talk about the logics of the left, we have to do so in terms of an 'altermodernity' capable of radically reviving the antagonist spirit of the socialism of yesteryear.

Neither the regulatory instruments of private property nor those of the public domain can fulfil this need for an alternative to the modern. The only ground on which the constituent process can be activated is now the common – the 'commons' conceived of as the land and other natural resources in which we share, but also and especially as the commons that is produced by social labour. This commons, however, has to be constructed and organised. Just as water is not common until a network of tools and devices is assembled to ensure its distribution and usage, so the social life that is based on the common is not immediately and necessarily qualified by freedom and equality. Not only must there be access to the common, but its management must also be organised and secured by democratic participation. Taken on its own, therefore, the common does not solve the problem of the future of the left, but it does show the terrain on which this can be rebuilt. The left needs to understand that only a new constitution of the common (and no longer the defence of nineteenth-century or postwar constitutions) can bring it back to life and offer the possibility of power. The constitutions we have today, as I said previously, are compromise constitutions that were inspired by Yalta rather than by the desires of the antifascist fighters of the time. They have not given us justice and freedom but have simply consolidated, through the public law of modernity, the capitalist structures of society. In the United States the left is caught in the same constitutional blackmail. It needs to overcome it. It must do so in order to go beyond the tragic periodical repetition of left governments that refinance the very banks that caused the crisis, continue to pay for imperial wars, and are unable to build a welfare system worthy of a great proletariat such as that of the United States.

What is needed today is a constitution of the common, and this factory of the common requires a prince. Nobody is suggesting that we should see this ontological principle and this dynamic *dispositif* in the same ways in which Gramsci or the founding fathers of socialism thought of it. Only from the new struggles for the constitution of the common will this prince emerge. Only a constituent assembly dominated by a left alternative will be able to bring it into being.

9
On the Future of the European Social Democracies

The European social democracies seem to be in a rather sorry state. This is probably because, in the last 30 years, they have failed to produce a political programme capable of matching the changing productive structures of capitalism. As we know, since the mid-1970s the global elites, both political and economic, have conducted a single battle on two fronts: on one front, the battle to move beyond the Fordist organisation of labour in order to dismantle the social regulation that had been imposed by the labour movement and by the social democracies since the 1930s; on the other front, the battle to introduce a model of 'limitation of democracy' designed to build new parameters of social control that would serve the aims of the free market and the social hegemony of big business. The technological innovations associated with the automation of industrial production and the digitisation of society were vital in making it possible to move on from Fordism. The massive financialisation of the economy, taken as the central criterion – of scale and orientation – in the reconfiguration of the social development of production, was the main element in organising the hard control of a society that was open to the power of capital and closed to any extension of democracy to the workers and to other minorities.

The social democracies were undoubtedly aware of these changes, which began in the second half of the 1970s, but had not seen their social and political consequences until much later. They were able neither to resist the offensive launched by Margaret Thatcher in Britain nor to change direction in response to the global fallout from Reaganism. The strategies implemented by neoliberalism were underestimated and, even when they were grasped at an intellectual level – in the major universities in London and Paris, which had for some time been involved in the social democratic project – there was no spark of an adequate political response to the neoliberal offensive.

First, it seems that social democracies have not proposed alternatives to those modifications in the organisation of business enterprise and of social production that have radically transformed the nature of work. Work has stopped being primarily material and has become increasingly immaterial, cognitive and communicative. The classic wage system has gone into crisis, and the precariat has begun to play an important role. This transformation should have been taken on board. On the one hand, workers' organisations should have been persuaded to take steps to deal with it; on the other, we should have seen the construction of new horizons of labour regulation, both in society at large (by investing unceasingly – in order to back up incomes from labour in welfare as a single mechanism capable of reorganizing labour 'beyond' the factory) and in the transformation of the work force (by investing unstintingly in schools, in research and in the rebuilding of services). We assume that the neoliberal revolution tended to block politically the level of the 'necessary wage', in other words of that (historically determined) measure of satisfaction of the needs of working-class families, which is necessary both in order to maintain a high degree of production and in order to ensure the reproduction of the labour force as a whole. The question (for the social democracies) was therefore not only to maintain or increase the quantity of, but also to qualify or to transform politically the struggle over the measure of the 'necessary wage' within the framework of the transformation of labour power. The development of capitalism and neoliberal ideology had removed the necessary wage from the realm of analysis of the timings of the working day and had made it subject to the laws of finance. The consequence was that the economic struggle for subverting the rules of the relative wage changed into a social and political struggle for subverting the rules of financial distribution, of income and welfare. The neoliberal revolution put a price on freedom and equality. They have a cost, as Thatcher and Reagan told us cynically; yes, they are absolute values but they also have a given economic foundation. One should have answered that yes, this is true in a sense but could be completely reversed. In fact, when labour becomes intellectual, freedom is an essential element of it; when labour becomes cooperative, equality is one of its qualifying elements: so without freedom or equality you can no longer have productive labour. Labour thus became more powerful in its confrontation with capitalist command. Why has politics not been built on this terrain?

Second, the social democracies did not understand that, in the new capitalist organisation of labour and production, finance had taken the upper hand over direct production. This occurred because financial and monetary values began to be able to circulate freely and to organize their relative autonomy in a market that was tending to become global. But this also created ambiguous effects: at the beginning, effects more in line with the bourgeois spirit of politics than with the capitalist spirit of industry; later, effects with perverse consequences. To put it succinctly, despite all rhetoric to the contrary, rent took priority over profit. This does not mean that the values of finance were only speculative: on the contrary, finance revealed itself to be symmetrical to social production, to such an extent as to represent its measure (that measure that the value of the working day is no longer able to constitute). In order to govern financialisation of this sort (which was not a parasitic deviation of quotas of surplus value but, as stated above, the new form of capital accumulation, symmetrical to the new processes of social and cognitive production of value), one would have had to reinvent democracy, build new rights of social ownership of common goods. So that is where intervention was needed, and that is what the social democracies failed to do. They should have set up a democratic policy for finance and should have moved to eliminate speculation, not in order to return nostalgically to the measures of industrial production – that idiotic fantasy that both the left and the right like to call 'real production' – but in order to achieve a concrete and correct financial dynamics of social production. Many analyses today take 'bioeconomy' as their subject, that is, the integration of life, society and production as a material base of economic analysis, but also (and especially) as a specific terrain of democratic intervention of control. When finance is left alone, when it is not regulated democratically, it becomes, unavoidably, a form of rent pure and simple: a parasitic phenomenon, private and genetically linked to ownership individualism, which claims it with arrogance – all the more scandalous as production becomes increasingly social. To this we can add that privatisations (so generously authorised by the social democracies), instead of supporting the expansion of investment, have constructed and permitted further rent possibilities.

Furthermore, since the 1970s, the social democracies did not even minimally understand the emergence of a new geopolitical framework, either on the institutional–intensive terrain of the crisis of national sovereignty or on the resulting political framework of international equilibria. What do I mean by that? We can take just one example: the question of Europe. The building, during the 1980s, of a new global geopolitical dimension (which became definitive after 1989) led, alongside the weakening of the concept of national sovereignty, to the urgency of fixing efficacious poles of international political organisation; for the European social democracies, a strong subjectification with global aspirations could only be achieved around the European Union as a political institution. Do you think that the social democracies did this? Absolutely not. Both before and after 1989 they stuck with the Atlanticist conception of Europe and never challenged – indeed, in the period of the Yugoslav Wars, they lauded – the importance of the slip knots with which the North Atlantic Treaty Organization (NATO) was throttling Europe. Eastern Europe was not conquered by ideals and by the European institutions but was annexed by NATO. All this has had disastrous consequences. The inability to construct in coherent fashion a European subject has stripped the social democracies of the last chance to save what could be saved for the benefit of workers, to maintain the social compromises of the period after the Second World War. Today the likes of Dany Cohn-Bendit can mock social democracy, brandishing the 'Europe fetish', calling it an interclass interest that is devoid of principles! And what a good thing that he does so – this way at least Europe will be able to organise itself within the global order, like a beautiful Switzerland, fat and impotent, just as the Swiss Confederation has been for a couple of centuries within the European order. The fact is that all of this, let alone the international scene, not only is not enough but also produces pernicious effects in Europe itself: it leads to a vile swarming of small local potentates, wishful thinkers, identity politicians and populists. These are the real foundations that sustain the Atlantic policy in Europe today; these are the forces that pre-empt any possibility of reinventing a global politics of Europe within the new world order (and in the crisis of US unilateralism). Social democracies seem to bear a heavy responsibility for this situation.

Leaving aside the related crisis of the principle of sovereignty, the social democracies have not even understood the 'crisis of government'. In general they still think that a national government made up of a set of structures institutionally and constitutionally guaranteed is enough to govern. Hence the fetishism for the administrative unity of the law, for constitutional traditions, for the independence of the judiciary, to mention just the most important issues. But today – and the social democracies seem not to have noticed it – government no longer takes place within nation-states; at best what is exercised is governance. So, when they are in the majority, the social democratic parties try to impose government and fail. When they are in a minority, they do nothing other than ideological opposition. But – one could add, by way of a minor paradox – being minoritarian in governance is, in a phase of crisis of representative regimes, almost better than being in government. In fact experience teaches that you can win elections with big majorities and not be able to govern: witness Obama. On the other hand, it is possible, through a shrewd use of available and relatively limited forces, to be continuously opening up focal points of resistance (in the face of the majority), both in trade union matters and in ecological matters, both in education matters and in social matters. It is entertaining to see how the German Greens, just like the French Greens, are able to be transversally effective precisely in the area of governance, both when they are in government and when they are not – and without any solidly established social theory or practice, simply by virtue of a deep-rooted opportunism. The social democracies have instead inappropriately dismissed any relationship of discussion, alliance or 'transmission belt' with the social organisations of the workforce and of society and thus have ended up being systematically incapable of attacking the forces of the right and those of the centre for their organic links with the national and transnational economic potentates.

We recognise that the reaction of social democracies to the crisis of the 1970s and 1980s was not linear or homogeneous. New Labour was ahead of the rest in anticipating the transformations that were under way. The Scandinavian social democratic parties have also moved consistently regarding the perception of the crisis of Fordism and the irreversibility of the social production networks defined by the new organisation of the firm, of the market and of finance. But the understanding of the transformation was followed only by political drifting. There was no confidence that this reality could be changed. The social democracies abhorred the risk, the very idea of getting themselves involved in the construction of the other, let alone producing a project of transformation. That explains why, after 1989, a real precipice opened. The strength that social democracies still managed to express as a prop to bourgeois power against the Soviet threat failed, their parliamentary and trade unionist function was reduced to a minimum. The great powers destroyed the watchwords of a social democracy that did not go beyond a proposal oscillating between a 'fairly regulated' market, public order, 'democratic' policing, and a 'morality' of political party mediation. Fine words, but, as always, in the absence of any kind of political line that stood against subjection to NATO and against a capitalist model considered to be unchangeable and insuperable.

So much for the past. And what about the future? We cannot know whether the social democracies will have the time to wake up from their disenchanted torpor, or rather from their postdogmatic slumber, but they seem to find themselves in the same position as Gorbachev when he was trying to shake the Soviet Union out of the Brezhnev ice age. By what means and with what ideas could social democracies today positively confront the crisis that is under way and that Brazilian President Lula has called 'a crisis of civilisation'? If (to proceed summarily) we were to confine ourselves to the points developed above, one could say that the social democracies should engage in the organisation of cognitive labour – neither more nor less: that is, in the organisation of the new proletariat that, around the immaterial and cooperative conditions of work, is the force that today produces every excedence of value. They should attract the trade unions into the orbit of the struggles on the new social productivity, beyond any corporate hesitation, within and against the processes of precarisation of jobs and wage differentiation, building values that are common to all workers (if there is one alliance that needs to be prioritised, it is that between blue-collar workers and cognitive workers). There is also the problem of organizing a new 'welfarist' distribution of income: a distribution that (like all true distributions) must operate on the processes of production. This is about building a policy for the 'production of humans for humans', namely tools and production objectives that focus on increasing the capacity of citizens to be free and equal.

Social democracies should also build a new democratic control over the financial system: not only over that part of it represented by the banks (which is something that has to be done for as long as the crisis continues), but also over the part related to the processes of investment and to the overall dimensions of the relationship between business and the market and between direct production and the social conditions of production. This means not only ensuring the proper symmetry of financial values with social production: the task is also one of reinventing democratic instruments of big government, making permanent the instruments that were used in the most acute moments of the crisis. Paul Krugman has repeatedly and correctly insisted on this step, and I think he is one of the few economists today who, in addition to economic forecasting, knows how to add a correct recognition of measures of political intervention and of 'exit politics' that will not lead, with the reproduction of privilege, to new accelerated cycles of crisis. But it is clear that the fundamental problem remains that of rent revenue: we have to destroy it and restore its values to the community; today this is the first condition for any basic democratic advance. Clearly, in this context, fiscal policies need to be completely rethought and reconfigured on the basis of social production – obviously without losing the great democratic achievements related to the principle of progressive taxation, but directing them towards the elimination of rent revenue. Social democracies should also put European unity at the centre of their political discourse. Without European institutions, at this stage in the crisis of American unilateralism, there is no possibility of political autonomy. Breaking the Atlantic link is vital in terms of security, energy supplies, and generally governance of production flows on the world market (not to mention the fight against poverty); and also – this is the most important thing – in terms of the reconstruction of a common political horizon for the peoples of Europe. There is no price that cannot be paid in this field. The cultural content of European humanism and the great progressive traditions of the labour movement can be innovated only at the European level.

And then the social democracies need to be capable of showing courage; and this is a crucial point. This is not to ask for the courage of a Lenin or a Roosevelt; all that is needed is the courage of common sense. To propose and to try to do the things outlined above does not take a lot of effort: simply listen to the world of work and to the world of knowledge. Then, as a first indication, from the perspective of constitutional theory, having the courage could mean giving up all models of a bipolar, left–right politics, which in the current situation is entirely inappropriate; and, from the perspective of governance, having courage could mean giving up all models of two-party politics, showing instead constitutional loyalty to the plurality of social and political drives for renewal. The point is to make a break with 'political science' and its conservative quibbles and to rediscover the broad lines of the production of subjectivity in the intellectual and social world of work. From a sociological point of view, thinking about the new forms and the new subjects of the class struggle will perhaps not be useless for social democracies; from a political point of view, to programme a clash on the social terrain will perhaps be useful and productive. Our social democracies should remember that, in Italy for example, without the events of July 1960 the country would never have recovered from April 1948.

10
Let's Start Reading Gramsci Again

Book review

Peter Thomas's book *The Gramscian Moment: Philosophy, Hegemony and Marxism* is important primarily because it translates the thinking of Gramsci from Italy to the world, and particularly in the way he frames Gramsci for the English-speaking world. The intention of Thomas's work is explicitly to open the debate on Gramsci within Anglo-Saxon Marxism, an environment that is central today in the development of Marxist philosophy. Needless to say, in so doing he develops a reading of Gramsci that not only takes account of the renewal of studies that occurred after the full publication of the *Quaderni* (Notebooks) and the *Letters* in the mid-1970s, but is also enhanced and given a new focus by a comparative reading of the relevant literature (Althusser and Anderson) which has, so to speak, been the basis for the *experimentum crucis* [decisive test] in Gramsci's transition across the Atlantic.

In what follows I offer a few remarks on Thomas's interpretation of Gramsci. I should say immediately that I am only partly convinced by his approach via Althusser. Both Althusser's initial heavy critique of Gramsci in *Lire le Capital* and his ambiguous rapprochement in the last phase of his thinking (the so-called 'philosophy of the encounter') take place within an epistemological system (typically French and connected to the critique of scientific language in the school of Georges Canguilhem) that is alien to Gramscian Marxism. However, we recognise that Thomas does not set much store by similarities; indeed he bluntly rejects them. But why the comparison, then? Because, in the view of some Althusserians, this episode – the encounter between Althusser and Gramsci – was 'the last great debate' around the definition of the 'philosophy' of Marx. But was that debate really of such importance?

Much more convincing is Thomas's approach to Perry Anderson's reading of Gramsci and his subsequent critique. Anderson (1976), in an important article titled 'The Antinomies of Antonio Gramsci', argued that Gramsci's researches in prison were characterised by a series of ambiguities that would give rise to a progressive transformation and reshaping of his theses, in particular those concerning the state and his central concept of hegemony.

According to Anderson, the error is in the approach, and it is at the origin of the subsequent ambiguous multiplicity of the uses of Gramscian thought. Gramsci's concept of 'passive revolution' in particular would be a move towards Kautsky; second, the concept of hegemony would express an excessive insistence on the potential [*potenza*] of civil society against state power (a thesis to which Bobbio had also subscribed, in Hegelian vein), and so on. So, although laborious, it is not hard for Thomas to deal with these interpretations, although they have become widespread and firmly held in Anglo-Saxon thought.

Now, Thomas denies, both philologically (essentially on the basis of the excellent contribution of Gianni Francioni) and politically, the critical reading that Anderson makes of these fundamental concepts, and instead paints a strong and substantially new picture of them. In this he is successful. (It is worth noting, incidentally, that in the intensity and the scrupulousness of his writing this book reproduces the great German and Russian tradition of Marx studies – a feature that adds to its scientific validity.) Thus I begin by selecting a few motifs from the book. I very much like the discussion of the concept of 'passive revolution' that we are offered, with resonances that go beyond simple reconstruction, moving us onto a terrain that is already 'biopolitical'. This means that here the 'passive revolution' of the bourgeoisie is shown through molecular passages that are fixed and reconfigured in time – passages that affect equally (and reciprocally, in other words dialectically) the structures and the subjectivities of the historical process. I am particularly partial to this definition of 'passive revolution' – a conceptual tool of which I was, more or less consciously, a user in my effort to describe the genesis of bourgeois ideology between Descartes and Spinoza and between the primitive accumulation of capital, the configuration of the absolutist state, and the republican alternatives.

Equally comprehensive and powerful is the analysis that Thomas offers of the concept of 'hegemony', when he constructs its originality both in relation to the prerevolutionary history of Russia and in relation to the experience of constituent Bolshevism, down to the period of the new economic policy (NEP). This originality lies in the radical refusal to consider hegemony as a general theory of social power and to relate it instead to the definition of the 'state form', as the latter had taken shape in the western world and in its revolutions. Reborn in the form of dictatorship of the proletariat, hegemony is a weapon to be won and to be applied in the process of fighting for the realisation of socialism. Here too Gramsci's analysis contains moments of great foresight in that he considers proletarian hegemony as rooted in a biopolitical context (the one arising out of the revolutionary experience of the working class) or, on the contrary, as an expression of the dictatorship of the bourgeoisie, of fascism – a hegemony that extends from the state to invest society as a whole, configuring it as 'biopower'. But only the former concept of hegemony, the class concept, contains that constitutive potentiality that makes it an ontological *dispositif*. In using Foucauldian categories here I don't think that I am fudging Gramsci's categories. On the contrary, I think that the reference to Foucault gives more actuality to Thomas's interpretative innovations; it really is about time that scholars started studying the thinking of Gramsci from a Foucauldian point of view.

So now: having carried through this work of redefinition of the basic concepts, Thomas goes beyond the existing interpretative traditions and tries to arrive at a definitive picture of Gramscian thought. Permit me to cite one of his concluding sentences:

> 'Absolute historicism', 'absolute immanence' and 'absolute humanism'. These concepts should be regarded as three 'attributes' of the constitutively incomplete project of the development of Marxism as a philosophy of praxis. Taken in their fertile and dynamic interaction, these three attributes can be considered as brief resumes for the elaboration of an autonomous research programme in Marxist philosophy today, as an intervention in the *Kampfplatz* of contemporary philosophy that attempts to inherit and to renew Marx's original critical and constructive gesture. (Thomas, 2009, p. 448)

It is therefore on the terrain of an absolute reduction of concepts to history that an open and translatable grammar for the hegemonic organisation of social relations becomes possible. It is in the field of immanence, in the rejection of all forms of transcendence that a social practice can be built as theory, or rather that it becomes possible to establish a mutual and productive relationship between theory and practice. And, finally, only an absolute humanism can lay the foundation for the creation of a dialectical–pedagogical work of hegemony: 'In other words, the notion of a new form of philosophy as an element in the development of an alternative hegemonic apparatus of proletarian democracy' (ibid., p. 450).

To conclude, one single observation. Why is it that this Gramscian thought, thus reconstructed, still has to be presented as a 'philosophy'? Or better still, can praxis and the thought that configures it within the parameters of historicism, of immanence and of humanism still be defined as 'philosophy'? Does not philosophy become rather an unsustainable illusion, a tool unusable once those criteria – historicism, immanence and humanism – are assumed as categories of reflection in praxis? Indeed, we may wonder what remains of philosophy once we have witnessed the destruction of its references to the transcendence of the theological–political and to the residual issues of secularisation. In my view, which a Thomas-style Gramscianism confirms, philosophy these days constitutes, for better or worse, a relic – a more or less reactionary variant of the bourgeoisie's attempt to understand its own destiny. But then, once thought has been relocated to the place where Thomas puts it, why would one want in the end to consider Gramsci a philosopher? Would Gramsci himself have been comfortable with such a qualification? The object of praxis is not philosophical but historical – immanent, human, and therefore revolutionary. As the Gramsci of 'Americanism and Fordism' puts it: 'In America rationalisation has determined the need to elaborate a *new type of man* suited to the *new type* of work and productive process' (Gramsci, 1996, p. 286). What praxis reveals to us is the continuous revolutionising of humanity.

11
Biopower and Biopolitics

Subjectivities in Struggle

Interview with Luca Salza

LUCA SALZA   Can you explain for us the reasons why the concept of biopolitics has taken a leading role in the development of radical political thought in Italy? In addition to your positions I am thinking of Virno, Agamben and Esposito. Presumably the theoretical and political stances of Italian feminism, the insistence on sexual difference, and the battle for the politicisation of the sphere of reproduction have played a decisive role in this regard. We could perhaps start from your specific contribution to the question: 'real subsumption' and 'biopower'.

ANTONIO NEGRI   I would say that as regards Italy, the issue should be considered in the light of the internal crisis of Marxist categories; in other words, as part of the analysis of the concept of 'real subsumption' – which is not simply a concept, but also a *dispositif* of the concrete analysis of capitalist development – and the position of the movements within that development. We should bear in mind that the concept of 'real subsumption' derives from the work done by the Frankfurt School on the global extension of capitalist domination, but it makes possible (in the name of its immediate Marxian determinations, and differently from what happens in Adorno and Marcuse) the rediscovery of 'class antagonism' within this globality. This permits us to move beyond the concept of 'alienation' and beyond the paralysis that this concept induced (throughout the 1950s and 1960s) in the analysis of political subjectivity. It is from these assumptions that the definition of a biopolitical field and appropriate *dispositifs* for political intervention are now beginning to mature. This all happened in the 1970s, in the context of going beyond the workerism of Tronti and *Quaderni Rossi*. The hypothesis was that you had to go beyond the factory; above all, and once and for all, beyond the party. So I would add this aspect to the ones you listed, for example those that revolve around gender difference. It was an event that followed the actual dynamics of movement: political theory followed the transition from the class movement that took place in the factories to the movements that developed in the metropolis. Those were the years of the first social centres, the first centres of aggregation of proletarian youth. There was also the women's movement, which at first was not simply a feminist movement, because, as the struggles developed, they turned impetuously, you might say, from the question of wages to that of income (whether of the family or not). There were also the movements of emancipation from the family and the first gay rights movements. What is strange is that biopolitics did not explicitly make its appearance in theoretical debates until the 1990s, 10–15 years after the start of these struggles, and when we started talking about biopolitics people assumed that this new language effectively relegated Marxism to the attic. In reality, what distinguishes the theoretical positions that you cite here is precisely their continuity with Marxism. Speaking for myself – but I could also cite Virno, Ferrari Bravo and others – I have always claimed a continuity with Marxism: the 'biopolitical', just like 'real subsumption', is taken on board as a *dispositif* of antagonism in the social struggle, as previously in the industrial class struggle. In the 1990s, when the theoretical *dispositif* of 'biopolitics–biopower' made its major entry into philosophical debate, in other positions there was a very marked shading off of the concept of class struggle within, and in relation to, the concept of biopolitics. This misinterpretation is absolutely characteristic of the weak conceptions of the postmodern period. In other instances one would have to check. Esposito for example sees himself as having a central and mediating position, but in my view he fears like the devil the re-emergence of an antagonistic subjectivity. In Agamben some antagonism does exist, but it is disengaged from any historically determined condition. There is an ideal–typical typology of antagonism that, in Heideggerian terms, is not given as singularity and invention–creation but as resistance *in extremis* and 'extreme nakedness'. In fact, on these margins there is no longer any sense of an alternative, and struggle and resistance are lost in an atmosphere that is demobilising, not to say mystical (the neutralisation of passion in the sublime and of being in nothingness).

LUCA SALZA   But along this continuous line you trace between the concept of biopolitics and Marx (and communism) there is also the presence of Foucault, which was decisive in those years.

ANTONIO NEGRI   Certainly, the method of antagonism appears in Foucault, where it is characterised as the production of subjectivity. From that we draw some consequences. Communism is no longer a horizon implicit in history; rather it becomes an endangered element. On the one hand, it is based on and embodied in concrete determinations, in historical necessities of production – the productive transformation of labour into intangible, communicative, cooperative and linguistic activity. On the other hand, it becomes, as a result, a new mode of production (with the intensity and extent that the term 'mode of production' implies in Marxism) – a real and proper social innovation. It is in the social qualification of labour that we discover the common substrate, the singular and productive relationship that arises between historical determination and the production of subjectivity. There is thus an ontological engine, a *vis* [force, strength, vigour] or a *potentia* [force, power] that organises the relationship between these two moments. Here Foucault is essential reading – the later Foucault, mind you, from the period of the Collège. In 1974 or 1975 I wrote a review of Foucault for *AutAut*, later to be republished in *Macchina tempo*, which I have also integrated in this volume (Chapter 12); in analysing the writings on the clinic, and *Discipline and Punish*, I realised that he had reached the limits of the Frankfurt School and that, having thus identified the terrain of *bios* [life] – where there is not only alienation but also physicality, strength, and constitution – he had to move beyond structuralism for good. And this is exactly what he was going to do. But during those same years we had Cacciari and others railing at Foucault and the 'mush' created by his 'vitalism'. And the other Italians who were learning from Foucault and beginning to translate his works were so frightened by his philosophical and political radicalism that, with a few exceptions, they did everything to restore the structuralist influences, to bring out the weak aspects of micropolitics and to ignore the testimony of militant activity. So we had the paradox that it was left to a young communist, Duccio Trombadori, to publish a powerful interview with Foucault in a small provincial journal and to offer it, just as it was, to the Italic public. We have to tell ourselves that the 1970s were difficult years and that the stakes were clear: either renew the political strength of the Italian movements (and of communism), calibrating them on the transformations that were taking place in production and giving voice to the new antagonist subjectivity (which was what Foucault was trying to do from his side), or strengthen the old alliances, repress the new, and promote the power of the party. As everyone knows, the second path was the one that was chosen – the outcome of a lack of intellectual and ethical courage that ended in the extinction of a glorious tradition.

In those same years another decisive authority was Spinoza, who became a reference point against the growing academic influence of Heidegger and the resulting conversion to Heideggerism of large contingents of academics and former Marxists. In contrast, choosing Spinoza meant, schematically, being for life and not for death, being on the side of the movements, within their proposal of resistance, rather than inside the academy and the institutions. In those years Alexandre Matheron, a former communist, was the first to discover the ontological and political density of the concept of power in Spinoza. (Those were the years of other fundamental books on Spinoza, from Deleuze to Gueroult.)

What was Matheron proposing? To open the analysis of Spinoza's concept of *potenza* to questions of time (duration, history, eternity), to themes of action (that is, political potentiality [*potenza*] and the production of subjectivity), and finally to themes of the relationship – powerful and constitutive – of body and mind (in which were embodied a dynamics of the passions and a *dispositif* of the common institutions). Materialism, under the logical and ontological lens of Spinozism, could here perfect its traditional pantheist status, assuming a project that was (at the same time) subjective and constitutive. Thus, around 1968, it responds to the call of the times and to the new form of the class struggle. This was a decisive line, in my view possibly more important than the one that passes between Merleau-Ponty and Foucault – the other great roadway on which it was possible in those years to break with classical Marxism, even in its Sartrian figure, on a terrain of revolution.

LUCA SALZA   A further line would be the one that Badiou was attempting to trace...

ANTONIO NEGRI   What we have in Badiou is above all an abstract line, a claim on utopia, the political (namely communism) understood as a logical and ideal principle. Starting from that position there is an abiding concern not to allow this idea, this sacral assumption, to be sullied by the dimension of the real. It is the logical consequence of a certain French 1968, mainly student-based and Maoist, which saw itself (and its own identity) as a revolutionary event, completely disarticulated from the determinations of the class struggle (this position looks like a perverted reflection of the dogmatics specific to the French Communist Party, taken as a basic polemical objective). Communism would here be something that has nothing to do with the wage-related, trade unionist, and political aspects of the movement and with the historical continuity of the class struggle. It is an ideal or, better, an explosion, an event that stands beyond it. Only with the destruction of the present will the sun of the future emerge. It is, in short, a vehement critique of the class struggle as such. In this position either the transcend-ence of the communist ideal takes place or there is no longer any chance of achieving it. We need to break the process of struggles over the wage and invent communism as a future reality. There will never be a homology between the contents of the present-day struggle and the building of communism. The relationship between proletarian *potenza* and the power of the bourgeoisie must be absolutely interrupted. The event is something that explodes. It is transcendent. Essentially the thinking of Badiou seems to echo that of Tertullian: 'I believe because it is absurd.' The principle becomes absurd because it must be stated in absolute discontinuity with the struggle and with concrete life. There is a complete lack of models of historic and material instrumentation in the transi-tion from the current struggles to communism. At the time of the riots in the *banlieues*, this is was what led Rancière and Badiou to say that those were not political struggles. It is Maoism in its rue d'Ulm version, where the political imperative is that you should not express, in the contents of communism, any relationship with the class struggle. Needless to say, all this requires a party and an intellectuality (external and vanguardist) to play the leading role, but on this terrain one has to wonder whether the 'cynical wit-nessing' of Foucault or Jameson's 'cynicism of reason' were not preferable to this 'pure politics'.

LUCA SALZA   Is there perhaps an analogy between the theoreti-cal and political split in the 1970s between 'workers' autonomy' (Negri, etc.) and the 'autonomy of the political' (Cacciari, Tronti) and the split that is currently taking shape between the Deleuzian biopolitical option and what Žižek has described as 'pure politics' (Badiou, Rancière)?

ANTONIO NEGRI   Not really. When Tronti and Cacciari spoke of 'the autonomy of the political', they were referring to the auton-omy or self-sufficiency of the party. They insisted on the continuity and the originality of the Italian Communist Party (PCI). It was, of course, an illusion, but an illusion fuelled by something that claimed to be political realism. What we have in Badiou is an operation that is entirely philosophical, in which the political appears as a concept of logic. Politics is understood only in terms of ideal concepts – none other than those of communism: only such Platonic assumptions could organise matters of revolution. This, of course, is not a resumption of anarchist positions; it is rather an attempt to take refuge in idealism. In fact there is a certain tiredness, plus a certain desperation (which make this operation understandable at a fraternal level) and, in my view, a solely rhetorical appeal to Plato: Benjamin and Debord, and a certain ethical and utopian Kantianism, are the inspiration behind this position – rather than Marx and historical materialism.

The 'political autonomy' of the postworkerist theoreticians in Italy – the 'entrists' in the PCI – as well as being a pure product of the crisis (or rather defeat) of groups that had believed they could reform the left from within, was also an opportunist decision. To hide it, Tronti (as well as Cacciari) turned this into a historical question, a reflection on the twentieth century, the end of the politics of modernity. There are ambiguous Nicaean accents throughout this debate, and above all a strange psychological effect: these theorists, former communists, still saw themselves as the centre of the world at a time when their party (which gave them a position, if not at the centre, at least somewhere) had vanished. All this crying about the end of modern politics is therefore a very foolish thing, because then we find ourselves with a surprise such as Obama on our hands and we discover that the political still operates.

LUCA SALZA The question of the political brings in the theme of the institutions of the common: what is the relationship between constituent power and institutionalisation (communism and democracy)? Perhaps you could clarify your relationship with the positions of Deleuze: in *Mille Plateaux* we have the proposal of a radical ontology of the production of the social. Does that remain a chaotic and indeterminate horizon, or is there already something more? More generally, I would like to touch on one of the more delicate points of your proposition, the question of organisation. You have often insisted on the need for a subjective moment, a moment of subjectification, which you have characterised in classical terms as 'decision'. This moment would consist in a shift from 'multitude' (resistances and differences) to the 'common'.

ANTONIO NEGRI In *Mille Plateaux* there is a capacity of hybridisation of the analysis that is absolutely fundamental. A Renaissance explosion, like Giordano Bruno's, a potential [*potenza*] for grasping, a 'grabbing' of reality and of the world as they are. But within this chaotic realism institutions still exist: they act within each historical situation, as within each singularity, and the hypotheses, projects and proposals that the historical movement determines in and of itself are always there, they constitute the multiplicity of the real. *Mille Plateaux* is not a machine that eliminates the problem of organisation but a track on which one can work for it. The term chaotic should not be taken with a negative connotation but, more precisely, as difference and complexity of differences. It is, first of all, resistance, and then it is productive emergence. (Here I would refer to Gilles Deleuze's 'Instincts et institutions' in Deleuze, 2003.)

So the problem of organisation has to be linked to the theme of the multitude because the concept of multitude is – albeit within the chaos that constitutes it – a concept of organisation, just as is the concept of class. Joining together multitude and organisation means, as we say, 'making multitude'. What does 'making multitude' mean? It means gathering together a series of chaotic elements and making them work so as to result in a new society, a new world, a new language, a new set of values. Build a machine that produces common life, organisation, and a constituent project that is always open. In all probability this step can take place through the rediscovery of the common. The common is the product of a multiplicity. But what the multitude produces is not simply a virtuality, a causal relationship of *potenza* and act: the virtuality endures. The common that organises the multitude is thus a matrix that singularities experience and express (in the sense acquired by 'express' in this new philosophy of Spinozan descent: to produce being and to put it into a shape). The problem of organisation then becomes the very *dispositif* of our common existence. It is a problem of ontological determination. This is why, in our discourse, we reject all political party alternatives; and this is not a question of adopting anarchist positions. What is absolutely central, then, is to bring the mediation process back within the real, when 'expression' is opposed precisely to 'representation'. In *Commonwealth* (the recently published book in which Hardt and I address these issues) we try to define the multitude precisely as an expressive concept – expressive because it is ethically productive (the common is the element that renders the multitude expressive in biopolitical terms).

LUCA SALZA So production and organisation, material level and political level need to be made to function together.

ANTONIO NEGRI 'Making multitude' means building one's own institutions. We live in an era in which the crisis of capital is deepening; we live in a revolutionary transition. We move on a terrain of freedom, in concrete terms – we have thus grabbed back the value of 'freedom' from capital. With the concept of the 'common' we are also saying that the future has begun. The exodus. Mao's army crossing the Yellow River – for me, this is the image of the exodus, but also of 'making multitude'.

LUCA SALZA Now I would like to touch on the issue of the poor [*il povero*], with reference to the notion of 'use without property rights', drawn from the tradition of Franciscan spirituality and from theological–legal dispute with the church. In what sense, today, is the poor the multitude?

ANTONIO NEGRI We are in absolute immanence; we live in a world that has no 'outside'; inside that world, all are producers. In this framework the poor person also embodies a form of resistance–reversibility. The poor are productive: they produce sociality, languages, anger and struggle, pity and welfare, and so on. In Latin America, if you study a city such as Rio, you realise that the half of the population that lives in the favelas is as productive as, or even more productive than, the half that lives in the white or *mulâtres* neighbourhoods. The favela is an impressive centre of activities. Here we have a paradox: the global order is not merely extensive; it is also intensive. In other words it invests all citizens, all subjects, and takes the poor into the heart of production. The liberalism of the second half of the twentieth century has pushed the factory worker (the bedrock of the socialist revolution) into poverty. But in this process the poor have taken the place of the industrial worker. The poor person 'covers' the worker and is the first representation of potentiality [*potenza*]. So we have to reverse the Platonic myth of the poor who seek wealth as an ideal. In fact we have always known that it is Penia who creates Poros:* poverty is the ontological producer of all wealth, of all being. In this same perspective, the other element that we introduce massively in *Commonwealth* is the experience of love, detaching its concept both from the religious and from the bourgeois and romantic interpretation... Love is the ontological force that stands at the foundation of every society. The multitude is refusal of solitude, and this rejection is sustained

---

* Translator's Note: Reference to the account of the birth of Eros from Poros and Penia in Plato's *Symposium*.

by love. Love is the key to the *potenza* of the poor. So poverty –
that poverty that seemed to have annihilated the workers – on
the contrary redeems them. The poor is a *potenza* that expresses
itself in terms of love. According to Machiavelli, the poor *ciompo*
who rebels in thirteenth-century Florence cries out: 'Strip all of us
naked, you will see that we are all equal. ... And when we realise
that we are equal, there is no longer power, there is only our
love' (Machiavelli, *Florentine Histories*, iii 13.122–3, 444–5; see
Machiavelli, 1971).

LUCA SALZA   Perhaps the moment has come to address the issue of
ontology, which we have already touched on. It would be useful
to explore the relationship between excedence and measurement,
between life and value. Viewed from a Nietzschian perspective,
the biopolitical means life as something that cannot be evaluated.
But from another perspective the biopolitical means techniques of
valorisation and devaluation of life set in motion by capital on a
global scale. In this sense, dealing with a political problem in the
postmodern means directly confronting an ontological problem.
But what kind of ontology are we talking about?

ANTONIO NEGRI   The concept of excedence is terribly important,
because that's what allows you, for example, to make the transition (which we theorise in *Commonwealth*) whereby 'what is one
divides into two'. This means that we are entering an era in which
reducing living labour under the command of capital, unifying
within capital intellectual, emotional, and generally immaterial
labour becomes increasingly difficult, if not impossible. The 'one'
– capital – breaks into two – living labour and command. In fact,
when we speak of excedence, we no longer speak of surplus labour
that can be transferred into surplus value and then into profit, and
thus into the construction of a class of exploiter bosses – and hence
the construction of a ruling class, of a state, and so on. Excedence
has here become something that is non-recuperable by power. This
is the excedence of immaterial labour in all its forms (cognitive,
affective, linguistic, etc.), but above all the autonomous excedence
of productive cooperation. Excedent means 'beyond measure',
where by 'measure' we understand the qualitative and quantitative
control of labour power (which creates value) in its subsumption to
the command of capital. In short, here measurement is blown out,
when measurement is the criterion that permits the recuperation
of human activity by power. Therefore the critique of the concept
of measure – and, consequently, of the concept of value and of
the law of value in Marxism and in general under capitalism – and

the practical verification of its historical and material crisis make it possible to make the assumption of a horizon of freedom. What will then always arise is the problem of defining a new measure of production and of the production of subjectivity when institutions might constitute themselves. This problem is never closed. In this openness of ours there is an undeflectable hostility to Plato and to all the representatives of knowledge and command enclosed within the walls of the great schools of Weimar, Oxford and, most recently (*si parva licet* – if one may compare small things with the great), Bologna. In any case, in *Kairos, Alma Venus, Multitudo* (Negri, 2000) I attempted a periodisation of the tropes of measure by defining ideal types: the 'human to animal', the Centaur, is the figure who, in ancient times, embodied a relationship of subordination to (measurement in relation to) nature; then, in the middle phase of modernity, it was the idea of 'human to human' [*uomo-uomo*], as Pico della Mirandola called it, that fixed the measure of value creation; and today there is instead a new ideal type, which I call 'human to machine'. I do not know whether this image works in the context of this proposal of periodisation (today I would rather call it 'human to excedence'). What matters, however, is the fact of reaffirming the idea of the metamorphosis of labour, which now connects directly to the excedence of value. Today, all this is machinic. As regards the production of value, resistance and reversibility live in a machinic regime. Against power's measurement, excedence is a lack of measure [*dis-misura*] that explodes all logic of capitalism, and yet keeps this logic and these breaks always open. Until the extinction of capitalism? It may be so. Here, at root, you can see my problem, which has always been that of the class struggle, that is, of the liberation of human beings through class struggle, until the destruction of class society – in other words until the extinction of capitalist valorisation. From this point of view, the multitude as excedence is class struggle in a winning phase. These are ontological principles.

LUCA SALZA But how will this victory of ours come about? Instead of dialectics, in the biopolitical regime there is the logic of reversibility, so is there no longer rupture, discontinuity? And in what sense does biopolitics change the direction of the relationship between reform and revolution? Are the institutions of the common the form that takes the place of governance, or do they embody a revolutionary break?

ANTONIO NEGRI I build my languages, and through the languages I build my life concretely. We must be realistic. Communism, *ce n'est pas n'importe quoi* [is not just any old thing]. Communism today is this concrete goal: the construction of my life, the relationship with my children, with my sisters and brothers, with others, outside any capitalist subordination, outside the dominion of humans over humans. Clearly, therefore, the relationship of reform to revolution, which had been set in the classical theory from Engels to Lenin, passing through Bernstein, now works differently. Because today things are being made. Because we are living a transition. The transition is ontological. The revolution stands inside the transition. It is neither its starting point nor its culmination. Revolutionary war, which was a key element in the classical theory of communism, is now an everyday fact, and not a catastrophic one (or at least catastrophic in a different sense). When we speak of 'absolute democracy' we mean the ability (through political instruments, struggles, building of movements, insurrections) to build a new world in which everyone works for everyone; or rather to build new spaces, spaces of the common, and to defend them. Examples abound: the commons are not only the natural resources – water, air, gas, forests, oceans and so on; the commons are also these spaces that are transformed for common use; the commons are also all those artificial goods (machinic, built by the machine–human) such as money (or productive finance), informatic spaces, educational and cultural institutions, and so forth... spaces where everyone should have access and in which there is a common availability. Here profit no longer reaches. Thus one sees the extent to which the distinction between reform and revolution is tenuous. Reform may be revolutionary when it goes in the direction of the common. If, then, under the question of the relationship between revolution and reforms, we want to raise the issue of the use (or non-use) of violence, this may be a vulgar and hypocritical provocation, but it is above all devoid of meaning: the communist struggle (whether reformist or revolutionary) is always violent, because those who own and have accumulated wealth and power always defend their possessions with violence (of weapons, or of the law). Now, the defence and the development of already existing institutions of the common, such as might be the university or welfare, for instance, are certainly a priority, but this is obviously not enough. The movements have to foster the emergence of the ability to create 'soviets', councils, or other instruments of democratic organisation that expand, organise and guarantee the spaces and institutions of the common. You can devise programmes for this. It is not a matter of 'hypotheses', but of deeds and facts. We need revolution in order then to make plans. The revolution does not come afterwards. The revolution lives every day in this going beyond measure of our relationship and in this organised pressure for the construction of the common. It is, then, a matter of grasping, especially in the crisis, the dis-measure of the relationship of exploitation, when the bosses are no longer able to exploit you. This is because it is hard for the organisation of knowledge, for the organisation of life, for the biopolitical dimension of production to be subsumed in capital. There is a new and revolutionary element in the capitalist relation of exploitation: 'what is one has divided into two', and I can now be successful in not commodifying any longer what I do; rather I can consider it as something I transmit, in common terms, to future generations through the institutions I try to build.

LUCA SALZA   What is the link between the common, communism and biopolitics in a crisis situation? How can the notion of the common become the conceptual medium between communism and biopolitics?

ANTONIO NEGRI   Let us dwell on the crisis and its interpretation. I think that, of all interpretations, you should prefer those, whether of the right or the left, that reject the ideas that locate the reasons for the crisis in the separation between finance and so-called 'real production'. Now, rather, we have to insist that financialisation is not an unproductive, parasitic diversion of increasing amounts of surplus value and collective savings, but rather the form of capital accumulation that is symmetrical to the new social and cognitive processes of production of value. The current financial crisis should therefore be interpreted as a blockage of capital accumulation rather than as an implosive result of a failed accumulation of capital. The blockage comes from the drives towards re-appropriation and from the rejection of cooperation exhibited more and more amply by the behaviour of the new globalised productive classes against the policies and practices of exploitation and neoliberal war.

How do you exit the crisis? On this issue, too, one has to express a communist radicalism matched to the depth of crisis. One can only get out of the economic crisis through social revolution. The fact is that today any New Deal that may be proposed has to involve building new rights of social ownership of common goods, rights that are clearly in opposition to the right to private property. In other words, if until now access to a common good has taken the form of 'private debt', if capital has foregrounded the sociality of exploitation by presenting itself – in a manner cleverly and wickedly mystified – as 'communism' (of the owners of capital, obviously), from now on it is legitimate to claim the same right in the form of 'social income'. Imposing the recognition of these common rights is the only correct way to exit from the crisis.

Part III

12
On the Method of Political Critique

The vulgar arrogance of *raison d'état* lives a continuous cycle of births and reappearances. Both before and after Marx. Before Marx, in the return to Hobbes; and after Marx, in the disenchanted memory of Stalin. But Hobbes and Stalin, in the physics of power that they assumed, registered a necessity, a *raison* of supreme conservation, the highest value of peace and, then, that of the nation, of the motherland [*patria*]. Leviathan and Ivan the Terrible. 'Politics above the economy', the 'autonomy of the political above interests of class', the 'dependence of economy on politics', all of this can only refer to those values: peace and the nation, *über alles* – at least if, in Neumann's usage, one opts for Leviathan and not Behemoth. Hobbes and Stalin act within a mechanicist horizon whose key they have to possess in order to impose the value that interests them, to lock the system in value. Even a physical horizon that is singularly open, such as that described by Hobbesian mechanicism and by its pulsations, by its potentialities, must thereby postulate a transcendentality of power [*potere*]. Power is a transcendental: the criterion of obligation is transcendental – so it is read by its interpreters – and irreducible to the mechanics of instincts. So here we discover power and define it as a moment that possesses an extraordinary intensity of alterity: an *other* that stands above to the extent that it is necessary to existence. Idealism is the ongoing existence of *raison d'état*, it is the motor that continually reproduces it. Idealism is the doctrine of value, of domination over passions, of their solution in transcendentalism. The truth of idealism is thus not different from that of the values it expresses and imposes: peace and *patria*, peace or *patria*.

People talk about *politique d'abord*, the 'autonomy of the political'. Well: what is the value that is being pursued? None other, they say, than the law of working-class dictatorship over development. Glory be! As if this were a mere trifle! But it requires at least one presupposition: that the workers want dictatorship and development, that they accept to subordinate the potentiality of their force to the transcendental of development, in the same way in which elsewhere it is subordinated to peace or to *patria*. The 'autonomy of the political' is a theory of the transition, a theory – assuredly 'Leninist' in a Third Internationalist sense – that affirms the *contents* of capitalist development in the revolutionary process under the *form* of the leap: a hyper-Leninism conceived in a zone of very high, sublime theoretical and historical rarefaction. Its concrete determination is thus a conception of development that must demonstrate a push towards this leap, to the qualitative change. And what if this is not given? No matter: the function of the political is reaffirmed; that's all that is required for the 'new type' of organic intellectual – the mystification of value is reintroduced, redefined, and assumed within the system. The political has to be separated from the economic because only this separation permits the restoration of value.

This kind of 'Lysenkoism' in political theory is no less characteristic than its counterpart in the theory of science. It is a system – inevitably it has to be systematic – of generic utilities – inevitably they have to be generic: the economy and not the class struggle – which postulate a sublimation (peace, nation, development) within the state. The banality of scientific 'Lysenkoism' is tempered, in politics, by a tradition that asserts, as a matter of principle, that politics should be disengaged from truth: truth is only that which concerns the totality of the value proposed, to which the truth of singular movements [*movenze*] has to sacrifice itself. Peace, nation, development: this is the final truth. Its relationship with reality is as an apology of the concrete, a dryness of intellect, a curial attitude (Machiavellianism. not Machiavelli, Hobbesianism and not even Hobbes... Togliatti and not – but why not? – Stalin). Lysenko is the autonomy of truth. The system of 'Lysenkoism' is a process that produces the leap beyond truth, the sacrifice to value, to conservation, to peace–nation–development. It is a system of homologies pushed to one single coherence: that of value, of its surreptitious domination, of falsity. It is a prostration before power, which transforms the problem of power into servilism and projects a technical solution for it: law-court techniques.

There are some who say, then: let us not accept these homologies and the necessity of the leap to the totality that consecrates and sublimates the process! Here – and this is the pure and simple opposite of the theories of the autonomy of the political – the transparency of the leap is negated so radically that power comes to be reinstated to its misplaced ideal self-sufficiency, to its fetishistic determination, to its originary non-truth, without having to take recourse to any dialectical function, to any formality. This interpretation of power poses it as an object to be destroyed. What needs to be destroyed is the 'Lysenkoism' – a model of input–conversion–output. Lysenkoism assumes a series of givens and produces absolute non-truth through a mechanism of conversion that operates on a system of mystified homologies. Power represents itself in 'Lysenkoism': in the point of view of power, and also in that of science, what counts is the totality – it absolutely precedes the real; sublimation controls truth. So this is the point reached by the denunciation – moralistic, if you like, but also solid and documented: the solidity of the facts and the stubbornness of reality against idealism of the political. But can we really bring the critique of power to a negation that verges on indifference? Is indifference adequate to the critique of idealism? Or does it not itself becomes an expression, a variant, a trick? When the *nouveaux philosophes* push the critique of power towards the crudeness of indifference, do they win or lose the battle on the terrain of truth?

I have this fact before me: 'Gulag idealism'. The manipulation of reality that derives from it follows the laws of the mystificatory dialectic of totality. The passages of this dialectic are all dominated, supported and directed by the indifference of value. Homologies can only exist inasmuch as the context on which they operate is that of indifference. But if I deny, resist and denounce this fact and its indifference, I am not – by that very fact – within indifference; on the contrary, there is difference, real determinacy and determination in practice. 'Human beings are not characterised by a certain relationship to truth; but they contain, as rightly belonging to them, a truth that is simultaneously offered and hidden from view' (Foucault, 2009, p. 529). I deny *that* power because I want (not that power, but) the power, the Hobbesian vital pulsation, that is a power of existing, producing and reproducing. If I deny every possible homology between my potentiality to exist and *that* power, I cannot deny it in indifference, indeed I have to affirm the universality of the problem of power. Critique cannot destroy the object – and this holds all the more as the problem is universal, all the more as the determinate reality of each subject is implicated in it. The approach of the *nouveaux philosophes* is valid to the extent that it confronts and poses the universality of the problem of potentiality [*potenza*] at the level of its present historical and sociological dimensions: social labour determines its antagonism in relation to the state; it does not confront a boss but the collective reality of the state, the ideational power of the collective boss – in all its monstrosity and its necessity.

On the other hand, it is true, it did happen that, in the face of a socialised labour [*lavoro sociale*], the homologies of the concrete and immediate labour process (those defined by the experience of the factory worker) have faded away in analogies, have been wiped away in a qualitative leap: the antagonism is no longer that of the immediate labour process but the antagonism that begins to take shape on the terrain of the socialisation of labour. If this is given, all the categories of antagonism need to be reformulated. The idea of the 'indifference of power' fails to reformulate anything except the terrain on which the problem is to be raised. But this reformulation in terms of indifference is in turn a mystification: a power that is identical and omnipresent, in the face of which we have, not a determined, but an undetermined potentiality, raises claims that are undefined and undefinable. Yet this criticism, both in what it says and in what it lacks, determines the problem, defines the need to deepen the research and to establish its articulations. However, neither the idealistic delight of renewed Stalinism nor the indifference of the totality of power – redefined or critiqued – satisfies us; and 'Lysenkoism' in political theory or the denial of the problem of power cannot remove the ideal reality of the mystification of power. However, breaking the horizon and going to the roots of the process that constitutes it, shattering it, opening an articulation of analysis that can follow the molecular articulation of the variables that are present – this is the priority task of the moment. Undoubtedly the *nouveaux philosophes* who have come to address this problem are important. But more important still is to live it from within, in its most brutal concreteness. I believe that this is possible.

Therefore analysis reacquires validity if it traverses the fabric of the being, of the historical being, of power, but in traversing it it destroys its figure, its articulation, its dimension – not the thickness, the weightiness, the actual skeleton. These, in fact, have to be rebuilt. What needs to be constructed here is an ontological analysis, a *Daseinsanalyse*: to the extent that you grasp the being, you destroy the false geometry of its image – you turn analysis into a weapon of excavation and demolition; science deconstructs power inasmuch as it reveals its constitutive dynamic and consequently unmasks its image. Power then reveals its necessity, starting from the dissipated and dispersed fabric of its constitutive threads. You can traverse these threads and follow them: you will never find in them grounded

truths, homologies and analogies, or an unbroken continuity of sig-
nifications or concretisations that are impermeable to action – no,
what you find here is labour, what you find here is a young power
that is constructing itself each time. This really is the opposite of that
romantic discovery that prompted Schelling – the young Schelling
– to cry out in front of the discovery of that historical hardening of
human reality, of the world, of its products: 'Here is nature!' But
here there is labour instead, there is human operativity. It is there as
long as we reconquer the immediateness of its discourse against the
stratification of images and the reality of mystification. Faced with
the objectivity of historical being, of its stratifications, of its institutions, we have a courage of truth that brings us ourselves entirely into
play: history is a complexity of tangents that resolve into a resultant,
of strategies that tend towards the result. The point of view is the
constitutive element of the historical project, but it is also the constitutive element of the archaeology of knowledge. The relationship
between sense [*Sinn*] and reference [*Bedeutung*] is reversed: it is the
reference that now explains the sense, not the reference – the brutal
consolidation into the given – that subsumes the sense. The scientific
deconstruction of the known world brings us to the origins of knowledge and of the world, and also to the definition of the conditions of
self-valorisation.

In Foucault a specific ontological tradition of French thought
becomes an operational horizon, scientifically effective, without
yielding to the blandishments of the philosophy of action. Thought is
accepted as an overall action; it is not to be confused with action but
cohabits with it. It is a unitary world, this world that presides over the
formation of analytical instruments: it had been defined as the fabric
of the imaginary (Foucault, 1954). The *Daseinsanalyse* of the imaginary interposes itself between anthropology and ontology and seeks
to be such as to overcome both the hermeneutics of symbols and the
mere horizon of decyphering: existential structures that are fundamental and not alienated have to be grasped in this first approach.
Further along, a philological work of continuous, ever closer scru-
tiny of the text permits us to positivise this scientific impulse: from
Rousseau to Spitzer, from Kant to Weizsäcker. Let us look at the
work that Foucault did on the latter two authors: you might consider
this a gross diversion but it is not, even though the texts taken into
consideration (Kant, 1964; von Weizsäcker, 1958) are not particularly significant and are even ambiguous. Nevertheless, it is not a
diversion but rather a process of homing in onto a profound unity
within which, and starting from which – from its anthropological,

biological and medical materiality – analysis can reconstitute itself in the face of totality. Build the synthesis where it is and do not seek it in what lies outside the immediacy of the real. Analyse, make distinctions within reality, to see it constituting itself not according to metaphysical schemata but according to concrete strategies, plans, projects and investments.

And struggles? When thought frees itself from Kant's 'schematism of reason' or from Husserl's 'functional intentionality', one finds oneself within a concrete horizon that has to be reconstructed as such: the horizon of strategy, of the complex of strategies, is the interchange between the will to know and concrete givenness, between rupture and limit of rupture. Every strategy is struggle, every synthesis is limit. Here there is more dialectics than in dialectics, there is more astuteness than in reason, there is more concreteness than in the idea. Power is finally related back to the network of acts that constitutes it. Certainly those acts come to be covered by the ambiguity that Power represents for itself. But this does not remove the fact that always, at every moment, the totality is split, a heteronomy of ends can become a reality, and the picture loses all unidimensionality. Because what changes is the point of view; what modifies and gives the research so much freshness is that being within reality, recurring within that act of existence and of separation that belongs to us and to all the subjects that move in history. Struggles are the containing space of needs and of points of view, of projections and wills [*volontà*], of desires and expectations. Synthesis is delegated to nobody and to nothing. Science liberates itself from its master to offer itself to action, to concrete determination and to determination in practice.

The fact that a simple, formal approach of this kind is sufficiently powerful to preserve us from Power and to avoid falling for the blandishments of 'Lysenkoism' or of 'indifference', to afford us an active conception of the historical project, and also of its science, is astonishing. Perhaps for the first time a historiographical methodology and its philosophical foundation put themselves in a position to transform the reality they are attacking. Transforming reality means avoiding the 'transformation problem': from comprehensive categories to other categories, according to the rhythm of structural analogies. Instead we get laws of dishomogeneity, of fracture, of separation, which strike the eye immediately. The problem of transformation – of value into price, of the real into the symbol, of the universal into the particular – seeks to structure reality definitively: the stamp of the process is its non-truth, *das Ganze ist unwahr* [the whole thing is untrue]. Transforming reality means rather destructuring it continuously, so

that the process – which is as liminal as you wish, but real nonetheless – of self-valorisation, of the emergence of needs, of the tendency
of desires, can take place. 'Put again into question our will to truth;
restore to speech its character of event; finally remove the sovereignty
of the signifier' (Foucault, 1981, p. 66).

Reversal, discontinuity, specificity, exteriority: the relationship that
presides over the desire to learn no longer finds easy – or indeed difficult – dialectical solutions. What runs through this methodology is
violence, it is always a determination of the conditions of possibility
of existence and discourse, taken together. 'Where there is work of
art [oeuvre], there is no madness' (Foucault, 1988, pp. 288–9). And
yet *Homo psychologicus* [the psychological human] is a descendant of
homo mente captus [the insane human].

> For Sade as for Goya, unreason continues to watch by night; but
> in this vigil it joins with fresh powers. The non-being it once was
> now becomes the power to annihilate. Through Sade and Goya, the
> Western world received the possibility of transcending its reason in
> violence, and of recovering tragic experience beyond the promises of
> dialectic. (Foucault, 1988, p. 285)

This is the violence that destroys Power; this is the violence of
self-valorisation that deconstructs Power; this insisting on physical
potentiality in Hobbesian terms unmasks the metaphysics of Power.
'Now, the study of this micro-physics presupposes that the power
exercised on the body is conceived not as a property, but as a strategy' (Foucault, 1979, p. 26). So

> this power is not exercised simply as an obligation or a prohibition
> on those who 'do not have it'; it invests them, is transmitted by them
> and through them [...] This means that these relations go right down
> into the depths of society, that they are not localized in the relations
> between the state and its citizens or on the frontier between classes and
> that they do not merely reproduce, at the level of individuals, bodies,
> gestures and behaviour, the general form of the law or government;
> that, although there is continuity (they are indeed articulated on this
> form through a whole series of complex mechanisms), there is neither
> analogy nor homology, but a specificity of mechanism and modal-
> ity. Lastly, they are not univocal; they define innumerable points of
> confrontation, focuses of instability, each of which has its own risks of
> conflict, of struggles, and of an at least temporary inversion of the power
> relations. The overthrow of these 'micro-powers' does not, then, obey
> the law of all or nothing; it is not acquired once and for all by a new
> control of the apparatuses nor by a new functioning or a destruction of

the institutions; on the other hand, none of its localized episodes may be inscribed in history except by the effects that it induces on the entire network in which it is caught up. (Foucault, 1979, pp. 26–7)

But is it true that this world of Foucault's tends to flatness? And that it tends – beyond single emergences – to project the richness of the dialectics of strategies onto a horizon that is only formally structured, to repeat it in the conception of a totality that is 'without a subject'? If this were true, political theory would yet again have killed its object. The mystified subject could have the upper hand over a methodology that is empty.

Foucault does not help us much in solving this problem. The progress of his discourse is provocative: his history of madness knows no mad people. On the terrain of ideology he then tends equally to render justice to indifference and to the interchangeability of discourses: Bentham and Rousseau, Foucault stresses in his Introduction to the edition of *Panopticon*, are complementary. Later on, when the problem is formulated expressly (for example, in a 1977 interview in *Révoltes Logiques*, 4), Foucault admits to the emergence of a subjective tremor in the history of systems, but this absence is liminal (and thus universal, an attribute of the species); it is dialectical (but better, one should say, residual, because produced by the mechanism of power); and then, finally, it is resistant... And thus in some sense powerful? Is the subject of strategies therefore real, is it not simply the point of intersection of the networks of existence? Foucault does not go beyond the hypothesis of a possible positive determination; he does not overcome but rather deepens the ambiguity, the elusiveness of his own approach. Baudrillard (1977) insists: this is not about ambiguity but about a new, sublime mystification. In Foucault the discourse mediates. Foucault himself had put us on our guard against this: 'the theme of universal mediation is [...] yet another manner of eliding the reality of the discourse' (Foucault, 1986, p. 159).

But now the author is prey to the danger that he denounces.

The nemesis of reality is powerless over discourse because the word [*parola*] is formally negated, substantially assumed to an exclusive horizon. This ontology of discourse is heavy, mediative, unresolvable. Baudrillard accuses Foucault of having deprived discourse of a subject and of having reduced it on the terrain of *circulation*. Here the problem of transformation does not exist, not because it is negated in the face of the productive force of transforming – as historical knowledge – but because the real (in its discontinuity and interruption) is not grasped as it is, but is already mediated by the simulated transparency of the discourse.

We have arrived at the heart of Foucault's ambiguity. His discourse is revolutionary from a formal point of view: reality is recognised to the extent that it is transformed by the complex of strategies that invest it. But, from a substantive point of view, the contents of the operation of transformation are mediated with respect to levels of reality that are stale and conservative. Pessimism of content, implacable optimism of transformational tendencies: but this definition of the *new* nature of circulation does not succeed in becoming a discovery of the *productive* nature of circulation. Reproduction is subsumed to circulation, not circulation to reproduction. And yet all the conditions for the former to happen were given. The productive force of knowing (and of the subjects of the strategies) was formally given. Now, instead, the whole does not reveal this productive force; it destructures but does not self-valorise; it carries out an operation that is *destruens* [destroying], but it does not organise the *pars construens* [building part]. Rather it negates the tension of the will to knowledge in the flatness of objective knowing. The world is a great mechanism of circulation in which everything goes around in respect of everything. Regularities, the series that are determined, are *wertfrei* [value-free] – not only in the sacrosanct circle of logic, but above all in relation to reality. Production of power, production of knowing through the means of knowing: going beyond structuralism repeats the stalest of its characteristics. Political Lysenkoism and the political theory of indifference take revenge (on the terrain of contents) for the defeat suffered at the level of methodology, of the apparatus of research. When analysis limits itself on the terrain of circulation, it does not succeed in expressing the potential that the process of foundation, the insistence on the force of transformation, the thickness of strategies had grasped. The materials are solid but the tower is fragile: the confusion of languages, their indifference become possible. The destruction of the structural homology constructs – or at any rate residuates – a structure of non-meaning – the interruption permits the reconstruction of every identity.

Why this internal aporia of Foucault's thought? Why is it that the productive axis that, starting from the methodological foundation and passing through the vitality of strategies, could have invested in a creative manner the circulation of knowledge and of the real limits itself to itself instead, and leaves us a horizon that is destructured and only passively defined? On what can the ideologies of power rebuild their will for power? Why is it that the richness of a project that, grounding itself in specificity and passing through discontinuity and the logic of the concrete, of separation, overflows the complex totality of the real and becomes a wretched thing, stripped of its productive thrust – which nonetheless seeks to present itself as universality (and this is crucial, because this is the question we are all asking ourselves, for better or worse)?

★ ★ ★

It is said that in France politics fulfils the function exercised in Germany by metaphysics and in Britain by political economy. So let us have a bit of fun with these comparisons! Actually, in examining whether the Foucauldian impasse does or does not correspond to some of the terminology of philosophical thought in the era of late capitalism, I have little interest in focusing on German metaphysics. Such an approach would risk multiplying the ambiguities, if it is true that Nietzsche holds a pre-eminent position in Foucault's meditations – as is the case for other representatives of French contemporary thought. But which Nietzsche? The fascist manikin who promulgates the absoluteness of *Wille zur Macht* [will to power]? Of course not; rather that irresoluteness of power and potentiality [*potenza*] that constitutes itself and cancels itself out, like tragedy, being individually, metaphysically unresolved around the historical diffusion of the emergences of being. But assuming this genealogy of Foucault's thought, or only one of its distinguishing philological resonances, does not explain anything: you end up repeating the problem raised by the Foucauldian impasse. Is the weight of the senselessness [*insensenzatezza*] of circulation, the emptying out of its productive meaning, somewhat Heideggerian? Such never ending paths lead me nowhere. So, once again, the impasse remains unresolved; it is simply jumped over by Heidegger, just as it is posed in extreme and paralysing terms in Nietzschean thought too. So this is not what interests me: the Foucauldian problem is that of transformation, and it remains an open problem.

So we have to look elsewhere to find meanings and experiences suited to the identification of this problem – in a place where the problem of transformation exists as reality, as a question in play.

Rather than looking at German metaphysics, perhaps we could take a look at English political economy. They say that one day Pietro Sraffa met Wittgenstein. The experience of the *Tractatus* had come to an end, and that terrain could no longer be pursued. What Wittgenstein was pursuing in the *Tractatus*, the final frontier of positivism, of empiricism, was, again, a problem of transformation.

Now every possibility of transformation is in crisis, the solutions do not satisfy him; a huge weight of experience and suffering negates them. Sraffa expresses himself with a characteristic comical gesture, a hand gesture, a sign of contempt – the Neapolitan version of 'up yours'. He ironically asks Wittgenstein for a symbolic translation. For Wittgenstein, they say (and I am not very interested in the truth of this anecdote, provided it works), the suggestion prompted the discovery of a new field of investigation: the *production* of signs by means of signs beyond the sphere of the pure circulation of signs, beyond the static unity of a universe of semiotic movement. A production of signs by means of signs... a production of commodities by means of commodities? When we consider what this story recounts, is it not the victory of a new political economy that includes production in circulation, is not the irrational proposed by Sraffa the winning element?

The production of commodities by means of commodities? That economic horizon that centuries of critical thinking had sought, up to this point, to ground systematically in a theory of value dissolves. All the relations, all the homologies, all the categories are subjected to retesting, and not one of them stands up. The reality of the market has changed so radically and significantly that every function that is not linear, not immediately grasped through a linear perspective, is removed. But not only the market (and the possibility of building there, no matter how, analogous networks) is removed; also removed is any determination of processes outside the terms of regularity, outside serial and statistical analysis. And, above all, the categories of production have to be critiqued as well: Where do we find now the link between labour and value? Where is it still possible to consider constant capital as a result of the development of living labour, when all the internal relations of constant capital are disrupted and, according to the law of the non-return of technologies [*la legge del non ritorno alle techniche*],* we cannot infer regular relations in any single case? So let us no longer talk of the law of value: the only image we can have of it is conclusive, resultant, Humeian. It is the effect of rejoining different images placed one on top of the other on a large screen. Its only existence is serial, but these series record only linear functions – and cannot do otherwise; they register no series that is linked to, or based on, the materiality of a real process of transformation. And so this

---

* Translator's Note: This formula is associated with, if not coined by, the Italian economist Pietro Sraffa.

economic world is reduced to a panoptic universe in which we must move according to sequences that are determined by structural relations and by changing dynamics, different from one moment to the next. Those serial regularities are themselves effects and conclusions.

It seems clear to me that here you find yourself before an analytical position that, with absolute consistency, presents a radical critique of the transformation problem. And the 'panoptic' character of this model also seems clear to me. But this does not mean that, in the work of Sraffa and his colleagues, the picture is painted only in formal terms. That science and critique can penetrate the level of production and of reproduction only by reducing it to that of circulation does not mean that one should doubt that production and reproduction still exist. Far from it: the panoptic level of circulation is constantly stimulated by the productive emergences, by the figures that preside over production and reproduction; circulation runs because it is continuously driven by small electrical stimuli. Of course, we only grasp the tip, the emergence of these stimuli, we only see them – and we can only see the fact that they organise themselves – as linear functions. Profit is a linear function of the wage; preconstituted relations do not exist, they are in the process of constituting themselves. The dynamism of the system is internal to the level of circulation. This does not mean denying the weightiness of the ontological problem of political economy. It only means avoiding that this weightiness becomes unbearable, that ontology becomes a hole into which we plunge impotently. This will mean that the dynamism impressed on circulation comes from another source, from another place; however, I register it as an effect, refusing to problematise the genesis beyond the limit of its experimentation. As the Sraffian theoretician of political economy will continue to explain, I shall seek my genealogies at this level of circulation, and in any event they will be *strong* genealogies if it is true that all categories, all conflictual content that is inserted in them, I now resolve at the level of circulation – following these tendential lines, the crossing points, the intersections and series, the results and the resultants ...

The production of commodities *by means of* commodities. Political economy is a strange science: it lives a direct complementarity with economic policy, which is a practice. The analysis of strategies turns into a practice of strategies. That solution of the problem of transformation, which is denied at the genealogical level, is obligatory at the political level. But the terrain of this practice has thus far been emptied out – at the analytic level – of all necessity. And not just of this: it has also been emptied out of any subjectivity. The schema is *sans sujet* [without a subject] – but that is not a possibility for practice. The schema has, additionally, stopped time (and can play on the transformation between diachrony and synchrony, and vice-versa) as an important lever of the analysis: this is not an option for economic intervention. Sraffa has invented a theoretical schema that may permit various algebras of planners *à la* Leontiev; but then, when these algebras are applied in space and time, a number of difficulties arise. Production of commodities *by means of* commodities, hegemony of circulation: fine, but what is meant by this 'by means of'? The instrument finds difficulty in matching itself to the analysis. The analysis has dissolved in front of me the spatial and temporal concreteness of the field of intervention; it has demystified for me every possible totality. So to what can the instrument now be matched, what totality will it have to create for itself? None, replies the economist. From the temporal point of view my units of intervention will become ever smaller: and as regards any long-term trends, I shall only be able to conceive of them as ensembles of many independent entities, as resultants of a chain of short-term situations. From the spatial point of view, my units of intervention will become increasingly more diverse and pluralistic: any theory that assumes a priori constant levels of long-term usage of any productive potentiality is of no use to me; I have to break with them all; I have no coefficients through which to deal with the big relationships of the cycle – on the other hand, the rigidity of the functions and magnitudes that I address can be at least as important as their fluidity, considered so far. This said, science has to be in command once again and economic policy is obliged to arrive at a conclusion, at a final determination. And in a situation where there is no norm of production and dynamic stimulus is given only as an external pulsion to a system that is loose and dispersed – well, here again the subjectivity denied to the ontological nexus comes to be surreptitiously reinserted as command, in, on, and of circulation. All ambiguity is dissolved. The destruction of every homology can only be resolved by the relation of force. The production of commodities by means of commodities becomes the production of commodites by means of command, the production of command by means of commodities, the production of command by means of command.

The paradox of the panoptic story of contemporary political economy lies in being its prey; that is, in the fact of moving surreptitiously from the destruction of the problem of the ontological foundation to the determination of an authoritarian validation, in the fact of developing a differential genealogical analysis and of concluding in a one-dimensional practice – which, however, inasmuch as it arises from these critical assumptions, is determined and can only be determined in terms of will, of specification of indifference. But this specification is in turn indifferent. The conclusion is prey to the indifference of the content. All production is in the end dominated by circulation. In this manner a highly mystified function comes to be affirmed, and a theoretical picture that, with Sraffa, had grasped the new dimension of economic becoming and had defined the horizon upon which the ensemble of forces was determining an entirely innovative relation (and series of relations)... that theoretical picture gets blurry and becomes both the basis and the result of an operation of transformation and manipulation of reality. Once again there is Lysenkoism, all the more seriously and tragically powerful as the field of economic reality was fruitfully dug at the start. Once again a political behaviour emerges that will determine the obfuscated and indifferent conclusion of the theoretical analysis. Once again the paths lead nowhere, except to a recognition of that and to the accompanying conclusion of an act of force, of a continuous rape of and against reality.

No, in Foucault production is not dominated by circulation. The analysis of circulation as a privileged terrain offered today by social capital, the analysis of the institutional circularity within which the existence of classes is given today – these do not negate but heighten the aspect of production. It is not production that is subsumed to circulation, but vice versa; the latter is invested by the former, according to an interplay of strategy and tactics, of structures and functions, of games and terms of reference that offer us both the freshness of the power [*potere*] of production and the new quality of circulation. Certainly, in Foucault this tendency often (indeed too often) becomes flattened. The analysis seems to get lost between the formalism of a traditional philosophy of action (without object) and the concrete quality of a traditional structuralism (without subject). We have grasped this impasse of Foucault; but in Foucault, unlike in my experience of other contemporary thought, I feel, beyond the impasse, a potentiality that is so powerful, an ontological thrust that is so alive, and a constitutive earnestness that is so strong that I find it difficult, if not impossible, to reduce his thinking to the level of a painful impasse.

Rather it is in the other direction that we need to proceed – namely to recognise the centrality of the terrain and methodological initiative proposed by Foucault. Is this new form of critique a new model of 'a priori synthesis', of action and structure, of will and matter?

Once again, no. It is rather an ontology that is renewed here; it roots itself in the complexity of the given historical reality and subsumes all the determinations of historical being – just as capital itself has come to be determined, at this outer limit of its social development. Critique, in addressing this area, extends over all aspects of the existent; it grasps the complexity of its articulations, their intersection, and the mobility of all factors; in the perspective of the social totality of the capital – and thus of power. Because, when the complexity of capitalist development has reached these magnitudes, the critique of political economy becomes the critique of capitalist society, therefore the critique of society, of institutions, and of the state, and therefore a critique of politics. The game played by the power of social capital has to be revealed: to analyse it is also to denounce it – this ontology of historical being is simultaneously a genealogy and a critical potentiality [*potenza*] of destruction. At this point Foucault's shortfalls do not matter, nor am I concerned about the weight of the impasse that his way of proceeding continually reveals, like an original stain that has not yet washed away. What interests me is rather the radicalness of the point of view and the truth of the definition of the terrain of analysis. It is this social potentiality [*potenza*] of capital that the viewpoint of inquiry, in its very foundation, reveals to me in its mystification, in the network of strategies to which it is constrained – in the potentiality of its impotence.

But this is not enough. And it seems that it was also not enough for Foucault. In his Préface to Bruce Jackson's *Leurs prisons: Autobiographies de prisonniers et d'ex-détenus américains* (Foucault, 1972b) he proposes a reading of the world as a world of the circulation of command, exclusion and violence; he offers a critical consideration of capital as a prison, but at the same time he is struck, astonished and excited by the formidable reality of rebellion, of independence, of communication and of self-valorisation inside the prisons. The idea and the reality of the power, of the law, of the order that traverses prisons and brings together, in the accounts of prisoners, the most terrible experiences, here begins to falter. The events, in their seriality and regularity, open onto new conditions of possibility. There is no dialectical link in all this: dialectics, in its false rigour, imprisons the imagining of possibilities. No static overturning. Instead, by contrast, a horizon that is open. To the extent that it is realised, the analytical *logic* of separation opens into a *strategy* of separation. The separation, the overturning become real only in strategy. A world of self-valorisation opposes itself to the world of valorisation of capital. Here possibility becomes potentiality [*potenza*]. But by introducing this Spinozan concept of possibility–*potenza*, are we possibly extending too far our interpretative take on Foucault?

Perhaps so. However, in Foucault the suspicion of indeterminacy is always alert. On the other hand his analysis 'seeks' – so to speak – not only critical outcomes but also probably a kind of stability in the effectuality newly arrived at. Yet that methodological 'mobility' that we like so much and that corresponds so well to the quality of intellectual labour determined by social capital, which is intrinsic to the modalities and the purposes of the revolutionary process today, poses a problem: will it or will it not be capable of standing on its own? Is it not necessarily led to embody the hard determination of the historical process, of *potenza* against Power, of the proletariat against capital? Here a problematic picture opens, to which only a real movement is able to provide an answer. But, even if Foucault achieved no more than to pose this set of questions, the real movement should be grateful to him.

From the point of view of a critique that marches with the movement, it is thus necessary to repropose the totality of these problems: from the critique of political economy to the critique of politics, from the critique of capital to the critique of power, as I have said. Here the method constructs itself in strategy and articulates itself to functions and contents. It cannot be otherwise, if every category has to be verified from the point of view of its genesis, if every institution has to be disassembled and revealed in the totality of its mechanisms, if every freedom – and above all that of critique – is to be incorporated into the potentiality [*potenza*] that the historical process and every possibility of separation produce. But here, above all, nothing is flattened. This single and exclusive field of analysis that is circulation, its necessary and inescapably political quality, remain nevertheless a field of production. Production that is labour, human activity geared to ends of reproduction and of happiness, of expression and of potentiality [*potenza*]. Production is requalified within the horizon of circulation, but production itself remains, as a hegemony of the historical being of the human against and above every other form of existence. All the categories of the critique of political economy need to be laid out anew, constructed, and strategically connotated. Their dimension is that of circulation and politics; their foundation is production – the human power [*potenza*] of transforming the world.

When Marx comes to his definition of the 'society of capital' – that is, to the intuition that the development of the capital overcomes by its own necessity all limits of possible historical prediction and by that fact imposes the modification of its own categories of operation according to a schema and according to dimensions that are 'social' – at that very moment he calls for the implementation of a *neue Darstellung*, of a new and adequate exposition. The *neue Darstellung* – in Marx's writing – is obviously not only a new exposition of contents; it must also be a new identification of subjects, and then *a new refounding of method*. Today we are in the middle of (and possibly beyond) that threshold phase glimpsed by Marx and absolutely required by his critical method of proceeding. *Today we are thus witnessing a first fertile upheaval of the scientific horizon of revolutionaries – and for this we must also be grateful in part to Foucault.* This upheaval of categories and this resolute innovative method thus become fundamental tasks. Tasks to be taken on directly, by insisting on the structural complexity of capitalist *Zivilisation* [civilisation]; on the radicality of the project for destruction; on the sectarian partiality of the scientific strategy that we are putting in place; and on the offensive character of the tactical consequences that derive from it. What is certain is that a lot of progress has already been made in this direction. *The intensity of the Foucauldian approach and the fertility of his method are among the things that have been done, and at the same time they are tasks to be undertaken.*

As always, however, the reasons for a choice or a task and the foundations of a method are certainly not sustained solely on the identification of a historical turning point. Ontology is more dense than *histoire* [history]. The method, as we have said, is required by the specificity of the exposure of the contents. But here, at this stage, we have to say more: the method requires, determines the specificity of the contents. The method seeks to be rooted in the 'ontologicality' of the grip on historical existence that is characteristic of this existence and reveals to us the world of this radicality. Try to read with the simplicity of the dialectical method and its strange alternatives some of the great problems of the (critique of) political economy and of politics: at best you end up with a handful of flies in your hand! Truth rather reveals its complexity today through the thousand paths that lead into the critical process of revolution. To follow them and to articulate – in the face of, and against, Power – the infinitely complex interconnections of autonomies and independences, of autonomy and autonomies, of possibilities and potentialities [*potenze*] – and to explain this process as both the source and the overturning of the enemy's domination: this is the method we need if we are to make this task possible for us; we need its ontological fullness. An adoption of this method and of its functional, multifaceted and diverse activity, of the complexity of the semantic function that it determines, the method of the critique of political economy and of politics proves itself today on this task, and that is thanks also to Foucault.

13

How and When I Read Foucault

In the last 1978 issue of *AutAut*, the journal that first took Foucault on board in Italy, I published an essay (already written in the previous year) entitled 'On the Method of Political Critique' (Negri, 1978).*
In that essay I discussed what, until that time (the last Foucault writing that I covered in the article was *Surveiller et punir*), had been the impact of Foucault's work on the thinking of the revolutionary left in Italy, in which I was then an activist. This was the period when I had resumed my work on Marx, and in particular on the *Grundrisse*; between 1977 and 1978 I had been giving my course on 'Marx beyond Marx' at the École Normale Supérieure at rue d'Ulm (Negri, 1991 [1979]).

I offer this information to the reader to point up a coincidence: my reading of Foucault was happening at the very moment in which I was presenting a university course that summed up a long 'revisionist' experience of readings of Marx. However, the reader should note that my 'revisionism' in those years developed within an attitude of adherence to the basic concepts of the critique of political economy and also as part of revolutionary militant activity, and not – as was often the case during that period – in a rejection of Marx.

Why did I start to get interested in Foucault? Because in those years the Italian Communist Party (PCI) and the trade unions, with which the movements were locked in polemic, were planning an alliance on

---

* Translator's Note: The article cited here has been integrated in this book as chapter 12 (the preceding chapter). In the present section Antonio Negri quotes rather extensively from it. Given the historical relationship between the two texts and its larger role in the author's development, the overlapping material is being left in place in this chapter.

the societal and parliamentary terrain with the forces of the right – the famous 'historic compromise' – advancing the notion that it was now possible for the proletariat to achieve sovereign power, that the forces of the left could not be picky when they engaged in this operation of difficult but necessary compromises, and that the political was autonomous and indifferent to values: only strength counted. For the PCI, the cult of sovereignty and the exercise of *raison d'état* – as we were soon to find out – slept under the same blanket. The problem was how to demystify this idea – a bizarre one for communists – that power and sovereignty were autonomous places and indifferent instruments. A real and proper 'transcendental'! And the idea that struggle could only take place, and that the political transition could only be built, by taking into account these transcendentals. We replied: on the contrary, the materiality of power and of the political constitution is clearly defined and well characterised from the point of view of liberal politics, and this condition is very far from indifferent. Consequently, when I deny, resist, and denounce that supposed indifference of power, I do so with good reason. In other words I adopt a point of view that is critical and determined. I deny indifference because I am *difference*, a difference that is itself determined, real, politically defined, and unable to show itself in a different way. We could say, with Foucault, that 'human beings are not characterised by a certain relationship to truth; but they contain, as rightly belonging to them, a truth that is simultaneously offered and hidden from view' (Foucault, 2009, p. 529).

This, however, was not enough to transform the rejection of a political disaster in the making – the disaster of the policies of the left – into the making of a new horizon of struggle. What was needed was to reorganise analysis and rebuild organisation. We had to give that moment of consciousness a capacity for expansion and the solid construction of a new theoretical foundation. This is why it was useful to think with Foucault.

From the beginning it was clear that Foucault was working within an 'ontological' tradition of French thought that did not succumb to the lure of the philosophy of life and action. Moving up, in my reading, from Foucault's (1954) essay on Biswanger, through his essays on Kant's (1964) *Anthropology from a Pragmatic Point of View* and on Weizsäcker (1958), to the *History of Madness* (Foucault, 2009) and the *Birth of the Clinic* (Foucault, 1976 [1963]), in the above-mentioned article I highlighted on the one hand the potency of the relationship that was proposed between anthropology and ontology and, on the other, the fact that in this work the construction of the historical object was extremely realistic: the object was no longer sought in the range of things outside the immediacy of experience. In this Foucault there emerged, as Althusser noted, 'absolutely unexpected temporalities' and 'new logics' (see in this regard Vilar, 1973). Freeing himself from the Kantian 'schematism of reason' and from the Husserlian 'functional intentionality', Foucault constructed within a horizon that was concrete – within a horizon of struggles and strategies.

Now:

> the horizon of strategy, of the complex of strategies, is the interchange between the will to know and concrete givenness, between rupture and limit of rupture. Every strategy is struggle, every synthesis is limit. Here there is more dialectics than in dialectics, there is more astuteness than in reason, there is more concreteness than in the idea. Power is finally related back to the network of acts that constitutes it. Certainly those acts come to be covered by the ambiguity that Power represents for itself. But this does not remove the fact that always, at every moment, the totality is split, a heteronomy of ends can become a reality, and the picture loses all unidimensionality. Because what changes is the point of view; what modifies and gives the research so much freshness is that being within reality, recurring within that act of existence and of separation that belongs to us and to all the subjects that move in history. Struggles are the containing space of needs and of points of view, of projections and wills [*volontà*], of desires and expectations. Synthesis is delegated to nobody and to nothing. Science liberates itself from its master to offer itself to action, to concrete determination and to determination in practice. (Chapter 12, p. 142)

★ ★ ★

What happens around this decision? There happens something that is as elementary as it is difficult – you have to push this experience from history to life, from the description of the *historia rerum gestarum* [history of events] to *res gestae* [events]: regain the totality in order to deny it (*das Ganz ist unwahr*) [the whole is untrue], but deny it because the totality, Power, could not encompass life, the point of view of the singularity, the *dispositif* that desire organises.

★ ★ ★

I had immersed myself in German historicism, *Historismus*: in fact this was precisely the topic of my doctoral research (Negri, 1959). I had focused especially on Dilthey – on that very singular *Kulturpolitik* [cultural politics and cultural policy] that constituted the terrain of his analysis. Burckhardt and Nietzsche were in there, much more than it seemed. 'Epochs' in which knowledge was organised unitarily, but that were always being broken – 'epochs' in a discontinuity. Might this process not also be called an 'archaeology', a sequence of *epistēmai*? And yet the 'epoch' of the analyses of *Historismus*, as also the *epistēmē* [knowledge, understanding] of Foucault, sometimes seemed more solid than the decision of constitution (which, however, traversed them) and than the ability to recuperate it. So, in that eventual blockage of the process, *Kultur* changed into *Zivilisation* among historicists; and, in parallel, life, the living *epistēmē*, and biopolitics were, in Foucault, absorbed into biopower.

Epistēmē: how difficult it was to understand it in a non-structuralist manner, in an epoch traversed by the flourishing of (until then undefeated) cultures and methods of structuralism in the humanities! That is how *Les Mots et les choses* was in fact interpreted (Foucault, 1966; but see also IMEC, 2009). The same fate was to loom over *Surveiller et punir*. Here it was the idea of the 'panopticon' that rigidified knowledge and movement. Production seemed to be dominated by a kind of unproductive circulation. The 'panopticon' invested production in order to subsume it, and Foucault's analysis seemed thus 'to get lost between the formalism of a traditional philosophy of action (without object) and the concrete quality' of the philosophy of the structure, 'a traditional structuralism (without subject)' (Chapter 12, p. 150). Between *historia rerum gestarum* and *res gestae* a circuit without an escape route was sometimes established. In many ways, therefore, the openings I described above seemed to be blocked.

Yet it is in *Surveiller et punir*, just where the blockage seems at its strongest, that the discussion reopens. The terms used by Foucault to give a name to this new economy of power (*panoptique*, 'all-seeing'), which is now based on the exploitation of life and on putting to work the physical strength of individuals, on the management of their bodies and the control of their needs, in short on the normalisation of what people do, are actually twofold: biopowers and biopolitics. Thus far we have used these terms indiscriminately, as if they were equivalent. In fact they are not.

So now we have this problem: as long as one maintains a lack of distinction between biopower and biopolitics, it seems no longer possible to have a resistance to the capturing of life and to its standardised management; there is no longer the option of an exteriority, and you can no longer even imagine a counterpower, unless you reproduce – inversely – that from which you want to be liberated. This is where 'liberal' readings of Foucault began to appear on the scene: that is, starting from the Foucauldian analyses of regulatory management of a living being [*un vivente*] organised into populations – from which derives the political image of an 'actuarial' (insurance-like) political management of life, of a classification of individuals within macrosystems that are regulatory, desubjectivating and homogeneous.

Otherwise, on the contrary, the biopowers are dissociated from biopolitics, and the latter becomes the affirmation of a potentiality [*potenza*] of life against the power over life. Or rather there is, located within life itself – in the production of affects and languages, in social cooperation, in bodies and in desires, in the invention of new ways of life – a place of creation of a new subjectivity that would also prove to be a moment of destruction of all subjection. In this regard, it could be objected that the opposition between Power and potentiality [*potenza*] owes more to Spinoza than to Foucault. It is certainly the case that my own thinking owes much to this derivation. In those years I was in fact beginning the work on Spinoza that would lead to my writing of *L'anomalia selvaggia* (Negri, 1991 [1982]). Yet I believe that Foucault can very much be located within this division between Power and potentiality. For instance, at the end of *Surveiller et punir*, when he wrote: 'In this central and centralised humanity, the effect and instrument of complex power relations, bodies and forces subjected by multiple mechanisms of "incarceration", objects for discourses that are in themselves elements for this strategy, we must hear the distant roar of battle' (Foucault, 1979, p. 308) – in short, when Foucault proposed that 'roar of battle' as the sound of a work in progress, he negated any possibility of reducing it to the noise of the panopticon – and thus that potentiality [*potenza*] could be flattened on power.

As regards the simple reduction of my analyses to the simple metaphor of the panopticon, I think that here one can reply at two levels. One can say: compare what they attribute to me with what I have actually written; here it is easy to show that the analyses of power that I have conducted are not in any sense reducible to this figure, not even in the book where they went looking for it: *Discipline and Punish*. In fact, while I show that the panopticon was a utopia, a kind of pure form developed in the late eighteenth century to provide the most convenient formula of a constant exercise of power that is immediate and total, and while I showed the birth, the formulation of this utopia, its *raison d'être*, it is also the case that I immediately showed that it was precisely a utopia that had never functioned in the manner in which it was described and that the whole history of the prison – its reality – consisted precisely in the fact of having bypassed this model. (Foucault, 1994a, vol. 3, text 238, p. 628)

Thus in *Surveiller et punir* this was already entirely clear. It was also entirely clear to me in provincial Italy, and in fact in my article of 1978 I quoted this long section from Foucault:

> Now, the study of this micro-physics presupposes that the power exercised on the body is conceived not as a property, but as a strategy. [...] Therefore this power is not exercised simply as an obligation or a prohibition on those who 'do not have it'; it invests them, is transmitted by them and through them [...] This means that these relations go right down into the depths of society, that they are not localised in the relations between the state and its citizens or on the frontier between classes and that they do not merely reproduce, at the level of individuals, bodies, gestures and behaviour, the general form of the law or government; that, although there is continuity (they are indeed articulated on this form through a whole series of complex mechanisms), there is neither analogy nor homology, but a specificity of mechanism and modality. Lastly, they are not univocal; they define innumerable points of confrontation, focuses of instability, each of which has its own risks of conflict, of struggles, and of an at least temporary inversion of the power relations. The overthrow of these 'micro-powers' does not, then, obey the law of all or nothing; it is not acquired once and for all by a new control of the apparatuses nor by a new functioning or a destruction of the institutions; on the other hand, none of its localised episodes may be inscribed in history except by the effects that it induces on the entire network in which it is caught up. (Foucault, 1979, pp. 26–7)

It was during this period that it was possible for a text such as my *Dominio e sabotaggio* (Negri, 1979), where the 'agonistic' and 'antagonistic' concept of power was strongly stressed, to emerge simultaneously with my research on Foucault but also within the hard-fought struggles that were taking place in Italy. And above all it was during that period, and on these theoretical bases, that the antagonism of the class struggles could begin to be interpreted through that social microconflictuality that socialisation (both that of capital and that of labour power) now entailed: and this in fact explains the emergence of the concept of the 'socialised worker' [*operaio sociale*].

So one has to go beyond the promises of dialectics; in other words one has to read power not as a property but as a strategy.

At that point, in that 1978 article, I made a long digression on what seemed to me to be the state of the critique of political economy in its more active schools: the Ricardian ones, which were already going beyond Keynesianism. And it was on Sraffa (1960) that I settled – on the potentialities that, in *The Production of Commodities through Commodities*, he showed were determining new value in order to produce innovation *from within* the movement of goods, thus updating the reading of the movement of goods and the transformation problem *chez* Marx. In recalling the theoretical importance of this Sraffian reading of Ricardian circulation, I remembered the anecdote of the encounter-confrontation with Wittgenstein, after the experience of the latter's *Tractatus* had reached its conclusion. Piero Sraffa suggested to his Cambridge colleague that the problem, at the level of logic and in the critique of political economy, was the same: How was it possible to identify a point of transformation (of innovative production) for the economist in the circulation of goods, and for the philosopher in linguistic circulation? Now, whereas for Wittgenstein

> every possibility of transformation is in crisis, the solutions do not satisfy him; a huge weight of experience and suffering negates them. Sraffa expresses himself with a characteristic comical gesture, a hand gesture, a sign of contempt – the Neapolitan version of 'up yours'. He ironically asks Wittgenstein for a symbolic translation. For Wittgenstein, they say (and I am not very interested in the truth of this anecdote, provided it works), the suggestion prompted the discovery of a new field of investigation: the *production* of signs by means of signs beyond the sphere of the pure circulation of signs, beyond the static unity of a universe of semiotic movement. A production of signs by means of signs... a production of commodities by means of commodities? When we consider what this story recounts, is it not the victory of a new political economy that includes production in circulation, is not the irrational proposed by Sraffa the winning element? (Chapter 12, p. 147)

And might we not take this anecdote as a parallel to the task that Foucault had already for some time explicitly been setting himself: 'to question our will to truth; to restore to discourse its character as an event; to abolish the sovereignty of the signifier'? (Foucault, 1981, n.p.).

★ ★ ★

But is all this enough? Is it possible to have truth without praxis, without resistance? This is how I answered that question in 1978:

> But this is not enough. And it seem that it was also not enough for Foucault. In his Préface to Bruce Jackson's *Leurs prisons: Autobiographies de prisonniers et d'ex-détenus américains* (Foucault, 1972b) he proposes a reading of the world as a world of the circulation of command, exclusion and violence; he offers a critical consideration of capital as a prison, but at the same time he is struck, astonished and excited by the formidable reality of rebellion, of independence, of communication

and of self-valorisation inside the prisons. The idea and the reality of the power, of the law, of the order that traverses prisons and brings together, in the accounts of prisoners, the most terrible experiences, here begins to falter. The events, in their seriality and regularity, open onto new conditions of possibility. There is no dialectical link in all this: dialectics, in its false rigour, imprisons the imagining of possibilities. No static overturning. Instead, by contrast, a horizon that is open. To the extent that it is realised, the analytical *logic* of separation opens into a *strategy* of separation. The separation, the overturning become real only in strategy. A world of self-valorisation opposes itself to the world of valorisation of capital. Here possibility becomes potentiality [*potenza*]. But by introducing this Spinozan concept of possibility–*potenza*, are we possibly extending too far our interpretative take on Foucault?

Perhaps so. However, in Foucault the suspicion of indeterminacy is always alert. On the other hand his analysis 'seeks' – so to speak – not only critical outcomes but also probably a kind of stability in the effectuality newly arrived at. Yet that methodological 'mobility' that we like so much and that corresponds so well to the quality of intellectual labour determined by social capital, which is intrinsic to the modalities and the purposes of the revolutionary process today, poses a problem: will it or will it not be capable of standing on its own? Is it not necessarily led to embody the hard determination of the historical process, of *potenza* against Power, of the proletariat against capital? Here a problematic picture opens, to which only a real movement is able to provide an answer. But, even if Foucault achieved no more than to pose this set of questions, the real movement should be grateful to him. (Chapter 12, p. 151).

* * *

In 1983 I returned to France after a long period of imprisonment in Italy. At around the time of Foucault's death I resumed contact with Deleuze. I discussed with him at length about Foucault, going beyond the reticence about Foucault that was common among Deleuze's closest friends and collaborators. So I was breathing from close up the air of that masterpiece (not of the history of philosophy – have you ever seen anyone further away from that horrid discipline than Foucault and Deleuze? – but of literature and of spiritual sharing) that was Deleuze's (1986) book on Foucault. It represented the definitive overcoming of that impasse between a 'subjectivity without object' and a 'structure without a subject' of which we have already described the topography in Foucault (and which should be read as a result of French philosophy's 'loss of identity' from the 1950s onwards) – that overcoming that is not an *Aufhebung* [sublation] and has nothing of the dialectical ('the idea of *universal mediation* is yet another way [...] of eliding *the reality of discourse'*, Foucault, 1981, n.p.) but is a definitive going beyond the tradition of French spiritualism, which on the matter of the subject-individual presses hard on the truth, paralyses action in love, and in psychology nullifies the positivity of existence. Indeed, well before narrating the history of the encounter between *epistēmē* and its innovation, Deleuze had offered its *dispositif* to Foucault. This was the reason why now he could speak of him so pertinently. As for us, in order to get the whole of the picture of this formidable going beyond of the French philosophical tradition – completed from within itself – and in order to become aware of that 'realisation' that was hegemonic on the (not only European) terrain of philosophy that Foucault and Deleuze made possible for it, we still had to wait for the publication of Foucault's lectures at the Collège de France. We had, however, understood that, if the twentieth century had become Deleuzian, the twenty-first would be Foucauldian.

★ ★ ★

Yet how many efforts have been made to get rid of the definitive conversion of Foucault's discourse – beyond biopower, through the biopolitical – to the production of subjectivity! I remember, in the early 1990s, at one of my seminars at the Collège International de Philosophie, a sharp exchange between François Ewald and Pierre Macherey. They clashed on the question of individualism, on the different determinations of freedom, and on the meaning of Foucauldian ethics; but both missed the fact that in Foucault the opposite of individualism was singularity, that ethics experienced a search for a freedom that was not only of the spirit but also of bodies, and that its ontology was productive. And so they missed the point that sovereignty, within which biopower was rooted in each of its forms (both liberal and socialist), was not the only fabric on which ontology could be constructed and measured. On the contrary: sovereignty was taken up by Foucault and then analysed and deconstructed, within biopolitics, in the relationship between various different productions of subjectivity.

> When one defines the exercise of power as a mode of action upon the actions of others, when one characterises these actions as the government of humans by other humans – in the broadest sense of the term – one includes an important element: freedom. Power is exercised only over free subjects, and only insofar as they are 'free'. By this we mean individual or collective subjects who are faced with a field of

possibilities in which several kinds of conduct, several ways of reacting
and modes of behavior are available. Where the determining factors
are exhaustive, there is no relationship of power: slavery is not a power
relationship when a man is in chains, only when he has some possible mobility, even a chance of escape. (In this case it is a question
of a physical relationship of constraint.) Consequently there is not a
face-to-face confrontation of power and freedom as mutually exclusive
facts. [...] The power relationship and freedom's refusal to submit
cannot therefore be separated. The crucial problem of power is not that
of voluntary servitude (how could we seek to be slaves?). At the very
heart of the power relationship, and consequently provoking it, are the
recalcitrance of the will and the intransigence of freedom. (Foucault,
2000, pp. 341–2)

This text is from 1980. Everything that Foucault develops subsequently will be entirely within this perspective. There will be an
uninterrupted deepening of the materialist character of the analysis
of the historical determinations, of the content of *epistēmē* in the
transition between 'archaeology' and 'genealogy', and also of the
potentiality [*potenza*] of the 'production of subjectivity', from resistance to rebellion and to expression, and to the critique of political
democracy.

★ ★ ★

Another page from my *AutAut* article of 1978:

When Marx comes to his definition of the 'society of capital' – that is,
to the intuition that the development of the capital overcomes by its
own necessity all limits of possible historical prediction and by that fact
imposes the modification of its own categories of operation according
to a schema and according to dimensions that are 'social' – at that very
moment he calls for the implementation of a *neue Darstellung*, of a new
and adequate exposition. The *neue Darstellung* – in Marx's writing – is
obviously not only a new exposition of contents; it must also be a new
identification of subjects, and then *a new refounding of method*. Today
we are in the middle of (and possibly beyond) that threshold phase
glimpsed by Marx and absolutely required by his critical method of
proceeding. *Today we are thus witnessing a first fertile upheaval of the
scientific horizon of revolutionaries – and for this we must also be grateful in
part to Foucault.* This upheaval of categories and this resolute innovative
method thus become fundamental tasks. Tasks to be taken on directly,
by insisting on the structural complexity of capitalist *Zivilisation* [civili-
sation]; on the radicality of the project for destruction; on the sectarian
partiality of the scientific strategy that we are putting in place; and on

the offensive character of the tactical consequences that derive from it. What is certain is that a lot of progress has already been made in this direction. *The intensity of the Foucauldian approach and the fertility of his method are among the things that have been done, and at the same time they are tasks to be undertaken.*

As always, however, the reasons for a choice or a task and the foundations of a method are certainly not sustained solely on the identification of a historical turning point. Ontology is more dense than *histoire* [history]. The method, as we have said, is required by the specificity of the exposure of the contents. But here, at this stage, we have to say more: the method requires, determines the specificity of the contents. The method seeks to be rooted in the 'ontologicality' of the grip on historical existence that is characteristic of this existence and reveals to us the world of this radicality. Try to read with the simplicity of the dialectical method and its strange alternatives some of the great problems of the (critique of) political economy and of politics: at best you end up with a handful of flies in your hand! Truth rather reveals its complexity today through the thousand paths that lead into the critical process of revolution. To follow them and to articulate – in the face of, and against, Power – the infinitely complex interconnections of autonomies and independences, of autonomy and autonomies, of possibilities and potentialities [*potenze*] – and to explain this process as both the source and the overturning of the enemy's domination: this is the method we need if we are to make this task possible for us; we need its ontological fullness. An adoption of this method and of its functional, multifaceted and diverse activity, of the complexity of the semantic function that it determines, the method of the critique of political economy and of politics proves itself today on this task, and that is thanks also to Foucault. (Chapter 12, pp. 152–4).

14

Gilles Felix

The How and When of Deleuze–Guattari

The preface written by Gilles Deleuze for Félix Guattari's *Psychanalyse et transversalité* (Guattari, 1974) had as its title 'Pierre-Félix'. Here Deleuze was playing on Guattari's two forenames to suggest that there were two personalities coexisting and interacting in the same thinker: the political activist and the psychoanalyst. I have titled this present article 'Gilles Félix' in the same way in which people use the term *Arabia felix* to refer to a productive space, a common prophetic topos – chaos or a desert that decision and circumstances require you to cross together – which these two thinkers – oh so different from each other – roamed together and lived together, in relation to each other.

A second point. In this article I shall try not to talk 'history of philosophy'. Like Deleuze, 'I belong to a generation, one of the last generations, that was more or less bludgeoned to death with the history of philosophy. The history of philosophy plays a patently repressive role in philosophy, it's philosophy's own version of the Oedipus complex' (Deleuze, 1997, p. 5). Also, like Deleuze and Guattari, I shall explore an approach that does not permit a reading of their 'doing philosophy' as part of the 'powers that be' that 'have an interest in communicating to us sad affects' – these 'powers that be' that 'need our sadnesses in order to make us slaves' (Deleuze and Parnet, 1977, p. 76). Rather I shall attempt to 'talk politics', starting from the particular political space in which Gilles and Félix met and where they embarked on a long – and felicitous – journey together.

This political space was *Anti-Oedipus: Capitalism and Schizophrenia* (henceforth *A-Œ*; Deleuze and Guattari, 1972). *A-Œ* was 'from beginning to end a book of political philosophy' (Deleuze, 1997, p. 170).

Before *A-Œ*, Gilles Deleuze had published *Logique du sens* and, notably, *Différence et répétition* – a *theatrum philosophicum* [philosophical theatre], a 'return' [*répétition*] in the form of 'a lightning storm', as Michel Foucault put it in his review of these two books: 'from an always-nomadic and anarchic difference to the unavoidably excessive and displaced sign of recurrence, a lightning storm was produced which will bear the name of Deleuze: new thought is possible; thought is again possible' (Foucault, 1977 [1970], online version). In fact things were more complicated than that, and Foucault could have held back a little on his enthusiasm. Here we need only note that Deleuze himself – between *Différence et répétition* and the work on *Spinoza et la théorie de l'expression*, which he was reading to his students at the same time – felt that he had not resolved the problem of how to move away from structuralism, of finding ways out of this 'structure without structure' into which his thinking seemed to be locked. In 1967, in an article that François Chatelet was to publish in 1972, Deleuze wrote that structuralism has five distinct characteristics: the fact of going beyond a static or dialectical relationship between the real and the imaginary; the topological definition of conceptual space; the differential relationship of symbolic elements; the unconscious character of the structural relationship; and, finally, the serial (or multiserial) movement of the structure itself. And it is clear that, even if the philosophy of *Différence et répétition* realised these *dispositifs* fully, this could still not open the way to a 'new way of thinking'. Because a new way of thinking has to be productive. How, then, is one to recover, within a defined field of immanence, a force, an ontological element that makes it possible to exit both from dialectics and from sterile structural epistemology, by building a relationship with the real that is in all respects positive? *Logique du sens* and *Différence et répétition* put an end to the two traditions that could be found in structuralism: on the one hand, a transcendental philosophy in the tradition of phenomenology; on the other, this empiricist logic that, since Hume, had considered perception to be the exclusive mode of knowledge and the 'common name' to be the sole definition of the concept. But all this is still not enough. Where does one find the place in which a symbolic, creative and active intersubjective force traverses both the real and the imaginary? Where is the figure that, starting from the symbolic, reactivates the spatial topologies and virtualises them? Where is the 'structuralist hero' to be found? Therein lies the problem.

It is worth stressing that this problem had an immediate political resonance in the philosophical debate of the time, a debate that concentrated on the critique of the mechanical relationship between *Unterbau* [substructure] and *Überbau* [superstructure] and on the notion of the reproduction of the social and its possible revolution. Thus we find ourselves in a philosophical debate that is largely dominated, even in its most original currents, by the 'left-wing' revisionists of official Marxism. Henri Lefebvre and Guy Debord cleared up a field that revolutionary surrealism had already shaken in the late 1930s. And major cultural institutions were attracted by this critical assemblage: they were headed first and foremost by the École Normale Supérieure in rue d'Ulm, where teachers and students were racking their brains to work out how to bend the structure to revolutionary innovation. But, unlike Lévi-Strauss, Althusser, Foucault and Derrida, Deleuze is not one of the École Normale crew. To solve the same problem, he switches track. This is where 'Gilles Félix' begins. It is here that the event occurs. The 'structuralist hero' steps forward, throwing Molotov cocktails: this was May 1968.

So it was on street corners in the Latin Quarter that Félix Guattari appeared. Up until that point Félix had been working on the unconscious, with explicit reference to Lacan. However, at that time he had entered a phase of breaking with the master. Drawing on some experiments that he had done with Tosquelles (who had also worked with Fanon for a long time), and especially with Oury, at the La Borde clinic and in the groups working on institutional psychotherapy, Guattari came to the conclusion that it was no longer possible to isolate the unconscious in language or to structure it on signifying horizons. On the contrary, the unconscious has to be related to the whole social, economic and political field. The objects of desire are determined as a reality that is coextensive with the social field (and consequently with the field defined by political economy). They reveal themselves to be a transversal flow that engages and disengages every relationship – and it is here that the 'libido' appears, undisguised, this essence of desire and sensuality. It is from this perspective that Guattari proposes the concept of the 'desiring machine'. It invests the chains of signification and causality and explodes them, by liberating their latent potentialities.

Deleuze:

> I was working only in concepts, and still very timidly. Félix talked with me about what he was already calling desiring machines: a theoretical and practical conception of the machine unconscious, the schizophrenic unconscious. So I felt that it was he who was ahead of me. (Foucault, 1972a, p. 6)

In effect, in his encounter with Deleuze, not only did Félix contribute his critique of Lacanism and his schizoanalytic inventions. He also brought in – and in this he was the one who was ahead – a complexity of work and a wealth of militant experience of the communist left of the 1950s and 1960s. That is where the 'desiring machine' was born: between resistance to the unnameable practices of the Comintern and the issue of the rebel struggles in Algeria, in the communion between working-class struggle and militant solidarity with Vietnam. It was within revolutionary practice that theory presented itself as schizoanalysis and group practice as the 'mass analyser'. Much has been made of the fact that this effort of Félix (taken up by Deleuze) included a radical critique of all dogmatic continuations of Marxism Leninism (not to mention the conception of bureaucratic centralisation and its repressive consequences). People have not sufficiently emphasised the fact that, for Deleuze and Guattari, by analogy with what was happening in the Freudian school, if doctrinaire 'third internationalism' was liberating but at the same time castrating the forces of revolution, then it was necessary to radicalise the violence of liberation and to push it to a 'fatal outcome' ['*solution fatale*']. In this episode there was more of Marx and more of Lenin than the arrogance of the history of philosophy would ever care to admit. It is no accident that in 1990 Deleuze was to write: 'I think Félix Guattari and I have remained Marxists' (Deleuze, 1997, p. 171). I would like to correct that, interpreting it to mean: I think that we have remained communists.

Let us return to the *A-Œ*. What comes out of it is a revolutionary tendency that has nothing to do with rancour, with the necessity of the dialectic, with teleology... It is a text that is absolutely anti-Platonic. To borrow from the language of Popper, 'Gilles Felix' is Plato's worst enemy. Eros is effectively desire. It no longer implies any transcendence. It is not half poverty and half wealth but the destruction of any medium, the recognition of a force that is immanent and constructive. Hölderlin's Empedocles triumphs over the flames of Etna. Communism is renewed as a desire of the masses.

All this combines to produce a political book – political in the proper sense – that was exceptional. Its subtitle was *Capitalisme et schizophrénie* [*Capitalism and Schizophrenia*], volume 1. This is part of a programme that would be completed ten years later, as *Mille plateaux: Capitalisme et schizophrénie*, volume 2 (henceforth *MP*) – the masterpiece of 'Gilles Felix' (Deleuze and Guattari, 2004 [1980]). In the *A-Œ* there is already a profusion of new concepts, and also of old concepts turned to new uses: desiring machine, body without organs, lines of flight, nomad, machinic, full body, decoding, immanence, consistency, transversality, refrain, signifying–non-signifying, flows, deterritorialisation, reterritorialisation, molar and molecular, and so on. But, as in all major political works, there is one basic concept that is constantly developed throughout: power is not order but productivity – potentiality [*puissance*], as in Spinozan politics; 'body without organs', once again as in Spinoza: 'After all, is not Spinoza's Ethics the great book of the BwO [body without organs]?' (Deleuze and Guattari, 2004 [1980], p. 170).

The anti-Hobbes flourished here, in a communist season.

Then, from these premises, there began a rereading of universal history, a rereading that took as its starting point the organisation of power: the primitive age, despotism, capitalist civilisation. I have to confess, to my great shame, that the first time I read these chapters of the *A-Œ* I wondered whether its authors were not raving. Today, rereading them (something I would recommend to my readers), I cannot fail to recognise that the views expressed there are of our time to an extraordinary degree and establish concepts such as globalisation of capital, flexibility of the movements of labour power, or development of planetary machines of domination, which have become commonplaces. And what was even more of our times was the resistance that 'Gilles Felix' proposed within this new field of analysis and struggle.

The *A-Œ* was, simultaneously, the overturning of dialectical Marxism and the overturning of Freudianism; it was also the overturning of the Freudo-Marxism that was flourishing at the time, that of Marcuse (among others), who for a while had been set up as 'the' thinker of 1968. It was a shameful Hegelianism, a determinism of alienation and repression that left hardly any ways out other than mysticism or aesthetics: the 'one-dimensional man'. Liberation and repression were the two key concepts of Freudo-Marxism: if repression was necessary, liberation became superhuman. Psychoanalysis, even of the Lacanian variety, spoke the language of big repression [*grand refoulement*] related to the Oedipus complex and to the signifying chain. The Marxists, for their part, were only capable of imagining revolution as a way of reorganising the forces of production. The arrival of *A-Œ* made everything explode: it wasn't looking for some kind of neat proletarian normalisation; rather it saw a creative principle in the maddest of madnesses – schizophrenia. Are we not all schizophrenics? That was the founding question that was proposed.

It's not that one should give up resisting, or that the concept of struggle had lost its meaning. Rather the programme and objective of struggle and resistance were profoundly changed: they were refocused on the question of subjections (*assujettissements*) with all that they implied: the concept of the production of subjectivity. All this was based on a new phase of analysis of capital: the one that is present and necessary today, and that is grounded in the definition of the predominance of immaterial capital. As a result, without the *A-Œ* it is impossible to understand the structure of labour today. Certainly today's politicians and intellectuals, like those of yesterday, do not understand it and rack their brains trying to figure out labour as a signifier. But the opposite holds: what is work, if not the expression of a desire? And what is exploitation, if not the control of desire?

Taking that as our starting point, we can see the *A-Œ* as the first 'new' philosophy, born of the conditions of May 1968, but of course 'new' not in the sense of the 'new philosophers' [*'nouveaux philosophes'*]. The *A-Œ* showed that May 1968 was not the end of a period, but the start of another phase. And the effects of the *A-Œ* continue to be felt: in antipsychiatric circles, among feminists and so on. They have also helped to construct a kind of common philosophy, a certain ethical intelligence, through which the critique of contemporary society has since then been formulated.

How would it be possible today to think, without knowing that the imperial machines that dominate us are rendered fragile by unconscious investments, ever more highly subjectivated? And how would it be possible to resist if one did not know that the 'naked full body', the 'body without organs', has the capacity to oppose itself to the overcodification of territories by the despotic machine? How could we act ethically if we were not able, after the death of the human, to build a new humanism, antagonistic to the cynicism and the piety of capital?

> Cynicism is the physical immanence of the social field, and piety is the maintenance of a spiritualised Urstaat; cynicism is capital as the means of extorting surplus labour, but piety is this same capital as God-capital, whence all the forces of labour seem to emanate. This age of cynicism is that of the accumulation of capital. (Deleuze and Guattari, 1983 [1972], p. 225)

And how would it be possible to hope, if we did not know that nomadism, hybridisation and mutation invest the bodies of the multitude and create a generation of barbarians more powerful than any lord?

The *A-Œ* is thus not only the event of May 1968, but also the point from which the critique of the structures of modernity tends to constitute itself into a critique of the postmodern: not in the 'soft' sense that the dominant ideology has restored to this concept for us, but through the insurrectional figure whose attacks have begun to be felt by the empire of globalisation: postmodernity as this new world of production and its antagonisms, as mobility and violence of powerful subjectivities that inhabit it and construct in it places of singularities as a true counterempire of desire.

After the *A-Œ* two conceptual figures begin to embody this strong postmodernity on the path taken by 'Gilles Félix': Kafka and Coluche. Kafka and Coluche are interchangeable characters on the radiant path of desire that Deleuze and Guattari trace against the new forms of subjection set in place by the 1970s, on the occasion of the defeat of the movement and after. They were true 'smugglers' [*passeurs*], opening up words, breaking things open 'to free earth's vectors' (Deleuze, 1995, p. 33).

Our two friends were working on *Mille plateaux* during this period; Coluche and Kafka have now become the 'heroes of poststructuralism' – the Jew who knows the impossibility of speaking German or Czech, and the Italian [*rital*, slang] who knows the impossibility of speaking French. Both of them experience the impossibility of not talking, and yet their 'creation takes place in choked passages' (ibid., p. 133).

But the real choking was political, the politics that was prefigured in the 1980s and took shape in 'soft' postmodernity, where any grip at the ontological level loses its potential and where control becomes unbounded globalisation, on the one hand through the rhetoric of 'human rights' and on the other through the frozen immobility of 'real socialism'. Only the delirium of Kafka or the *lazzi* [clown routines] of Coluche manage to demystify this machine of sadness; with them desire disguises itself or undergoes metamorphosis in order to produce truth – in a manner that is theatrical and yet ontological in this new theatre of the absurd.

We are now in an intermediate space between the *A-Œ* (with its violent reclaiming of libido) and *MP*. How shall we give ontological substance to desire? The theatrical *monstruum* leads on to metamorphoses, where metamorphosis begins to reveal itself as an ontological procedure of desire. And we – we, precisely – have a need for these monsters that embody the field of immanence and give reality to the arborescences of desiring rhizomes.

Is it possible to give ontological substance to desire? It was at this conjuncture, and in replying positively to this question, that Gilles and Félix produced *MP*. In other words, 'on the ontology of desire', or 'on desire as metamorphosis'. A gallery of *monstrua* marks the transition to postmodernity: we have to deal with them. How? By recognising them for what they are; by resisting, by derailing their machine. But above all by laughing. 'On Laughter', this is what one could call this introduction to *MP*. Already Bakhtin, one of the favourite authors of Gilles and Félix, had understood this when he sought the excess of life that gives meaning to language in the earthiness – or, better, in the belly – of humans. This space remains essential for anyone who is crossing through desert or chaos or has to pass through institutions and prisons, through the history of philosophy, or through psychoanalysis, political economy and theology. And if they still have a breath left in their body, they laugh at all this. To laugh is to detach oneself; it is to take one's distance. 'I laugh therefore I am.' One identifies the conceptual person, above all, through that person's laughter; the glance is always ironic. Thus the sad powers can be defeated forever.

Laughter grasps the gap between what is significant and what is not, and highlights the gap between structure and desire – but this gap is not only epistemological, it is also invested by desire: thus it is real – ontological and powerful, as the *A-Œ* taught us. This is where the roots of *MP* lie: it is a book that works precisely on this gap, reveals its potentiality [*puissance*] by proceeding to an initial ontological construction; a 'bottom-up' ontology, determinedly anti-Platonic, not analytical but synthetic, not deductive but inductive, an ontology of metamorphoses. Thus a political work, insofar as politics is defined – as it always is with 'Gilles Félix' – as ontology, or rather as an intervention on being, designed to identify another virtual form of it, which is always possible. So *MP* too is, 'from beginning to end, a book of political philosophy' (Deleuze, 1995, p. 170).

I referred earlier to three fundamental political problems posed by the *A-Œ*: (1) reflection on the objective of social struggles, in other words, on the shift from struggle against exploitation to struggle against subjection; (2) the shift of the *dispositif* of transformation from centrality to multiplicity; (3) the anticipation of the deterritorialisation of movements, in other words the critique of the spaces of power (nation-state) and of the imperial perspective. These problematics are abidingly present in the field of analysis contained in *MP*.

It is with the theory of expression and of assemblages that the theme of subjection comes to the fore. The plane of consistency of expression proposed here is in effect coextensive with that of the production of subjectivity. So the singularity is the *primum*, and the whole machinic process cannot be followed except around its deployment. Being and history are thus conceived as both production and products of subjective assemblages. The thematic of 'exploitation', which always implies an 'outside' that determines it, thus finds itself emptied of all substance, lest it pertinently reformulate it within the relationship between subjectivities and signs of potentiality [*puissance*].

The shift of the revolutionary *dispositif* from centrality to multiplicity is proposed through the theory of the rhizome and networks. Space is dominated by the rhizome. The rhizome is a force, a phylum that opens onto an unmasterable horizon of arborescence – and in this process singularity becomes increasingly singularised. We thus find ourselves immersed in a set of systems that produce signs, systems that are in a state of permanent mutation. The future is the outcome of the innovation that arises out of the magma of expression; it is in some sense the solution of war, but there remains the fact that situations of conflict are reopening. It is only by coming to terms with this context and by reappropriating it that transformation becomes possible.

Finally, in this field where every subjectivity and every event have genealogy as their frame, every determined space is shattered. Now there is only one single surface before us: a surface that is full of crevices, ruptures, constructions and reconstructions; a territory that is perennially folded and refolded. One single direction, one single teleology: the growing abstraction of relationships, which is conjugated with the complexity of arborescences, with the development of rhizomes, and with the expansion of conflicts. The old categories of sovereignty (but also of the class struggle within national dimensions) are here completely surpassed. What is being described here is a new world. A postmodernity that is absolute: neither weak nor smooth nor one-dimensional – on the contrary, a world of caverns, of folds, of breaks, of reconstructions, where subjectivity applies itself to understanding above all its own transformation, its displacement, there where the highest abstraction rules. And this abstract field is the field of a new desire.

But *MP* is not only a reprise, a development, the grand fresco of the draft of the postmodern that we find already in the *A-Œ*. In this scenario *MP* focuses mainly on the subjectivation of resistant singularities. *MP* finds its specific dimension in transforming this description into a perspective of rupture: that is, in constructing the war machine that dissolves phenomenology into ontology and models ontology on the pragmatic mechanisms of the production of subjectivity.

Pragmatics and micropolitics constitute themselves in nomadology. This means that the horizon of war is delimited by pragmatic potentialities [*puissances*]. The historical world, constituted as a geology of action, sets itself free beginning from a geology of morality in the true sense of the term, which is tireless and incessant. Produced on the basis of conflictual arborescences, subjectivities are nomadic – that is, free and dynamic. As we know, subjectivities organise themselves through machinic assemblages – hence like war machines. War machines represent the molecular fabric of the human universe. Ethics, politics, the sciences of the mind [*sciences de l'esprit*] become here one and the same thing: war machines interpret the project, they constitute the human world by operating the discrimination between desire and antidesire, between freedom and necessity. And this is, once again, rhizomes and arborescences – but endowed with meaning. It is choice in war that determines the direction of historicity. But what is direction on this completely immanent horizon, on this stage that is absolutely non-teleological? It is the expression of desire, it is the enunciation and organisation of desire as event, as discrimination vis-à-vis all transcendence, as hostility to any blockage of becoming. Politically the war machine defines itself as positivity because it takes position against the state. Deleuze and Guattari reinvent the sciences of the mind, while at the same time attacking the last vestiges of historicism and Hegelianism and of their conception of a spirit that sublimates itself in the state. Faced with the state, and particularly the state in late capitalism, molecular order spontaneously organises a molar *dispositif*, it necessarily becomes a counterpower: society against the state, or, even better (a lot better, in fact), the entirety of desiring subjectivities and their infinite arborescences, moving, in the nomadic rhythm of their appearance, against every machine that is fixed, centralising and castrating. In reality, it is only from the pragmatic point of view that we can understand and appreciate subjectivity and the direction of historicity: the point of view behind nomadology is a veritable 'philosophy of praxis'. To be nomadic in the order of history that is produced and fixed means continuously to produce machinic assemblages and assemblages of enunciation that open onto new rhizomatic arborescences and constitute the real, pure and simple. Politics thus becomes a setting into place of microassemblages, a construction of molecular networks, which allow desire to deploy and, by a permanently ongoing movement, make it the matter of pragmatics. The pragmatic in micropolitics and *of* micropolitics, this is the only operative point of view of historicity: pragmatics as praxis of desire, micropolitics as a terrain of subjectivity, ceaselessly travelled and to be travelled, indefinitely. This alternation of points of view and this convergence of constructive determinations are never at rest. The aim of the molar order is to absorb the force of desire and to reshape the *dispositifs* with the sole purpose of blocking the pragmatic flux of the molecular. On the other hand, molecular flux is ungraspable, it constantly seeks to overturn the *dispositifs* of blockage and to open the way to historicity. But what is revolution? It is to turn this infinite process into event. The political line of *MP* is one that brings the molecular *dispositif* of desires to resist the molar order, to avoid it, to get around it, to flee it. The state is to be neither reformed nor destroyed: the only way of destroying it is to flee it. A line of flight, organised by the creativity of desire, by the infinite molecular movement of subjects, by a pragmatics that is reinvented at every moment. Revolution is the ontological event of the refusal and the actualisation of its infinite power [*puissance*].

MP constructs the terrain on which the materialism of the twenty-first century is redefined. *Qu'est-ce que la philosophie?*, the explicatory essay published by Deleuze and Guattari in 1991 as an appendix to *MP*, sheds light on this. The synergy of analyses on science, philosophy and art that was displayed tirelessly in *MP*, with an exuberance worthy of the ontological material that was its subject matter, is here transformed into educational illustration, into a popularisation of the conceptual mechanisms that are the basis of the process of exposition of *MP*. In this attempt at popularisation, the methodological, theoretical and practical functions are spelled out with maximum clarity. I believe it is possible to identify here (in *MP* seen through the lens of *Qu'est-ce que la philosophie?*) the founding elements of a renewal of historical materialism, in relation to the new dimensions of capitalist development, namely the level of maximum abstraction (the 'real subsumption' of society to capital) to which it leads and in relation to which social struggles are today reformulating themselves. Without ever forgetting that, in the philosophy of the sciences of the mind as pursued by 'Gilles Félix', as also in historical materialism, we find the same ethical and political requirement for the liberation of human potentiality [*puissance humaine*]. So what is the productive context in which we are evolving and the starting point from which historical materialism can and must be renewed as the basis of the sciences of the mind? What is the fabric that underlies this manifesto?

MP gives an explicit answer to this question. Through the extent and complexity of the analyses that it develops, it outlines the same level that Marx tendentially identified in the 'Fragment on Machines' in the *Grundrisse* and defined as the society of 'general intellect'. This is a level at which the interaction between the human being and the machine, between society and capital, has become so close that the exploitation of wage labour, material and quantifiable in time, falls short and is incapable of determining a valorisation; a miserable base of exploitation in the face of the potentiality of the new social, intellectual and scientific forces on which the production of wealth and the reproduction of society now rest exclusively. *MP* registers the realisation of the tendency analysed by Marx and develops historical materialism within this new society. It addresses the construction of this new subject, which reveals the power [*puissance*] of labour, both social labour and intellectual and scientific labour; a subject-machine that is also a force of production; a plural and disseminated subject that, however, unifies itself in the constitutive pulsion of new being – and vice versa, and in all directions. Fundamental here is the total displacement of the valorisation of production in the passage from the sphere of direct material exploitation to that of political domination on the social interaction between the development of collective subjectivity and intellectual and scientific power [*puissance*] of production. In this displacement, social interactivity is itself subjected to the molar contradiction of domination – it too is exploited – but the antagonism is carried to its highest level; it acts through a paradoxical involvement of the exploited subject. In addressing Foucault's analyses of power, Deleuze emphasises the passage from 'disciplinary society' to the 'society of control' as a fundamental characteristic of the contemporary state form. Today, in this context, which is the one referred to in *MP*, domination, while remaining constant, is as abstract as it is empty and parasitic. Raised to its highest degree, antagonism is, so to speak, emptied out; 'social command' has become useless. The control of productive society is thus a mystification from the start: it no longer has even the dignity bestowed by the organizational function, which is in some senses connatural with the figure of the exploiter, in disciplinary society and in the disciplinary state form. If this is how things are, the productive labour of the new social subject is immediately revolutionary, always liberatory and innovative. It is on this basis that historical materialism finds itself renewed, implicitly in the phenomenology of *MP* and explicitly in the methodology developed in *Qu'est-ce que la philosophie?*.

Above all, historical materialism as science. This little book tells us that scientific activity is formed starting from 'partial observers' who assemble 'functions' on 'planes of reference'. Can historical materialism be anything but what promotes the 'proletarian point of view' and makes the critique of contradictions a plane of reference? Can it be anything but the displacement of a partial subject within a tendency that translates materially a grid of reading of the real? And, in the case in question, within capitalist development as a global referent of the totality of contradictions determined by the movement of abstract labour? Plane of reference: this is, again, the world of real subsumption, of the complete submission of society to capital. Labour, this is the rhizome that produces the real, is the passage from molecular order to molar order in the course of development, traverses irresistibly war and, during war, defines liberation. The plane of reference is the *Umwelt* [environment] of social labour and of its contradictions.

This is where the place of philosophy lies – inasmuch as it is pragmatic, ethical and political. The 'partial observer' of science here becomes the 'conceptual character' of philosophy. This conceptual character, can it be anything other than the new figure of the proletariat, general intellect qua subversion – that is, a new figure of the proletariat, which is all the more reunified as social and intellectual potentiality of production as it is diffuse in space (a Spinozan 'multitude' in the proper sense of the term)? The philosophy of Deleuze and Guattari acts out the new reality of the modern proletariat; it scans the trope of its necessary subversion. Thus on the one hand the conceptual personage duplicates the real, makes it appear in its conflictual dynamism and in the realisation of its tendential movement. On the other, in presenting itself as desire, as an unmasterable utopian production, the proletarian conceptual character operates an implacable and ongoing rupture of all the material references to which it is subjected. The 'plane of immanence' that philosophy constructs is an ongoing project of insurrection, effected through an absolute overview of the real, by the radical untimeliness of the contact between molecular order and molar order, by the actual non-actuality of resistance.

Art (because there is also an art of revolutionary thinking) collaborates in an essential way in this dynamic of transformation and subversion of the concept, by composing the various planes of the imaginary and by always referring them to the urgency of praxis.

The didactic schema of *Qu'est-ce que la philosophie?* evidences the directing threads built into the Dionysiac phenomenology of *MP*. But with what a richness of content! What I mean is that a comparison between the two works in no sense implies that the latter was only a chapter of the former. On the contrary, it is important to mark the differences, which are all to the benefit of *MP*. For (despite the functional reduction that we have effected here) the *MP* constitutes not only a phenomenology (of an extraordinary richness) of the conceptual personage of general intellect – half machine, half subject, entirely machine, entirely subject; it constitutes also a revolutionary experience. Along the recapitulation of this extraordinary series of events that only great revolutionary episodes are able to offer, one can find gathered both 'the years of desire' and the *Erlebnisse* [experiences] of 'the changing of life' that followed 1968. People say that there is no book that succeeds in encapsulating 1968. This is not true! That book is *MP*. This is historical materialism in action in our time, it is the equivalent of Marx's *The Class Struggles in France 1848 to 1850*. Although the text has no ending and does not permit itself the satisfaction of final conclusions, this is because, just like its equivalent in Marx's thought, it identifies a new subject, whose mechanism of formation has not been completed but that has already acquired a substantive presence in the plurality of micro- and macroexperiences realised – ethical–political experiences that are in all respects significant. *MP* is the pulsion of a collective body, of a thousand singular bodies. The politics that is expressed here is that of the communism of the Spinozan *multitudo*, that of the devastating mobility of subjects on the stage of the recently established global market; it is the politics of the most radical democracy (of all subjects, including the insane), directed as a weapon against the state as the great organiser of the exploitation of workers, of the disciplining of the insane, of the control of general intellect. *MP* makes explicit reference to the diffuse and autonomous social struggles of women, youth, workers, homosexuals, marginals, immigrants... within a perspective according to which all the walls have already fallen. This richness of the movement is the framework in which the scientific point of view and the definitive construction of the concept are now possible. For this concept is event, and the system of concepts is the fracture in the geology of action across a genealogy of the event-desire.

The conditions for a reconstruction of the *Geisteswissenschaften* [sciences of the mind, humanities] in the perspective of a theory of expression and in the framework of a historicity that is at once the very movement of being and the point of incidence of the subject are thus given. One example of this, just one: the treatment of the history of philosophy in *MP* and in *Qu'est-ce que la philosophie?* and the methodological hypotheses that are developed there. The historiographical continuity of the history of philosophy is dissolved here, as is also its ontic teleology – philosophical historicity is thus treated as historicity *tout court*, understood as a singular confrontation between thought and the current problematic of being. The history of philosophy itself can only be understood, can only be reconstructed as event, as untimeliness, as present inactuality. Philosophy is always a Spinozan scholium to the deployment of the real. The schema of the sciences of the mind will thus always be horizontal, articulated to the event, interdisciplinary, stratified by the interrelations of its multiple elements. But what about the past or what it has produced, where is that? In fact machinic phyla, which are both results and residues of the past, oppose the rhizome of the present and of creativity. But the science of the mind is born where these machinic phyla are consumed in the determination of a new creation, of a new event. The material determinations, their accumulation, the opaque depth of the past, are a set of dead things that only living labour revives and that are reinvented by the new machines of subjectivity. When this does not happen, the past is dead, it even becomes our prison. *MP* is the materialist theory of social labour, understood as a creative event of a thousand subjects that open themselves to this present reality on the basis of a machinic conditioning that this same labour has produced and that only living and actual labour can again valorise.

If vitalism thus revised, the theory of expression, and absolute immanentism are the basis of the reconstruction of the sciences of the mind, what is it that makes it possible, on that horizon, that one does not stray again into scepticism or into some form of weak reading of value? Nothing is further from *MP* than the temptation to absolutise any element of the internal process, be that being itself, to avoid drifting into relativisms. On the contrary, what allows the science of the mind to be reborn, to renew the logical and ethical power of materialism, is the concept of the surface, ontology that is open to historicity, taken as present subjectivity. Let us look back for a moment: when Heidegger represents the overturning of the ontic into the ontological, of historiography into historicity as ineluctable, he at the same time makes this overturning, this logical rupture, this refusal of destiny the only meaning of the existent. The Heideggerian operation is a blockage of life. It pushes the metaphysical approach to the limit, to a point of arrival. Heidegger is a Job who – in contrast to what happens to the biblical Job – when he sees God is blinded by him. In *MP*, on the contrary, to see God in the manner of Spinoza is to effect anew the methodological overturning of the ontic into the ontological, in a new perception of being – of being that is open. Not to reaffirm God, but to exclude him definitively; not to grasp an absolute, but to consider the construction of being to be *omnino absoluta* [wholly independent]: going from the labour of the singularity to the creative work [*oeuvre*] of human labour. Rhizomatic, focused on the present, the human sciences can thus be rebuilt – the sciences and therefore the planes of reference; philosophy and therefore the planes of consistency; the human sciences and therefore the convergence of these approaches, approaches to the event, ethical charges that traverse the ontological machines, subjective combinations [*agencements*] that are more and more abstract. There is no other way of considering being other than being it, doing it.

Ten years on, one can still see *MP* as a phenomenology of the present that is completely operational; but above all we have to see in it the first philosophy of the postmodern. A philosophy that, sinking its roots into the alternative, immanent and materialistic option of modernity, sets out the foundations that might enable the rebuilding of the sciences of the mind. And, because *Geist* [spirit] is the brain and the 'brain' has become general intellect (with the crisis of capitalist, transcendentalist and idealist modernity, as Marx had predicted), *MP* announces the rebirth of a historical materialism that is worthy of our time. This materialism awaits the revolutionary event that will verify it.

Having reached this point, it remains only to ask ourselves: how was it that, through the course of their journey, the differing positions of these two authors were able to coexist? How was the thinking of each of them able to nourish itself on the encounter of their singularities?

Nobody can deny that their philosophical positions were different. We have already discussed the dissimilarity of their paths at the point when they met, and the differences in their methodological approaches and their disciplines. These differences continued and each of us can recognise, even in their jointly produced works, sections that represent different positions. Even towards the end of their collaboration (and of their lives), their differences never diminished. Starting with *Pli* (and he highlighted this in the collection *Critique et clinique*), Deleuze brings to the surface the Bergsonian ancestry to his thinking – an element that on other occasions had been, if not forgotten, at least passed over in silence. As for Guattari, in *Cartographies analytiques* and in *Chaosmose* he seems to allow himself to set off once again on adventures as a seeker of signs in the realm of the unconscious – which a constant nostalgia for his early research into autism made liable to return from time to time – and into the wild experience of coining new words: a thirsty inner drive to decipher the connection between the word and the dream, which he manifested unceasingly. But all this has no importance, in my view, except for those historians of philosophy who, like grocers of thought, are forever striving to separate Deleuze from Guattari, to save Deleuze from the abyss

towards which Félix pushes him, so that he may be reinserted into
that damnable history of philosophy. But this petty game is of relatively little interest, because in 'Gilles Félix' it is impossible to create
separations at the level of thought; the differences feed the unity;
critique and the clinic act according to the same *dispositif*. In the
Homeric poems, who can separate between Achilles and Odysseus?
'If the hero of the Iliad is a hero of form and therefore of force, the
hero of the Odyssey is a hero of the event and as such of intelligence'
(Diano, 1994, p. 49). Who will be able to separate the Ulysses–Gilles
from the Achilles–Félix? But there is more: we shall not even be able
to tell them apart, because the path they took together was a prophetic path. I say 'prophetic' in a Spinozan sense, in other words like
the action of 'one who creates a people'. In these three or four books
that together they left us, they created a people of concepts that make
a radical break with the present and prefigure the future; they built
dispositifs that allow language to move within being; and, above all,
they reopened ontology to the political. Thus utopia began to live in
the pragmatics of desire and in the joy of the construction of being
in thought. Thus the outcome of the road taken by 'Gilles Félix' is a
desiring multitude, which is no longer 'city', or 'people', or 'democracy', or 'state of law' but precisely multitude, a prophetic people.
Finally, let us look around us, let us contemplate, as philosophers,
the poverty of present-day politics, and let us do what one does *chez*
'Gilles Félix': let us laugh a Pantagruelian laugh.

Acknowledgement

This article, originally written in Italian, was published in a French
translation made by Gisèle Donnard and revised by Éric Alliez. The
present translation renders the French version.

15

Observations on the 'Production of Subjectivity'

On an Intervention by Pierre Macherey

Co-authored with Judith Revel

The key chosen by Macherey to identify the concept of production (and of a productive subject), retracing it from Foucault to Marx, is conceptual – namely that there is no case for going to look for direct references to Marx in Foucault; rather one has to reply, via Marx, to a few questions posed by Foucault; to interpret, via Marx, some of the conceptual machinery that Foucault constructed. First, one has to understand whether the structural *dispositifs* of Foucault's theory of power find a correspondence in Marx, or maybe even their source. Second, we have to understand whether the Marxian concept of 'living labour' is similar to, or even the same as, Foucault's conception of production and the productive subject. Third and finally, having answered 'yes' to these two questions, Macherey sets out to compare the reading of Foucault's figure of power, or rather of biopower, with how it operates in the contemporary world, stressing the fact that here its definition (which is consistent with Marx's presuppositions) broadens its descriptive power to encompass the new social figures, in which capital (its power of exploitation of the whole of society and its ability to represent itself as state) expresses itself in our present times.

On the first point, Macherey points out in general terms that, although the word 'class' is not present when – at the end of the *Leçons sur la volonté de savoir* – Foucault defines biopower (as a force that determines social hierarchy and segregation – or 'the social division of labour' – and guarantees relationships of domination and effects of hegemony, understood as the social and statal organisation of exploitation), nevertheless this is the selfsame framework that, in Marx, characterises capital as a structure of domination over the forces of production. To determine the concept of power, Foucault too fixes economics as a place of 'final instance'. 'Here Foucault seems to come close to flirting with Marx's analyses in *Capital*, in the attempt to locate power in a perspective that is positive and "productive"' (Macherey, unpublished manuscript).*

Macherey then follows, in *Capital* (in the chapters in which value and surplus value, absolute surplus value and relative surplus value are discussed), the path taken by Marx's research, observing that the definition of power in Foucault finds its most solid support there. We shall not follow Macherey in this effective and evocative in-depth analysis: we shall simply note a few points where, particularly strikingly, Foucauldian discourse – in the account given by Macherey – integrates and develops the thinking of Marx (and thus does not just 'flirt' with it). Such an 'overinterpretation' gives fruits that are important and often unexpected. The first consists in considering 'living labour' exclusively as a productive force and in defining its 'excedent' character in relation to all causal or physicalist, Aristotelian or positivist, in short, deterministic interpretations of the concept of 'force'. The force of production consists in fact in the ambiguity of living labour, because it permits the latter to manifest its 'excedence' simultaneously 'inside' and 'outside' the relationship that binds it to capital: it is 'inside' because capital appropriates that excedence to itself, making use of the legal contract that imposes the expropriation of the producer; but it is 'outside' because the excedence of living labour is unique and powerful, and brings living labour to life beyond the capitalist capacity of exploitation. This gives rise to a concept of power that is always inclusive of a balance of power. Indeed, just like the concept of power in general, capital too is a relationship. Every substantialist conception of power and of capital is thus voided. Around the concept of power, which is central to political theory, Marx and Foucault coincide. The second effect of the 'overinterpretation' is to show living labour as a determination intrinsic to the machine of power that commands it. The force of living labour is not only opposed to capital but also intimately connected to it, so much so that it creates its overall structure [*assetto complessivo*]. Moreover, in exercising itself as the source of surplus value, inserted within the system of machines, labour power not only produces capital but also composes and organises a society: it is over this society that the machine of power extends – commanding it,

---

* Translator's Note: The source text, presented in November 2004, was at https://www.univ-lille3.fr/set/machereynegri.html, but is no longer available.

organising it, and disseminating its contradictory potential. And from this a further effect follows: from the factory to society, this machine of command progressively extends itself, dominates every space, permeates populations and is, for this reason, subjected to a constant movement and tendency to rupture.

This interpretative framework can generally be drawn from Marx and Foucault. But, after taking this first analytical glimpse, I have a question to put to Macherey: Why does this enlargement, this intensification of the reading (via Foucault) of *Capital*, still hold for him (Macherey) – despite his having internalised labour power within a capital that is in expansion and having grasped the overlap between the organisation of economic exploitation and the organisation of political command? Why, then, does this excedence of 'living labour' remain extrinsic to its self-constitution as a subject, and thus to the production of subjectivity in this story?

The result of this extrinsic determination is that Macherey captures just a first stage, the one in which exploitation is transformed and consolidated into a *habitus*: discipline in the form of life. However, continuing his investigation, Macherey goes deeper. First of all he returns to the concept of labour power as a force of production and studies the grids within which it is constrained into producing capital under the command of capital. Production here is entirely enclosed within capital. We could talk, or so Macherey seems to say, of a narrow and insuperable technological connection between labour and capital. In fact labour power is so internal to the system that it can only express itself in the capital relation – in a manner that is actual but also virtual (that is, with an ontological intensity that expands its effects into future time): this is a dimension that Macherey captures perfectly (Marx would say that the power [*potenza*] of living labour is present in the continuity of the machinic operation). Intensifying the question, however, it seems that, for Macherey, one should conclude, from the internalness of labour power within the 'technical composition' of capital, that labour power itself is, so to speak, 'preconstituted' by capital.

Should we not rather ask what were the effects of a dual concept, open and polemical, of the power relation? And what was the figure (and the actual numbers) of the different subjects of and within the balance of power? It is certain that, in Foucault, at least up to *Surveiller et punir*, exploitation subsumes the whole of society in its effectuality; and, if the whole of society is exploited, little space remains for the genealogy of subjectivity. Rereading these pages, we can certainly recognise in them many ideas drawn from the critical theory of the

Frankfurt School. Discipline and authority are seen as one, and the same seems to be the case for alienation and exploitation. On the social terrain exploitation is directed; in the subsumption of society in capital it is no longer possible to distinguish between structure and superstructure and so on. But it is precisely in these pages, alongside the definitive recognition of the socialisation of exploitation, the definitive passage of critique from the factory to society, that Foucault (with great insight, as Macherey recognises) also accentuates his critique – and initiates the process of relativisation – of the absoluteness with which the concepts of norm, of discipline, and so forth, had been constructed up until that point. In contrast, what comes out of Foucauldian critique is that there is always resistance. The double nature of the power relationship is here restored to its truth. In the double nature of the power relation, that subjectivity that seemed to have been dissolved and set aside thus enters definitely into play. Instead there is resistance: the concepts of rule and discipline collide with practices of resistance, with logical revolts built on ontological ruptures. Temporally valid resistances, which work on spaces that are regional, micropolitical...

Macherey moves further forward into this field. Now it is no longer the pages of Marx that interest him, but increasingly those of Foucault, in relation to contemporary reality, to the reading of that book that today's ethics and politics force us to read. Foucault, according to Macherey, puts us in a position of having to read the concept (and the reality) of power for what it has truly become: it is now a network in which the economy, the regulation of labour, the extraction of profit and so on are collected under the term 'political despotism' (exactly as Marx said). Looking at today's world, we understand this despotic qualification better than Marx himself could do. It is very powerful, the system in which we are caught. Productivity is social, as is productive cooperation, too. There is no longer a specific space for ideology: there is no longer separated space, there is no longer given a world independent of consciousness *in se* [intrinsically] and per se, because capitalist exploitation has invaded everything – and the metaphysics of this social physics of production permeates everything. Macherey's notes on the 'physicality' of capitalist metaphysics of value are really good in their finesse and precision, but they are not enough. Yes, let us fix the articulations and catalogue the internal divisions of this machinery in which we are immersed. And yet, once we have made our distinctions and specifications, we still find ourselves in there, inside the machine. At this point the essence of being human is directly exploited by capital.

Here I stop. Macherey seems to have arrived to the place where I was waiting for him. After having described his approach – so thorough and so important for the recovery of the power relationship through the analysis of living labour in its opposition to capital – I ask him why one cannot, at least on two counts, conclude with *dispositifs* other than those he has tracked here. The first count is that, if capital is a relationship and if, in the given conditions, the struggle between 'living labour' and 'dead labour' has never ended, nothing compels us to believe that this process cannot be interrupted. The emergence of subjectivity within the process of exploitation, or rather within the very concept of capital, forces us to admit it. The 'excedence' of 'living labour' is not prefigured by the capacity of subjection and exploitation of capital; it is not – by definition – 'commensurate'. Rather it produces elements of hardness and resistance in relation to capital, and the 'resistance' is always an expression of freedom as well as of production. The second count consists in showing that, if this relation is currently controlled from above, by the command-imposing accumulation of 'dead labour', no determinism obliges us to think that it cannot be controlled from below. We should not pin our hopes on future catastrophes, or entertain mystical hopes for concretising logically this path from below. We need only think that, if within biopower there are forces in struggle – just as they struggle in capital and struggle in the process of producing (they produce through struggle) – then they do not produce only capital. First and foremost they produce, of course, their adversary – a capital that accumulates power until it's able at times (not only in a sort of reformist compromise) to foreshadow those same productive forces that dialectically produce it. But when there is no meeting between two reformisms (that of capital and that of the subjected producer), the confrontation remains open – then, within this clash, there is always a production of subjectivity, because that power relation is not symmetrical, indeed it is always an intransitive relation, and it creates asymmetry now here, now there – sometimes on the side of the capital, at other times on the side of living labour. And when it is on the side of living labour, when the asymmetry is overdetermined on that side, production becomes a production of subjectivity and is revolutionary – without forgetting that the path to the liberation of living labour is from the bottom to the top.

16

Marx after Foucault

The Subject Refound

1

The question that I shall ask today is simple: how was it that, in my work, I tried to read Marx together with, and after, Foucault (and how did I feel about the possibility of doing so)? I would like to offer a brief account of that experience. It involved setting down some axes of possible readings of Marx that could be organised around a *dispositif* of subjectification and could then be read in terms of Foucault. I shall try to demonstrate the possibility of this being applied to our current realities: it imposes a corresponding ontology. If, conversely, reading Marx means nourishing a radical desire for a transformation of historical being, I think that Foucauldian subjectification needs to be read in terms of that determination.

(A) It seems to me today that, on the basis of Foucault's insights and conclusions, the strongly historicised tone and style of Marx's critique of political economy should be articulated in a precise manner to a materialist approach. And this obviously is not just a question of reading Marx's historical texts together with his other works (especially those engaged in the critique of political economy), but one of deepening and developing genealogically the analysis of concepts – opening them up to the present. Foucault's approach has thus enabled us not merely to grasp but also to insist on the subjectification of the class struggle as an agent of the historical process. Naturally the analysis of this subjectification will always need to be renewed and matched to the transformative determinations that concepts undergo during the historical process. All this happens within the ambit of Foucault's invitation – beyond any dialectics and teleology – to assume historical subjectification as a *dispositif* that is neither causal nor creative, but determining: a historical materialism for our times, *à la* Machiavelli. Here are two of the many possible examples:

• When, in *Capital*, Marx defines the transition from the extraction of absolute surplus value to that of relative surplus value, correlating this transition with the working-class struggles for the reduction of the working day, the historical dimension of the struggle, the specific class subjectification here becomes essential, in the event, to defining the ontological transformation of the structure of capitalist value creation – not to mention the transformation of the relationship between the technical and the political composition – by which I mean innovation – of the workers' subjectivity. In short, the struggle makes possible both the event and the ontological transformation itself.

• When Marx passes from the analysis of 'formal subsumption' to that of the 'real subsumption' of labour under capital, this is primarily a hypothesis on the historical development of the capitalist mode of production. Now, from the description of this step (which involves the process of surplus value and its transformation into profit), Marx draws various possible figures of the extraction of surplus value. On this basis, historically founded, he introduces the analysis of a continuous configuration of the categories of exploitation during different periods of capitalist development. In this framework it becomes possible, for example, to subject to criticism the very concept of the working class, which transforms itself and is consolidated into different forms in the transition from 'manufacturing' to 'large scale industry' – and now from industrial capitalism in its Fordist incarnation, more or less socialised, to financial capitalism. The concept of 'multitude' could be appropriate here for describing the present determinations of 'living labour' in a 'cognitive', singular, plural and cooperative sense. Thus the idea is not to eliminate the concept of the working class but to redefine it.

(B)   In a theoretical perspective that is firmly Foucauldian in origin, you can then take Marx's concept of capital (especially when considered in its historical development, from 'manufacturing' to 'large scale industry' and from the form of 'social capital' to that of 'finance capital') in close connection with the concept of power, as defined by Foucault – that is, as the product of a relation of power, as an action on the action of another, as an effect of 'class struggle' with ontological implications. It is the characteristics of the new proletarian subjectification – resistant and active as a (singularised and cognitive) force of production – that make it possible to relocate class struggle at the heart of capitalist development, as its engine. And also at the heart of its possible final crisis. And by the way, whenever people talk about a possible end of capitalism, let us stop accusing them of historicist teleology... Quite the contrary, it is analogies such as these that allow us to re-launch the meaning of 'class struggle' as a *Begriff des Politischen* ['concept of the political'].

(C)   In this context one can also move forward – and this is the third point that I would like to consider – in the analysis of the transformation of the 'technical composition' of labour power, highlighting the relationship that antagonist subjectification opposes to capitalist command. In a Foucauldian perspective, of analysis of the 'technologies of the self', the efficacy of living labour can be increased when this labour appropriates quantities of 'fixed capital'. This means that labour power not only undergoes the subjugation of the capitalist mode of production but also, subjectivating itself at the level of cognitive capital, reacts by constituting new forms of living labour. These forms appropriate fractions of fixed capital and thus develop a higher productivity. Around this theme it is today possible to grasp the characteristic 'excedence' of cognitive living labour and make a deeper analysis of its biopolitical productivity. That form of *capital* and that form of *power* that are always interactive in the relationship of force that constitutes them are also always interactive in the relationship that governs the processes of subjectification. Here perhaps we should take up the Simondon experiment, using and developing it not simply in terms of intersubjectivity and transindividuation, but in (Guattarian and Deleuzian) terms of a *machinic* transformation of corporality and subjectivity. If the antagonistic element of subjectification is sometimes lacking in Deleuze, even in this machinic perspective, it can very well be recovered if you stay with Foucault's intuitions. Just as there is class struggle traversing the organic composition of capital, so also there is – and increasingly will have to be centrally taken on board – a machinic element, moved by the class struggle, which belongs to the technical composition of antagonist labour power. After Foucault, this development of Marx's discourse becomes possible. In the class relationship (studied after Foucault) the ontological dimension is not a background but a productive machine. The common operating, the productive hegemony of the common, stem not only from the transformation of labour into a cognitive machine but above all from the anthropological transformation that underpins it, from the pipelines by which it is fed, from the new technological potentiality [*potenza*]. While they find their roots in classical antiquity, the Foucauldian technologies overflow of their own accord into a new anthropology that has no naturalistic and identity-related characteristics – but that configures the human after the 'death of the human'. Foucault's work began from the analysis of the 'accumulation of people', which characterised the primitive accumulation of capital – whereas now the question is to deepen, with the technical composition of labour, the transformation of productive bodies, of ways of life. This is about stating loud and clear that 'ways of life' are becoming 'means of production'.

(D) Finally, a fourth point, and I put this one very schematically. When you take the Marx–Foucault relationship starting from Foucault's theory of subjectification, communism will have to be seen as the process that puts together the production of the common and democratic subjectification, in other words the individualisation of the multitude. It is here that productive ontology meets the concept of the common.

2

Now, having explained how Foucault was useful to me in reading Marx, I would like to go back and restart the analysis from a less subjective standpoint, to establish more transparent foundations for the kind of reading that I was developing. Running through the century that separates Marx from Foucault and analysing the diversity of the forms of exploitation, of struggles and of ways of life, let us first fix some points that define the differences. These are broad-brush differences, and undoubtedly limited, but they are at the centre of the political lexicons of both writers, and they give the impression of a considerable distance. We shall see later whether and how these important differences can be reunited within a common perspective. This is obviously my hypothesis. But for the moment let us take a look at the differences.

First difference: in Marx, the unity of command maintains itself in the figure of sovereign power. Governance is unified in the will of capital. In Foucault, the unity of power is rather looser, and within 'governmentality' we find articulated a plurality of different and diffuse productions of power.

Second difference: in Marx, domination is assumed in capital, and the historical dynamics of social development follow the rhythm of the different 'subsumptions', in a univocal perspective of 'capitalisation' – not to mention 'statisation' – of the social. In Foucault, biopower is decentralised, its diffusion takes place via different germinations, and the articulations of power become singularised. We have here a 'socialisation of the political'.

Third difference: in Marx, communism is organised through the dictatorship of the proletariat, and this alone can build the transition from capitalist society to a classless society. In Foucault, the political regime of liberation is organised in subjectification; it singularises itself as liberty; it places the construction of common happiness in production, unconstrained.

Can these manifest differences be corrected or brought together? Is it possible for the conceptual divisions that exist (albeit on the basis of a similar ontological line) to be removed? They could probably be rendered less important than they seem to be. For example, as regards the first difference, the organic conception of the state and of command is significantly attenuated in Marx, at the political level, by the historical analysis of the behaviours of social classes, by the interpretative device of 'class war' and of its transient and multiple effects, and then by the communard hypotheses (and critiques) developed in his various historical writings. It is, however, especially in the area of the critique of political economy that his conception is profoundly modified, when Marx passes from the analysis of productive and reproductive processes – in forms that are highly centralised and abstract – to an analysis of the social circulation of commodities, relating production processes back to processes of value formation and then going back down to the analysis of the wage and hence to the description of social classes and ways of life. The multiplication and diffusion of the mechanisms of power then define large spaces – when society becomes factory, the processes of power multiply and become differentiated, and on these differences they literally set themselves pulsating.

As for the second difference, in the face of the 'capitalisation' or 'statisation of society' (which presents itself extremely violently in 'primitive accumulation'), a degree of 'governmentalisation' or 'socialisation of the state' can also be found in Marx: it appears in the process of transformation of the capitalist mode of production from 'formal subsumption' to 'real subsumption'. Roberto Nigro in particular has stressed these analogies of subsumption between Marx and Foucault, while Macherey has tried to grasp, through analysis of these changes in society, that change of the 'subject as product' into 'productive subject' that, for Foucault, stands at the centre of the problem of subjectification. As for the third difference – which relates to the communism of Marx, to the dictatorship of the proletariat and, on the other hand, to its ontological shift into the theory of subjectification in Foucault – here perhaps one can establish some similarity, bearing in mind the pages on communism, the general intellect, and the 'social individual' in the *Grundrisse*. This similarity became obvious in Foucault's *Lessons* from 1978 – probably this was the result of discussions with friends, colleagues and associates in Foucauldian circles at that time – and certainly in the currency of a Marxist-originated historiography – I am thinking particularly of the work of E. P. Thompson.

To conclude on this point: these similarities bring our two authors close around a number of themes that are central to modernity (state, society and subject); but they permit us to position them only in the dissolution of the modern and not in the development of a new ontology. It should be noted, however, that, in emphasising these differences (and similarities) between Marx and Foucault, I am referring to Foucault in that phase of his work that led up to the biopolitical turning point of his lecture courses of 1977–8 and 1978–9. At this stage the analogies remain confusing. The concepts are treated ambiguously. In Marx's case we need only think that, in the first and second examples, each discursive accentuation is not given in terms of singularisation but rather of extreme 'abstraction'. The opposite is the case with Foucault.

3

I believe that, if we study Foucault by taking his classes of 1977–88 as a starting point and by reading his writings and his lectures when, after 1984, this was possible, and by making him ours not only as a philosopher but also as a militant (the classes at the Collège de France have a tone that permits this kind of reading), we shall be able to define a basis that goes beyond superficial convergences between the thinking of Marx and Foucault on governmentality, biopolitics and the subject and will enable us rather to identify in both writers a common that is grafted into an ontology of the present.

In the years that interest us Foucault moves ahead in the articulation of politics and ethics, defining a 'relationship to oneself' that is – against every individualising operation and every resumption of the Cartesian subject – a collective constitution of the subject and of its immersion in the historical process. What comes out of this is a 'dethroning' of the subject, which presents itself as the excavation of the 'we' – of the relationship I–we – not only as becoming but as a practice of multiplicity. The 'we' is a multitude and the 'I' is defined in relation to the other. When we analyse the 'care of the self' – on which Foucault dwells so much – we note that it is not reducible to individual practice, nor is it (and here I quote Judith Revel at http://www.materialifoucaultiani.org/it/materiali/altri-materiali/59-forum-qmichel-foucault-e-le-resistenzeq/153-materiali-foucaultiani-judith-revel-1.html, in the online journal *Materiali Foucaultiani*):

> an individual response to a power that tends to create and shape the figure of the individual according to its own needs. To put it brutally and schematically, the Greek self is not the Cartesian I and, all the more, it is not the individual created by the economic and political liberalism whose birth was described by Foucault in 1978 – rather, it is the singularity defined by Deleuze.

Ethics emerges at this intersection of being and doing. There follows decentralisation in the process of subjectification, which is entirely political. This is where the cynics triumph and where *parrhēsia* becomes clear, not simply as the will to speak the truth but as a terrain of truth. But, in order to say this, one has to stress not only the power–resistance pairing, which introduces a dissymmetry between the two terms – even though the one is not conceivable without the other – but above all the ontological character of this difference. This character is revealed by the intransitivity of freedom, an unconditional element even when it is subjected to a relationship of power. That is exactly what happens with living labour, an intransitive potentiality in the capital relation.

Truth is built on a *poietic* terrain that produces new being. Liberation struggles, for example, develop an intransitive practice of freedom, of a freedom that creates truth. In the debate with Chomsky, when the question arises of the proletariat's desire for truth, Foucault says:

> I would like to reply to you in terms of Spinoza and tell you that the proletariat doesn't wage war against the ruling class because it considers such a war to be just. The proletariat wages war against the ruling class because it wants, for the first time in history, to take power. And it's because it wants to take power that it considers such a war to be just. (roarmag.org at http://www.desrealitat.org/2013/05/foucault-chomsky-full-version-transcript.html)

Finally, it is clear that the development of such processes of subjectification leads to a continuous reformulation of the grammar (and of the practices) of power. If archaeology recognises the difference that exists between yesterday and today, and if genealogy explores the possible difference between tomorrow and the present day, all this can only be done through an accurate investigation into the present, through 'a critical ontology of ourselves'. And it is this critical ontology of ourselves, planted in the present, that gives the possibility, or rather the necessity, of shaking up the categories of modernity. Many examples could be adduced to this end, but those that seem fundamental above all others are the problematics regarding the new quality of 'living labour' and the new dimensions of its productive capacity; and, second, the exhaustion of the dimension of 'private' and 'public' and the emergence of that 'common' terrain that the I–we relationship – the production of the I in the work [opera] of the we – brings about.

Now, the important thing about this sequence of history, ethics, and making politics is to constitute the projection, or rather the dispositif, of an open ontology, of a real and actual production of being. It is perhaps curious but nonetheless relevant to recall this Foucauldian position, developed at a time when the latest findings of Sartre's existentialism had imposed themselves even within the revolutionary left. Now, as against Sartre, in Foucault there is no freedom of the subject and no necessity of the fact, but a necessary determination of the ontological context and its openness, freedom of ethical being and doing.

4

In the postmodern, after Heidegger, ontology is no longer defined as a place of the founding of the subject but as a linguistic agencement, practical and cooperative; as the fabric of praxis. In short, it is an ontology of present being that has broken the continuity of transcendental philosophy, as it had been established beginning with Kant. This ontology literally tears itself away from the ontology of modernity and from its Cartesian roots, from the centrality of the subject, and implants itself in the new materiality of 'ways of life'. This is where the epistemological screen is knocked down as a necessary bridge to reality. Heidegger is the one who proceeds on this terrain, but Heidegger is also the one who paradoxically renders it impracticable when technical doing [l'operare tecnico], which now constitutes the world, comes in collision with the work [opera] itself.

The threat to man does not come in the first instance from the potentially lethal machines and apparatus of technology. The actual threat
has already affected man in his essence. The rule of enframing [*Gestell*]
threatens man with the possibility that it could be denied to him to
enter into a more original revealing and hence to experience the call of
a more primal truth. (Heidegger, 1977, p. 28)

In Heidegger, where being is not productive, technology thus drowns
production in an inhuman destiny, which introduces into the genesis
of the new ontology a sign of perversion. Technology gives us a world
that is ravaged, a 'waste land'; and here, inevitably, the ghosts of the
subject reappear, well represented in the existentialism of Heidegger.

Between Nietzsche and Foucault, however, another path seems to
define itself. They assume the being of the world for what it is; and
they excavate it in order to find out what it has become, to manipu-
late the detritus of the past, the compactness of the present, the
adventure of what lies ahead – grasped in its material reality and open
in its temporality. For them, all that is needed is a push to fill ontology with history, to establish linguistic relationships and performative
dispositifs, genealogical reconstructions and wills to truth, so that (by
interacting) they produce new being. They extend every relationship over machines that are constitutive of world. Transcendental
epistemology is set to one side – it cannot give a guarantee of knowledge for that ontology of the present within which our life produces
itself. Unlike in Heidegger, in the new ontology a decisive bifurca-
tion is thus produced that opens to the common pulsation of life.
The production of being is given neither in the profound nor in the
transcendental, but is organised in presence, in actuality, in the care
of life. I use the word 'pulsation', but there should be no ambiguities
here. There is nothing vitalist in it; we are in social and political life,
not in a life that is naturalised or biologised. Life is always social and
political.

In Foucault is expressed, in the highest manner, this being that is
immersed in a new ontology of the present – a common being, where
the mutual and multilateral dependence of singularities constructs
the only terrain on which it is possible to pose the cognitive question
and seek truth. Foucault's books are, from the start – as Macherey
observed – located

at the beginning of a season of great debates that marked the complete
renewal of the modes of thinking and writing of the immediate postwar
period, when realism in literature, the philosophy of the subject, and

the notion of continuous historical progress of dialectical rationality were being simultaneously questioned. (Macherey, 1992, n.p.)

Freeing oneself from that culture means getting rid of the sovereign subject and of the concept of consciousness – and with them of all historical teleology. It means conceiving ontology as a fabric and product of collective praxis. In the mid-1970s, reading what Foucault had written up until that point, I felt that he had reached an impasse and I wondered whether it might not be overcome by moving beyond the structuralist cult of the object and spiritualist fascination with the subject, by a drive to subjectification, to the ontological construction of the 'to come' [*a-venire*]. This began to happen at the end of the 1970s.

In Marx we find an identical form of ontological rooting: a rooting in and of the historical presence and its continuous reconstitution. There is no metaphysics of the subject. The ontological fabric is the same as the one that thus far we have termed the 'new ontology'. Taking on this ontological immediacy does not mean ignoring the diversity of historical periods and, consequently, of the 'forms of life' under consideration, for example in Marx and Foucault, but simply having the ability to compare them on a consistent basis.

So we have to move ahead on the four points that I defined at the start of this chapter and that I summarise as follows: a radical historicisation of the critique of political economy; recognition of the class struggle as the motor of capitalist development; subjectification in the struggles of labour power, of living labour, and the adjustment of producer bodies to the change in relations of production; and, finally, the definition of a subjectification open to the common.

5

Often in French circles, counter to what I have outlined above, there was an attempt to advance on this terrain by developing the idea of a desubjectification of ontological discourse; and to this end the thinking of Althusser was used as a mediation. Indeed he had been strikingly radical in advancing this position. Now, there is no doubt that Althusser had laid the basis for critique on this terrain:

> the individual is interpellated as a (free) subject in order that he shall submit freely to the commandments of the Subject, i.e. in order that he shall (freely) accept his subjection, i.e. in order that he shall make the gestures and

actions of his subjection 'all by himself'. *There are no subjects except by and for their subjection.* (Althusser, 1971, p. 182)

We are well aware of this. The fact remains, however, that in this process, in his keenness to undermine subjectivity, to cut down the tree of any possible spiritualism, Althusser paradoxically ended up cutting the branch on which he was sitting. Étienne Balibar corrects the matter by observing that 'it is in the historical process understood as a process without subject that the "constitution of the subject" can have meaning' (Balibar, 1993, as quoted by Nigro, 2008, p. 104).

The Marxist critique of the subject cannot in fact be translated into a non-qualified or indeterminate form of antihumanism. The historicity, the potentiality [*potenza*] that is expressed from it, needs to be recovered. Perhaps in the ontology of the present we have the resurgence of a humanism that is required after the 'death of the human being' [*'la morte dell'uomo'*].

References

Althusser, L. 1971. 'Ideology and Ideological State Apparatuses (Notes towards an Investigation)', trans. B. Brewster. In L. Althusser, *Lenin and Philosophy and Other Essays*. New York: Monthly Review Press, pp. 127–86.

Anderson, P. 1976. 'The antinomies of Antonio Gramsci'. *New Left Review*, 1(100): 5–78.

Balibar, E. 1993. 'L'Objet d'Althusser'. In *Politique et philosophie dans l'œuvre d'Althusser*, ed. S. Lazarus. Paris: PUF, pp. 81–116.

Baudrillard, J. 1977. *Oublier Foucault*. Paris: Galilée.

Colletti, L. 1960. 'Prefazione'. In E. V. Ilienkov, *La dialettica dell'astratto e del concreto nel Capitale di Marx*. Milan: Feltrinelli.

Deleuze, G. 1986. *Foucault*. Paris: Minuit.

Deleuze, G. 1995. *Negotiations, 1972–1990*, trans. M. Joughin. New York: Columbia University Press.

Deleuze, G. 2003. 'Instincts and institutions'. In G. Deleuze, *Desert Islands and Other Texts (1953–74)*, trans. Mike Taormina. New York: Semiotexte, pp. 19–21.

Deleuze, G. and Guattari, F. 1983 [1972]. *Anti-Œdipus: Capitalism and Schizophrenia*, trans. R. Hurley, M. Seem and H. R. Lane, pref. M. Foucault, intr. M. Seem. Minneapolis: University of Minnesota Press.

Deleuze G. and Guattari, F. 1991. *Qu'est-ce que la philosophie?* Paris: Minuit.

Deleuze G. and Guattari, F. 2004 [1980]. *A Thousand Plateaus: Capitalism and Schizophrenia 2*, trans. and intr. B. Massumi. London: Continuum.

Deleuze, G. and Parnet, C. 1977. *Dialogues*. Paris: Flammarion.

Diano, C. 1994. *Forme et événement: Principes pour une interprétation du monde grec*, trans. from Italian P. Gernet and M. Valensi. Combas: L'Éclat.

Dilthey, W. 1976. *World-Intuition and the Analysis of Humanity since the Renaissance and Reformation*, trans. H. P. Rickman. In W. Dilthey, *Selected Writings*, vol. 2. Cambridge: Cambridge University Press.

Foucault, M. 1954. Introduction. In Ludwig Biswanger, *Le Rêve et l'existence*. Paris: Desclée de Brouwer, pp. 9–128.

Foucault, M. 1966. *Les Mots et les choses*. Paris: Gallimard.

Foucault, M. 1972a. 'Les Intellectuels et le pouvoir: Entretien Michel Foucault–Gilles Deleuze'. *L'Arc*, 49: 3–10.

Foucault, M. 1972b. 'Préface'. In B. Jackson, *Leurs prisons: Autobiographies de prisonniers et d'ex-détenus américains*. Paris: Plon.

Foucault, M. 1976 [1963]. *The Birth of the Clinic: An Archaeology of Medical Perception*, trans. A. Sheridan. London: Tavistock.

Foucault, M. 1977 [1970]. 'Theatrum philosophicum', trans. D. F. Bouchard and S. Simon. In *Language, Counter-Memory, Practice: Selected Essays and Interviews*, ed. D. F. Bouchard. Ithaca, NY: Cornell University Press, pp. 165–196. [Online modified translation at http://www.generation-online.org/p/fpfoucault5.htm, accessed 18 June 2016; French original of 1970 in *Critique*, 282: 885–908.]

Foucault, M. 1979. *Discipline and Punish: The Birth of the Prison*, trans. Alan Sheridan. London: Penguin Books.

Foucault, M. 1981. 'The order of discourse: Inaugural lecture at the Collège de France, given on 2 December 1970', trans. I. McLeod. In *Untying the Text: A Post-Structuralist Reader*, ed. Robert Young. Boston, MA: Routledge & Kegan Paul, pp. 48–78.

Foucault, M. 1986. 'The discourse on language'. In *Critical Theory since 1965*, ed. Hazard Adams and Leroy Searle. Tallahassee: University Presses of Florida, pp. 148–63.

Foucault, M. 1988. *Madness and Civilization: A History of Insanity in the Age of Reason*, trans. R. Howard. New York: Vintage.

Foucault, M. 1994a. *Dits et écrits*, vols 3–4. Paris: Gallimard.

Foucault, M. 1994b. Le Sujet et le pouvoir'. In M. Foucault, *Dits et écrits*, vol. 4, texte 306. Paris: Gallimard.

Foucault, M. 2000. 'The subject and power'. In Michel Foucault, *Power*, ed. James D. Faubion, vol. 3 of *The Essential Works of Foucault 1954–84*. New York: New Press, pp. 326–48.

Foucault, M. 2009. *History of Madness*, trans. J. Murphy and J. Khalfa. London: Routledge.

Foucault, M. 2011. *Leçons sur la volonté de savoir: Cours au Collège de France, 1970–1971*, ed. F. Ewald and A. Fontana. Paris: Gallimard.

Gramsci, A. 1996. 'Americanism and Fordism'. In A. Gramsci, *Selections from the Prison Notebooks*, ed. and trans. Q. Hoare and G. Nowell-Smith. New York: Orient Longman, pp. 277–320.

Guattari, F. 1974. *Psychanalyse et transversalité*, pref. G. Deleuze. Paris: Maspéro.

Heidegger, M. 1977. *The Question Concerning Technology and Other Essays*, trans. W. Lovitt. New York: Garland.

Ilyenkov, E. V. 1982. *The Dialectics of the Abstract and the Concrete in Marx's Capital*, trans. S. Syrovatkin. Moscow: Progress Publishers.

IMEC. 2009. *Les Mots et les choses de Michel Foucault: Regards critiques, 1966–1968*. Caen: Presses Universitaires de Caen.

Kant, E. 1964. *Anthropologie du point de vue pragmatique*. Paris: Vrin.

Macherey, P. 1992. 'Foucault/Roussel/Foucault'. In M. Foucault, *Raymond Roussel*. Paris: Gallimard, pp. iii–vi.

Machiavelli, N. 1971. *Istorie fiorentine e altre-opere storiche e politiche di N. Machiavelli*, edited by A. Montevecchi. Turin: UTET.

Marx, K. 1933. [First German edition of the unedited Chapter VI of *Capital*, with Russian translation; title unknown.] *Arkhiv Marska i Engel'sa* [*Marx and Engels Archive*], 2(7): 4–229.

Marx, K. 1968–70. *Lineamenti fondamentali della critica dell'economia politica*, 2 vols, trans. E. Grillo. Florence: La nuova Italia.

Marx, K. 1969a. *Il Capitale: Libro I, capitolo VI inedito: Risultati del processo di produzione immediato*, trans. B. Maffi. Florence: La nuova Italia.

Marx, K. 1969b. *Theories of Surplus Value: Part 1*, ed. S. Ryazanskaya, trans. E. Burns. London: Lawrence & Wishart.

Marx, K. 1971. *Teorie sul plusvalore*, trans. G. Giorgetti. Rome: Editori Riuniti.

Marx, K. 1972. *Capital*, vol. 3. London: Lawrence & Wishart.

Marx, K. 1973. *Grundrisse: Foundations of the critique of political economy, rough draft*, trans. M. Nicolaus. London: Penguin.

Marx, K. 1975 [1845]. *The Holy Family or Critique of Critical Criticism: Against Bruno Bauer and Company*, vol. 4 of *Marx–Engels Collected Works*. London: Lawrence & Wishart.

Marx, K. 1975. *Theories of Surplus Value*, vol. 31 in *Marx–Engels Collected Works*. London: Lawrence & Wishart.

Marx, K. 1977 [1863–7]. *Capital: A Critique of Political Economy*, vol. 1. New York: Vintage Books.

Marx, K. 1981. *Capital: A Critique of Political Economy*, vol. 2. New York: Vintage Books.

Marx, K. 1990. 'Appendix: Results of the Immediate Process of Production'. In K. Marx, *Capital: A Critique of Political Economy*, trans. B. Fowkes. London: Penguin, pp. 940–1084.

Marx, K. 1993. *Grundrisse: Foundations of the Critique of Political Economy (Rough Draft)*, trans. M. Nicolaus. London: Penguin.

Marx, K. 1997. *Capital: A Critique of Political Economy*, vol. 2, vol. 36 in *Marx–Engels Collected Works*. London: Lawrence & Wishart.

Marx, K. and Engels, F. 1975. *Letters*, vol. 42 in *Marx–Engels Collected Works*. London: Lawrence & Wishart.

Merleau-Ponty, M. 1974. *Adventures of the Dialectic*, trans. J. Bein. London: Heinemann.

Michaud, J. C. 1960. *Teoria e storia nel* Capitale *di Marx*. Milan: Feltrinelli.

Napoleoni, C. 1972. *Lezioni sul Cap. VI inedito di Marx*. Turin: Bollati Boringhieri.

Negri, A. 1959. *Saggi sullo storicismo tedesco: Dilthey e Meinecke*. Milan: Feltrinelli.

Negri, A. 1978. 'Sul metodo della critica della politica'. *AutAut*, 167/8: 197–212. [Reprinted in A. Negri, *Macchina tempo*, Milan: Feltrinelli, 1982, pp. 70–84.] [= Ch. 12]

Negri, A. 1979. 'Capitalist domination and working class sabotage'. In A. Negri, *Working-Class Autonomy and the Crisis*, trans. E. Emery and J. Merrington. London: Red Notes. pp. 92–137.

Negri, A. 1982. *Macchina tempo*. Milan: Feltrinelli.

Negri, A. 1986. *The Politics of Subversion: A Manifesto for the Twenty-First Century*, trans. J. Newell. Cambridge: Polity.

Negri, A. 1991 [1979]. *Marx Beyond Marx: Lessons on the* Grundrisse, trans. and intr. H. Cleaver, M. Ryan and M. Viano. New York: Autonomedia.

Negri, A. 1991 [1982]. *The Savage Anomaly: The Power of Spinoza's Metaphysics and Politics*, trans. M. Hardt. Minneapolis: University of Minnesota Press.

Negri, A. 2000. *Kairos, Alma Venus, multitudo*. Rome: Manifestolibri.

Negri, A. 2005 [2006]. *Books for Burning: Between Civil War and Democracy in 1970s Italy*, ed. T. S. Murphy. London: Verso.

Nigro, R. 2008. La Question de l'anthropologie dans l'interprétation althussérienne de Marx. In *Althusser: Une lecture de Marx*, ed. J.-C. Bourdin. Paris: PUF, pp. 87–112.

Rubin, I. I. 1972 [1928]. *Essays on Marx's Theory of Value*, trans. M. Samardžija and F. Perlman. Detroit: Black and Red.

Sraffa, P. 1960. *Production of Commodities by Means of Commodities: Prelude to a Critique of Economic Theory*. Cambridge: Cambridge University Press.

Thomas, P. 2009. *The Gramscian Moment: Philosophy, Hegemony and Marxism*. Leiden: Brill.

Vilar, P. 1973. 'Histoire Marxiste, histoire en construction: Essai de dialogue avec Althusser'. *Annales ESC*, 28(1): 165–98.

Virno, P. and Hardt, M. (eds). 1996. *Radical Thought in Italy: A Potential Politics*. Minneapolis: University of Minnesota Press.

von Weizsäcker, V. 1958. *Le Cycle de la structure*. Bruges: Desclée de Brouwer.

Origin of the Texts

Chapter 1 Why Marx?

Translation of 'Perché Marx', posted on EuroNomade, 'Dossier Marx', on 18 March 2013: http://www.euronomade.info/?p=682

Chapter 2 Reflections on the Use of Dialectics

Translation of 'Alcune riflessioni sull'uso della dialettica'. Presentation at the conference 'Critical Thought in the 21st Century', Moscow, June 2009, first published on UniNomade on 24 February 2011: http://www.uninomade.org/alcune-riflessioni-sull%E2%80%99uso-della-dialettica. Two previous English translations appeared in the online magazines *Chto Delat* (https://chtodelat.org/b8-newspapers/12-47/some-thoughts-on-the-use-of-dialectics) and *Transeuropeennes* (http://www.transeuropeennes.eu/tr/articles/315)

Chapter 3 Thoughts Regarding "Critical Foresight" in the Unpublished Chapter VI of Marx's Capital, Volume 1

Translation of 'Spunti di "critica preveggente": Capitolo VI inedito (Capitale, I libro)'. Posted on EuroNomade, 'Dossier Marx' on 18 May 2013: http://www.euronomade.info/?p=641

Chapter 4   Acting in Common, and the Limits of Capital

Translation of 'L'agire comune e il limite del capitale'. Posted on EuroNomade, 'Dossier Marx', on 18 November 2013: http://www. euronomade.info/?p=1075

Chapter 5   Is It Possible to Be Communists without Marx?

Translation of 'È possibile essere comunisti senza Marx?' Posted on EuroNomade, 'Dossier Marx', on 18 May 2013: http://www.eurono-made.info/?p=686

Chapter 6   An Italian Breakpoint: Production versus Development

Translation of 'Una rottura italiana: Produzione vs. sviluppo'. Published on UniNomade on 13 October 2010: http://www.unino-made.org/negri-una-rottura-italiana

Chapter 7   On 'Italian Theory'

Translation of 'A proposito di italian theory: Note sullo stato della filosofia italiana'. Presentation at the international colloquium 'L'Italian theory existe-t-elle?' Paris, 24–25 January 2014, posted on EuroNomade, 'Povero Yorick', on 8 February 2014: http://www. euronomade.info/?p=1670

Chapter 8   The Constitution of the Common and the Logics of the Left

Translation of 'La costituzione del comune e le ragioni della sinistra', co-authored with Michael Hardt. Published on UniNomade on 24 December 2011: http://www.uninomade.org/ la-costituzione-del-comune-e-le-ragioni-della-sinistra

Chapter 9   On the Future of the European Social Democracies

Translation of 'Sul futuro delle social-democrazie europee'. Published on UniNomade on 4 November 2010: http://www.uninomade.org/sul-futuro-delle-socialdemocrazie

Chapter 10   Let's Start Reading Gramsci Again

Translation of 'Ricominciamo a leggere Gramsci'. Review of Peter D. Thomas, *The Gramscian Moment: Philosophy, Hegemony and Marxism* (Historical Materialism Book Series, Vol. 24, Brill, Leiden–Boston, 2009). Published on UniNomade on 5 February 2011: http://www.uninomade.org/ricominciamo-a-leggere-gramsci. Also published in Il Manifesto of 19 February 2011.

Chapter 11   Biopower and Biopolitics: Subjectivities in Struggle

Translation of 'Biopotere/biopolitica: Soggettività in lotta'. Unpublished typescript of an interview with Antonio Negri conducted by Luca Salsa in Paris, July 2009.

Chapter 12   On the Method of Political Critique

Translation of 'Sul metodo della critica politica'. Originally published in 1978, in *Aut Aut*, 167/8, pp. 197–212, and reprinted in Antonio Negri, *Macchina tempo*, Milan: Feltrinelli, 1982, pp. 70–84.

Chapter 13   How and When I Read Foucault

Translation of 'Quando e come ho letto Foucault'. Published on UniNomade on 21 November 2010: http://www.uninomade.org/quando-e-come-ho-letto-foucault-2. Also published in French ('Quand et comment j'ai lu Foucault') in P. Artières, J.-F. Bert, F. Gros, and J. Revel, eds, 2011, *Michel Foucault*, Paris: L'Herne, pp. 199–208.

Chapter 14   Gilles Felix: The How and When of Deleuze–Guattari

Translation of the French version of an Italian original titled 'Gilles Felix: Come e quando ho letto Deleuze–Guattari'. The French translation was published under the title 'Gilles-felix' in 1998 in *Gilles Deleuze: Immanence et vie* (special issue of Rue Descartes, 20), Paris: PUF, pp. 77–92.

Chapter 15   Observations on the 'Production of Subjectivity': On an Intervention by Pierre Macherey

Translation of 'Osservazioni su "produzione di soggettività": A proposito di un intervento di Pierre Macherey', co-authored with Judith Revel. Published as postface to P. Macheray, 2013, *Il soggetto produttivo: Da Foucault a Marx*, Verona: Ombre Corte, pp. 83–95.

Chapter 16   Marx after Foucault: The Subject Refound

Translation of 'Un'esperienza marxista di Foucault'. Posted on EuroNomade, 'Dossier Marx', on 30 December 2014: http://www.euronomade.info/?p=3903